100 Most Beautiful Cities of the World

A journey across five continents

REBO
PUBLISHERS

© 2002 Rebo International b.v., The Netherlands/HVK Hamburger Verlagskontor GmbH

This 2nd edition reprinted 2004

Publisher and editor: Manfred Leier

Original text: Winifried Maas (pp 8-21, 80-81, 120-121, 138-187),

Anne Benthues (pp 22-37, 42-79, 88-95)

Hanns-Joachim Neubert/ScienceCom (pp 38-41, 82-87, 96-119, 122-137, 188-207)

Translation: Stephen Challacombe and Suzanne Walters for Bookpros UK

Graphic design: Bartos Kersten, Printmediendesign, Hamburg

Picture editing: Stefanie Braun, Natascha Brüggemann, Annette Cordes, Dirck Möllemann/Picture Agency Schapowalow

Documentation: Dr. Onno Gross

Proofreading: Jarmila Skranakova

ISBN: 90 366 1485 6

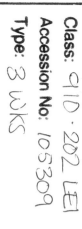
Foreword

Dear reader,

The world's 100 finest cities? While even the greatest of explorers in previous centuries could only visit a few of the world's famous cities, modern air travel has brought even the remotest corners within reach. First to those prima donnas among the metropolises. No other branch of tourism is so popular as the city destination - a sign that city living and culture with its historical buildings is particularly attractive. New York is a modern legend and equally the hub of our present world but almost every country has its own capital that has left behind traces of its history and the inhabitants create a distinctive atmosphere and life style. The historical monuments, the former palaces, and the imposing parliamentary buildings of today, the cathedrals, and the streets in the old towns, the bazaars of the Orient, and the markets of the west, the grand squares in which people meet one another, and the viewpoints across the city - all evoke something within us when we think of traveling to these exciting cities across five continents. Which city will stimulate us most and which we find most beautiful depends on our personal subjective expectations. Nevertheless, the map provides us with some criteria on which to base our selection of the "100 finest cities". It is the people who live there who have formed the nature of their city in their own special way. Without the magnificent buildings of the rulers of yesteryear, without the temples or the towers of their churches, without the alleys of the workers' district, or the colorful life on the grand boulevards, these cities would be devoid of the atmosphere that people adore and that opens people's eyes to the beauties of the world. But the subjectivity of these feelings too makes every selection subject to dispute. And that is equally true of our selection of the world's 100 finest cities.

The Publisher

LISBON

Hill of the old town beneath the Castle of São Jorge by evening light
PAGE 8

NEW YORK

View from the Empire State Building of the ravines of streets of Manhattan
PAGE 104

Contents

JERUSALEM

**Panoramic view of the Mount of Olives
above the holy city**
PAGE 138

SYDNEY

**The modern opera house is a symbol
of the metropolis**
PAGE 188

MARRAKESCH

**From Jemaa-el-Fna Place one enters
the bazaar through a gateway**
PAGE 192

EUROPE

Lisbon's golden luster
Stony witnesses recall the age of the great voyagers

Anyone who has not seen Lisbon has not seen beauty, or so say the Portuguese. The finest thoroughfare in this beautiful city is the Tagus estuary (Rio Tejo) that leads to the Atlantic and forms an inland sea known as Mar de Palha that is one of the most magnificent natural harbors of the world from which great voyages have set sail. On the sun-kissed hills of the northern bank Lisbon proudly displays her palaces, churches, and enchanting old streets across seven hills that are faded reminders of a golden age.

The first to anchor in these waters were the Phoenicians in 1200 BC. They named this anchorage Alis Rubbo or "peaceful harbor" which later became Lisboa or Lisbon. The city was developed by the Romans and the Visigoths, followed by the Moors who conquered the city. The green banner of The Prophet flew over the city's fortifications of the Castle of St. George (Castelo São Jorge) for four hundred years. The city was conquered by Christian crusaders led by King Alfonso I in 1147. A decisive act in the battle for the city was the sacrifice of Martim Monez who was killed inserting himself between the gates of the Castelo São Jorge so that the Christians were able to storm the citadel.

Treasures of seafaring
The city's treasury now began to fill. Ships from Lisbon dominated trade with Africa and there was business to be made too in the overland routes. When Vasco da Gama discovered the route to India in the late fifteenth century and Pedro Alvarez Cabral created the colony of Brazil the capital city became one of the richest European metropolises and the kingdom of Portugal was a world power. A tangible sign of this golden era is the highly-decorated Torre Belém watchtower on the Tagus. The treasures from the great voyages of gold, silver, gem stones, silk, spices, exotic plants and animals such as live rhinoceroses were unloaded close to the tower.

King Manuel I had six elephants and a tame panther accompanying him when he paraded for special occasions. To thank God for all the bounties he had bestowed King Manuel had the massive friary (Mosteiro dos Jerónimos) built. It is a fine example of Manueline architecture – a blend of Gothic, Moorish, and Indian architecture. It took sixty years to build this church of gray-white sandstone with its triple-vaulted nave.

The Friary is one of the few major buildings to have survived Lisbon's greatest tragedies. An earthquake, three seaquakes, and the associated great fires virtually destroyed the entire city on All Saints Day 1755. Thirty thousand inhabitants were killed by falling walls, drowned by the tidal waves, or burned by the fire storm. Fifteen thousand buildings were destroyed together with three hundred palaces, and 110 churches.

Square shaded by oaks
The grand scale of Lisbon owes much to the modern views of the Marqués de Pompal who was responsible for rebuilding the city. Pompal had the 35,000 square meter (0.01 square mile) Praça do Comércio laid out on the site of one the royal palaces alongside the Tagus which is now one of the brightest jewels of Lisbon. A triumphal arch at its northern side leads to the equally newly created Baixa or lower city which has wharves that are laid out symmetrically. A fire here in 1988 destroyed eighteen buildings.

At the Rossio adjoining the Baixa, that today is Lisbon's most lively square, an alleged heretic was burnt alive as recently as 1820. Just a few steps from here is the magnificent boulevard of the Avenida da Liberdade offering shade beneath oak and jacaranda trees or the sun shades of the sidewalk cafés. Many Lisboners enjoy a cat nap here during the Siesta despite the cacophony of car horns, while exhausted tourists plan the rest of their day's itinerary as they browse their guide books.

There is no shortage of things worth seeing in this city of 850,000 inhabitants. You can climb the steep steps to the Castelo São Jorge, visit one of the forty-two museums, or try one of Lisbon's cast-iron elevators that connect the lower and upper parts of the city.

Alternatively you might drink an espresso (Uma Bica) in the ancient Café Martinho da Arcadia and watch as the world passes you by or eat spiny lobster in Ribadouro followed perhaps with a glass of wine in Mascote de Atalaia while listening to Fados – songs of love and death of such sweet melancholy that the Lisboners call Saudade.

GETTING THERE
Lisbon has an international airport

ACCOMMODATION
Bed & breakfast and hotels in every category

BEST TIME
Mid-March to early June, September to early November

TIPPING
5-10 % of the bill. Tips are generally expected for tourist and other services

EXCURSIONS
Half-day trips to Estoril and Cascais. Whole day trips to Sintra, Coimbra, and Óbidos

TYPICAL FOOD
Bacalhau, the local fish for which there are 365 different ways of cooking it

The Castelo São Jorge seen by the evening light from the hill of the old town (top)

The tramway replaced the earlier and unusually steep route of the cable cars or Elevado da Bica (bottom left)

The Torre Belém on the banks of the Tagus

The sweet smell of Porto

Wine and sardines made the city on the Douro prosperous

From the clearly Romanesque of the oldest church to the finest Jugendstil of the Café Majestic there is hardly an architectural style that is not expressed in Porto. Portugal's second city admittedly did not have access to the colonial riches but did have ambitious city fathers, holy princes, and civic patrons who contributed greatly to the great aesthetic beauty with which this city was built.

Just under four miles inland from the mouth of the river into the Atlantic Ocean the Romans established a trading post here on the northern bank around 200 BC which they called Portus Cale or Cale port which also later gave rise to the country becoming Portugal. The town of Porto slowly became established overlooking this natural harbor. The Visigoths later made the town a bishopric and after three centuries of Moorish rule, Porto emerged as the capital of the then earldom of Portugal.

Settlement of the Medieval heart of the city was hard-going, with the building plots for the five storey high town houses having to be created on terraces chiseled from granite. The cathedral was erected at the top level

in the twelfth century and its double-sided towers have dominated the neighborhood like a siege castle ever since. The architecture was initially Romanesque but Gothic predominated later. The oldest church of Porto – the Romanesque São Martinho de Cedofeita – was completed a few months earlier. Its name of cedo feita or "quickly made" honors the speed of construction.

An Englishman's recipe

The city's construction was financed by the flourishing trade in wine from the upper Douro river. The red wines had been highly regarded from Roman times and were sought after in Great Britain. In 1860 an English trader mixed some ordinary red wine with a little spirits to improve its keeping properties, with unexpected results. The British customers were delighted with this new aperitif, resulting in the creation of Port. Of course the recipe was later modified, the sweetness varied, but sales continued to rise. Meanwhile British, Dutch, and German wine shippers established huge warehouses to store their Port in the southern suburb of Vila Nova de Gaia, from where a seductive sweet smell drifts over the Douro and the neighboring old town on days when there is no wind.

The export of preserved sardines and cork was also of great importance from the early days of the city, and in more recent times there has been a flourishing textile industry. The west of the old city is predominantly a modern example of town planning with contemporary business and living areas thrusting upwards, separated by handsomely formed places, avenues, and park land. Famous engineers such as Gustav – builder of the Eiffel Tower in Paris – participated in the construction of the new bridges across the Douro. The Ponte de Dom Luis I was celebrated in 1886 as a technical wonder with its twin roadways at 33 and 221 foot high (10 and 67 meter) to connect the city center with the wine trading district.

Porto's success is ascribed to civic pride, doggedness, and liberty. Following bad experiences with the aristocracy the citizens acquired a privilege in the later Middle Ages whereby no nobleman could become established in the city. Repeatedly there were rebellions against encroachment by au-

thority. Napoleon's soldiers were furiously repelled in 1808. As Portuguese capital, the city was anti-monarchist in 1891 and was not a supporter of the dictatorship of Salazar (1889–1970).

European City of Culture

The 330,000 inhabitants of Porto fail to understand why Port wine is more famous world-wide than their beautiful city. This changed somewhat – at least within Europe – with the naming of Porto in 1994 as a European City of Culture. This designation also helps increase tourist trade. They gladly show off historical buildings such as the supposed birthplace of Henry the Navigator (1394–1460), who did not undertake any voyages himself but as patron supported development of

new types of ships that were more seaworthy and maneuverable than previous vessels.

Most tourists enjoy the picturesque districts like the narrow streets and the Ribeira place and also the sweet scent of Port wine. Meanwhile one can taste from two hundred different Ports at the Institut Solar Vinho do Porto.

The steel Dom Louis I bridge with its twin road decks carries traffic over the Douro between the old town and Port wine district (above)

The picturesque streets on the old town attract tourists (bottom left)

Shallow barges like the Barco Rabelo (bottom right) were the most suitable form of transporting wine from the Douro region for a long time

See Madrid and enjoy

Chance is the best tourist guide to the Spanish capital

Anyone who attempts to plan a visit to Madrid's sights of interests soon realizes there are too many. A little planning perhaps is wise but Europe's most sensual capital is best enjoyed if left to a chance wander through the streets and lingering a while at its sidewalk cafés and tapas bars.

Right from the trip into town from the airport one is aware of Madrid's cosmopolitan character. The journey is along wide avenues lined with green, around mainly circular grand places, and past grandiose architecture. There is the main post office in wedding cake style, classical triumphal arches, banks decked out like Renaissance castles, but also post-modernist skyscrapers like the twin towers of Puerta Europa, completed in 1996, that intentionally lean together.

Madrid's original history once began at the western edge of the old city where the monumental royal palace now spreads itself. This is precisely where the Moorish conqueror, Emir Mohammed I, built an Alcázar in 852, on the banks of the Rio Manzanares, that was his fortified Mayrit palace. After the expulsion of the Moors in the eleventh century the Christian kings used the Alcázar as a hunting palace and the name Mayrit was adopted for a small settlement that became the Spanish capital of Madrid in 1561.

The king escapes through a window

The Alcázar served as residence for the Catholic king for two centuries until burned down in 1734 and replaced by the royal palace, a monumental château that is ten-times bigger than London's Buckingham Palace. One frescoed ceiling, gilded plaster, and massive chandelier gives way with apparent infinity to another. The last royal resident was King Alfons XIII, who escaped to his exile through a terrace window out of fear of republican demonstrators. The present king only uses the building for state receptions.

The pictures by the court painters portray their majesties who previously lived at the palace with fine and noble faces. More realistic countenances gaze down from the walls of the Prado. Velasquez, for example, portrays one of the Habsburg kings as pale and decadent. Titian depicts Charles V at twenty-seven as an ailing old king. The group portrait of

the family of Charles IV by Goya in room 32 is more exposing than idealized.

From their windows, royalty and their retinues watched executions, bullfights, and the burning of heretics on the Plaza Mayor – the finest of Madrid's grand squares. The aristocratic villas surrounding the open space now serve the Madrilenas as an ideal place to take the air, seated at a café on one's own, or with an aperitif, reading a newspaper, chatting with friends, or silently watching what goes on around them.

Something of every style

Whichever direction you leave the Plaza Mayor you will encounter an interesting neighborhood. Close by there are the shopping streets, gateways, small staircases, and bijou squares of the old town. Many houses still have facades in the style popular with the Habsburgs and might just as easily be in old Vienna or Salzburg, like the Palacio Santa Cruz, once a prison but now the foreign ministry.

Madrid is an open air museum of architecture. The old town del Obispo chapel with its robust Gothic awaits and one of the finest Iberian Baroque portals can be admired at the old hospice that now serves as a museum of the city's history. The Teatro Español is pleasing with its noble classicism at the easygoing Plaza de Santa Ana, while the Plaza de Cibeles offers the "candy" Venetian Renaissance of the Bank of Spain. For unadulterated Art Deco there is the grand cinema Palacio de la Música in the Gran Via and the Spanish motor sport organization's building provides Art Nouveau.

Anyone who has taken in all this within a few hours is ready for some refreshment. Fortunately by no farther than the next corner there will be a bar or taberna serving every type of drink and little snacks known as tapas. These can incorporate mussels, a piece of tortilla, cheese, ham, olives, or special delicacies of the house. These are intended to bridge the gap until dinner which the city's restaurants do not serve before ten in the evening.

GETTING THERE
International flights

ACCOMMODATION
Hotels in every price range. Expensive but close to the center and Prado: The belle-époque Hotel Palace and the famous Ritz

BEST TIME
Spring and Fall

TIPPING
About 5 % of the bill

EXCURSIONS
The cloistered palace of El Escorial, completed in 1584. The medieval towns of Segovia and Toledo

An area of the old town was demolished at the beginning of the twentieth century to make way for the Gran Via. This splendid street is home to many great names and also where the night spots are (top)

The eighteenth century Palacio Real was home to Spanish kings until 1931. Today the enormous building is a museum and also used for state receptions (bottom left)

The Plaza Mayor is Madrid's largest and finest square. Cafés and restaurants entice one to linger in the traffic-free area (bottom center)

The Naked Maja by Goya in the Prado

Fortunate times in Córdoba

A forest of columns recalls a glorious past

GETTING THERE
Nearest international airports are Seville (78 miles/125 km) and Malaga (121 miles/195 km)

ACCOMMODATION
Wide choice of hotels of every category including small bed & breakfast places. Specially recommended: Hotel Amistad on the old city walls

BEST TIME
March to June, late September to October

TIPPING
Up to 10 % of the bill

Just half a century after the conquest of Andalusia by the Moors a young, highly educated man rode at the head of a mounted army into Córdoba in 756. This was Abd ar-Rahman I, son of the last Umayyad caliph of Damascus who was a Berber. This led to the old trading town becoming one of the most liberal and wealthy metropolises of the old world.

Escaping a bloodbath

Six dramatic years lay behind the caliph's son. Persian Abbasids had slain his father and other members of his family to annex the throne. The twenty-year old escaped the bloodbath and hid with his mother's Berber tribe in the Atlas mountains. Later he went from North Africa with a horde of nomadic horsemen who were loyal to him to southern Spain where he killed the governor of Córdoba and many of

his soldiers in a victory at Seville. Self-confidently, Abd ar-Rahman took control of the province of Córdoba and created this as an independent emirate that preceded the later caliphate of al Andaluz. One of the ringleaders of the assassination of his father was captured and beheaded, with his embalmed head being sent to Baghdad.

Although war-like towards external threats Abd ar-Rahman ruled his emirate with tolerance and generosity. Although he was a devout Muslim he permitted religious tolerance.

The multi-cultural inhabitants consisting of Arabs, Berbers, Jews, and Visigoths gave rise through the wide range of talents to a rapid rise in commerce and industry. New crafts such as silk-weaving achieved great success. The production of artistic glazed tiles flourished, waste land was turned into oriental gar-

dens, or became citrus groves or exotic vegetable plots.

Debates of the elite

After the death of Abd ar-Rahman in 788 his Umayyad descendants continued to make Córdoba an economic and spiritual center of the old world. The elite studied various areas of culture, debating Arabic and Judaic philosophies. Unrestrained by religious dogma doctors were able to dissect corpses in the quest for knowledge. Córdoba's hospitals were the most advanced of the age.

In the tenth century Córdoba had a population of around one million inhabitants, three-times more than today. It had superb palaces and mosques. The main streets were paved and lit at night by torchlight. With its 113,000 houses, eighty schools, at least fifty hospitals, nine hundred bathhouses, a number of libraries, and some

In the Jewish-Moorish quarter

Close by lies the Jewish-Moorish quarter Juderia with its medieval houses, wonderful inner courtyards, and artistically tiled walls. The synagogue, Arabic baths, and patrician Palacio de Viana have been preserved. The Medina Azhara (town of flowers) on the other hand is now only a pile of ruins. This was the enormous palace facilities that Abd ar-Rahman III built for his 20,000 servants and soldiers.

The religious and spiritual freedom ended in 1236 when the "Holy King" Ferdinand III re-conquered Córdoba for Catholic Christendom.

View across the Guadalquivir to the old town of Córdoba, with the Great Mosque onto which the later cathedral was grafted (top left)

Quite plain on the outside the Moorish interior with its "forest" of columns comes as a surprise (bottom)

Flamenco dancers at one of the old town bars (top right)

Turn of the century architecture at Córdoba's elegant Plaza de las Tendilles

80,000 workshops, the capital of al Andaluz outshone every other royal seat on the continent. "Córdoba, the luminous jewel of the world, shines over the west," wrote the German abbess Roswitha von Gandersheim in a contemporary poem.

The most important sacred building of the era of the Andalusian Umayyad people is the Great Mosque or Mezquita, the most monumental Islamic building of the Occident. Modest in form externally, the interior of the Mezquita impresses one through its complete harmony of form, expressed by a "forest" of 856 columns beneath double round and horseshoe arches.

Gold and silver for Seville

The Andalusian capital symbolizes classical Spain

Seville (Sevilla) is the most Spanish of all Spanish cities. Here lie the remains – presuming they are genuine – of Christopher Columbus. Here stolen Inca gold was landed, Murillo painted his blissful holy faces, and Don Juan, Carmen, and the barber of Seville lived in the fantasies of poets. Bullfighting also has a long tradition in this Andalusian capital and nowhere else in this country celebrates Fiesta in such a devoted and colorful manner.

The greatest spectacle is in the Semana Santa or Holy Week before Easter when fifty-seven Catholic brotherhoods bear giant floats with enormous holy representations from their own church to the cathedral and back. In the procession following the floats there are barefooted penitents bearing crosses on their shoulders and iron chains around their feet, drummer boys, and disguised figures with the tall pointed hats of the Inquisition.

The Crusades

Seville has celebrated the Crusades or holy war by the Christians against Islam since the Middle Ages. The Moors ruled the city for half a millennium until defeated by King Ferdinand III in 1248. The monarch, who was beatified after his death, expelled 300,000 Muslims and shared their houses and land among his entourage. In desperation many Moors were baptized in order to keep their property ignorant of the risk of later being condemned to death and burned at the stake by the Inquisition.

King Pedro's love nest

In spite of the expulsions Moorish architecture is the symbol of Seville with its Giralda minaret visible from afar. Hence the Christian King Pedro III, who together with his beloved was fond of Moorish architecture and garden design, had the Alcázar palace quarters built in the heart of the city. With their pointed Moorish arches, fanciful battlements, filigree plaster decoration, and secluded courtyards these oriental showpieces have since become one of the most popular attractions of Seville.

The first major Catholic building was decided upon with the thought of the men behind it in 1401 of: "Let us built a cathedral so big that everyone who sees it thinks we are insane." In the space of a century the Santa Maria cathedral rose from the site of a mosque to become the third largest church in Europe, externally Gothic but with greater Renaissance influence in its interior. Since its completion, with its five-partite nave supported on mighty pillars, the cathedral has been the most admired building of Seville. Here too is the sarcophagus of Christopher Columbus, borne by four life-size kingly figures, assuming it is genuine since the great seafarer might also be buried in Santo Domingo.

Thanks to the discovery of the New World and the exploitation of the Inca kingdom by Pizzaro, Seville was the richest city of Europe in the sixteenth and seventeenth centuries. A fleet of Spanish galleons brought gold and silver to the city's port twice each year by means of the Guadalquivir. With the help of a monopoly on trade with the new colonies, Seville pocketed a cut of the treasure every time.

Corrida in 1750

A little of this new prosperity reached the people, whose numbers had dropped significantly with the expulsion of the Moors, followed by the persecution of the Jews, and an epidemic of the plague in 1349. In the picturesque Barrio de Santa Cruz the occupants decorated their atrium houses with colorful Azulejos tiles and artistic wrought iron grilles. Bullfighting also conquered Seville and has been a passion ever since. Gold braided Andalusian toreros first headed for the Corrida in 1750. Soon after this Seville built the finest bullfighting arena in Spain, the Plaza de Toros de la Maestranza with room for 12,500.

Bullfights are part of Seville's greatest fun festival, the annual Feria de Abril held in April each year. This is celebrated in 450 marquees along the Barrio Los Remidos. The highpoint is the procession by the prosperous landowning families with riders and in carriages. The Caballeros (men) wear short jackets and round black hats, the Señoras and Señoritas dress in ruffled frilly clothing with red carnations in their hair. For seven days the strong Andalusian wine flows, people everywhere dance flamenco and the more cheerful Sevillana, and the party lasts until daybreak. Viva Sevilla!

Seville's Plaza de España has served as a perfect example of Andalusian architecture since 1929. Alongside the semi-cruciform building are other examples with typical architectural features such as a colonnade, and wide promenade, and a canal with ornamental bridges (top)

In Holy Week before Easter churches such as Santa Macarena are starting point for magnificent processions (bottom left)

Highpoint of the annual Feria de Abril festival is the procession by horsemen and fine carriages.

The Alhambra is the glory of Granada

The most visited monument of the Moorish era

Eager for booty, the Berber prince Tarik Ibn Ziyad and his North African horsemen crossed the Straits of Gibraltar to Spain in 711 with dozens of ships. Within a few weeks he had conquered Andalusia and opened the way for the following Moorish marauders to subjugate almost the entire Iberian peninsula.

Soon after his arrival the Berber prince occupied the area of the future city of Granada. He found an insignificant Romano-Celtic settlement on a high plateau that was broken by three small hills and the Jewish community of Garnath Alyehad, but the landscape entranced him. To the southeast the snow-capped Sierra Nevada mountains tower upwards to more than 9,800 feet (2,987 m) while fertile valleys spread out to the west and south.

There was no longer a question of quickly plundering the land and moving on. The African horseman wanted to stay here. He had not brought any women with him in his marauding party but there were blonde Christian and dark Jewish women here. The Moors, as these people became known, established families, built houses, and later also schools for their children. They also built mosques and fine palaces. By and by the hill of Albaicín had a terraced settlement built on it that formed the first and only town created by the Moors in Spain: Garnata (pomegranate) or Granada.

A beating for the prince

Political unrest made things more difficult for the Moorish family man. The Berber prince Tarik Ibn Ziyad was punished with a beating by his Arabic war lord Musa Ibn Nusair for unauthorized actions and various army commanders resigned their allegiance to the Caliph of Damascus for whom they had originally joined the fight. For a time strict Islamic rule held sway in Granada. Eventually as elsewhere following 300–500 years of rule the Moors were driven out by Catholic crusaders and the settlement began a lustrous new era.

In 1238 Muhammed al-Ahmar elevated Granada to the capital of his kingdom and himself to monarch. He founded the Nazari dynasty of Moorish sultans who managed to rule for two and a half centuries through skillful tactics towards the Catholic rulers. Granada acquired city walls, trade, and the crafts flourished in this period and a Moorish elite of artists, architects, and craftsmen sought haven from the re-Christianized areas in Granada. Outstanding doctors established hospitals, bathhouses were opened, and weaving was also started.

Retreat with tears

The hill fort developed into an ambitious example of high Moorish culture and a royal residence. Within the fortified walls in the course of a century arose a fine assemblage of glorious buildings that oriental culture has provided the occident. The brilliant centrepiece is the Alhambra royal palace which stirred the Arabic poet Ibn Zamrak to enthuse: "The Stars themselves long to spend time there (the Court of Lions in the Alhambra) instead of moving eternally in the Heavens."

Moorish rule finally ended on January 2, 1492, with the young King Boabdil, twentieth Nazari king. Christian knights had besieged the city for many months, leading to hunger and the city ready to be stormed. To prevent a bloodbath and protect the Alhambra from destruction, Boabdil handed over Granada without a fight to the care of the Catholic King Ferdinand II and Queen Isabella I and departed in tears. Some consolation for the vanquished was the promise of the Christian king to preserve religious freedom for Granada's Moors. This did not last long though and Arabic books were burned and their owners were forcefully baptized.

Half a millennium later the Alhambra of Granada is the most visited Spanish monument. Around 20,000 visitors daily throng the grand chambers, gardens, and courtyards of the royal palace – too many to wonder at the timeless simplicity, the fairy-tale stalactite arches, and the magic of columns reflected in the water rills at leisure.

GETTING THERE
Flights from Madrid or Barcelona to Granada

ACCOMMODATION
Hotels up to four-star category. Ideal choice: Parador Real de la Alhambra (in the Alhambra estate) and Palacio Santa Inés (with a view of the Alhambra)

BEST TIME
Spring and Fall

TIPPING
Up to 10 % of the bill in bars, restaurants, cafés, and hotels. Extra tip for special services

WORTH SEEING
The Generalife Garden, Moorish old town, Albaicin. The cave dwellings of Sacromonte.
The cathedral with the tombs of the Catholic kings

The Alhambra stretches out above the roofs of Granada like a foothill of the snow-capped Sierra Nevada. It the Moorish fortified palace of the Nazari kings (top)

The outward appearance of the buildings contrasts starkly with the interiors with their magical display of oriental architecture as in the main hall (bottom left)

The gardens of the Alhambra are also masterpieces. Their creator wanted to give the living a foretaste of paradise.

Barcelona - stage for a zest for life

The Catalan capital gets more interesting year on year

The heart of Barcelona beats in the Ramblas. Between morning and midnight almost everyone in the city will find themselves at some time in the avenue lined with plane trees that links the massive Plaza de Cataluña with the harbor. Bird sellers, flower women, and newspaper vendors have their pitches on the 1 1/4 mile (2 km) long and almost 150 foot (46 m) wide promenade. There are also sidewalk cafés, ice-cream kiosks, and bars for a beer. The Boqueria with its enormous fish market opens at five in the morning, in the evening the middle classes throng the magnificent opera house that is always sold out in spite of five thousand seats and high prices.

The visitor to Barcelona finds a cosmopolitan atmosphere, a blend of zest for life, an urge for freedom, and joy of art. The Catalan capital still feels itself tied to Europe north of the Alps. Within its walls lived Visigoth and Frankish kings such as Charles the Bald, credited with creation of the Catalan coat of arms. During the defense of Barcelona against the Moors he is said to have dipped four fingers in the blood of the wounded hero Guifré el Pilós and marked four red stripes on the dying man's shield: four red stripes on a golden ground.

The king eavesdrops

The city with its harbor was founded by the Romans and achieved prosperity and power as royal residence of the Franco-Catalan kingdom of Aragon in the Middle Ages. The Barrio Gótico or Gothic Quarter retains the stern lines of Catalan Gothic in its fine residences and imposing cathedral. In the simple beauty of the Generalitat ("chamber of the one hundred") the city's first autonomous city government gathered in the fourteenth century, suspiciously spied upon by the Catalan king through a hole in a drape who gave away his hiding place when he gasped at a disagreeable speaker.

Columbus – known in Spanish as Colón and in Catalan as Colom – is revered in Barcelona as if he was a protecting saint. Prominent people escorted the discoverer of America from the harbor to the palace of the lords of Barcelona in 1482 where he was awaited by the two enthroned monarchs: Isabella of Castile and Ferdinand of Aragon. Later an almost two hundred foot high memorial

column was erected next to the harbor. Nearby is moored a faithful reproduction of the Santa Maria in which Spain's most famous seafarer discovered the New World.

Tourists flock along the Columbus route from the harbor, up some 750 yards (640 m) to the Ramblas and then a right turn to the Plaza del Rei at the front of which steps lead up to the Palau Reial Major. Here in the Salón del Tinell the voyager paid his respects to the monarchs accompanied by a group of native Americans.

Picasso in ancient palaces

Many medieval buildings now play valuable new roles in the cultural life of the city, such as museums. Three palaces alone are dedicated to the exhibition of the work of Picasso. From time to time the solid Catalan cooking can also be tasted within ancient vaults such as Can Culleretes or Los Caracoles.

More modern times have also left their impression on Barcelona. Amid the housing of the ordinary people one can admire the Golden Square with its array of some 150 Modernist buildings. Architects of distinction such as Antoni Gaudi created five-storey homes here with cave-like entrance halls, wavy roofs, and sculptural chimneys that conjure up fairy-tale images. This is also true of Gaudi's sacred work, the Sagrada Família church, under construction since 1882. When Gaudi died in 1926 only one of the present eighteen towers had been completed.

After the explosion of Art Nouveau and Modernism at the turn of the nineteenth and twentieth centuries fresh architectural impetus was given to the city through the World Exhibition of 1929 and the Olympic Games of 1992. A collection of modern galleries and futuristic sporting facilities arose on the 700 foot (213 m) high Montjuïc hill. Here too the architect Josep Lluis Sert built a museum to display the work of the outstanding surrealist Joan Miró (1893–1983). The master immortalized himself with the sculpture Dona i Ocell (Woman and Bird) that is as high as a lighthouse and with his colorful sculpture on the Ramblas.

The promenade of the Ramblas leads from the Columbus column to the city center.
The oldest part of the city, the Barrio Gótico (Gothic Quarter) with its imposing cathedral is on the right of the plane-tree lined avenue (top)

The up to 150 foot (150 m) wide and almost 1 ¹/₄ mile (2 km) long Ramblas is a pedestrian's paradise (bottom left)

Antoni Gaudi's famous Art Nouveau Sagrada Familia church has been under construction since 1882

21

View of Paris and the River Seine from Notre-Dame. The Rive Gauche on the left and in the background the Eiffel Tower (top)

Chinese architect I. M. Pei constructed a glass pyramid in front of the Louvre that is one of the new sights of Paris (bottom left)

The Place du Tertre is the center of the artistic quarter of Montmartre. Behind soars the church of the Sacré-Coeur

Paris and its boulevards

The French capital acquired its present image in the nineteenth century

BEST TIME
Spring, Fall, and Winter

ACCOMMODATION
Many "grand" famous and expensive hotels such as the Ritz. Budget hotels are between the Gare du Nord and Opéra

FESTIVALS
Festival of Paris (opera, concerts, ballet) May-June. Bastille Day national holiday, July 14 with military parade along the Champs-Elysées.

SOUVENIRS
Fashion, antiques, delicacies

CULINARY
Oysters, truffles, caviar but also entrecôte (steak), tripe, and blood sausage

SPECIAL TIP
Brasserie Train Blue in the opulent style of the Belle Époque on the Place Louis Armand

The poet Heinrich Heine wrote of Paris: "Living is so fine, so sweet on the banks of the Seine in Paris," and Ernest Hemingway described it as a "moveable feast." No other European city is so exuberantly loved as Paris and none other provides such an escape from reality. From a major appearance at the opera, through a picnic by the Seine, lunch at Brasserie Lipp, to sunbathing on the steps of the Sacré-Coeur, this city provides pleasure in abundance.

The low, protected islands on the Seine tempted the Celts in the third century BC to settle in the heart of present-day Paris and the Romans too later appear to have found Lutetia Parisiorum as an ideal place for a settlement. The invading Franks started the rise of the city in the third century AD and in the tenth century it became a royal residence and acquired its principal role at the heart of France even after Louis XIV moved his court to Versailles. With a population of more than one million, Paris was at the very center of the French Revolution. The city on the Seine is one of the most popular tourist destinations in the world with its art and culture, but also its haute cuisine and haute couture.

Many visitors want to spend some time on the Boulevard St. Germain-des-Prés, or perhaps in heated existentialist debate in the Café de Flore. The area, that was formerly a monastery, attracted artists and writers and the arts are celebrated here with a unique diversity of galleries.

Rebellious Sorbonne
The neighboring Quartier Latin is devoted to education and it was here in 1968 in the narrow streets around the Sorbonne that the spirit of resistance led to the Students Revolt. The Rive Gauche or Left Bank is synonymous with a philosophy and the same is true of neighboring Montparnasse with its exclusive streets and the legendary Brasserie La Coupole.

But in spite of the colorful life on the Rive Gauche half-way through this story one is dropped off on the right bank where the Louvre towers as a symbol of royal power. The palace, that became a museum following the Revolution, today houses some 400,000 art treasures such as La Joconde, better known as the Mona Lisa. The gardens of the Tui-

leries run from the Louvre to the Place de la Concorde. This was known as the Place de la Revolution in the months following the storming of the Bastille and was the site for the guillotine with which the executioner (Monsieur de Paris) beheaded more than one thousand of the aristocracy, including Marie Antoinette. A straight axis leads from here along the Champs-Elysées with its expensive stores and offices to Napoleon's triumphant Arc de Triomphe, built to celebrate his victory at the Battle of Austerlitz.

The old luster of the Marais
If you take the road towards the Opera from the Place de la Concorde you will pass the Place Vendôme with its well-proportioned town houses that form a giant space under the sky. The Place de la Opéra is huge in contrast with the intimate Place Vendôme and comes into its own during the evening.

For newcomers to Paris the up and coming quarter of the Marais is a surprise with its businesses and courtyards but also grand mansions and the elegant Place des Vosges. That frequently celebrated diversity of life can also be found in Montmartre, particularly when you discover it on foot. Steeply climbing streets with greengrocers stores, bars, and fantastic milliners lead to the Mons Martyrium or "Martyr's hill" surmounted by the white church of the Sacré-Coeur, that provides one of the best places to view the city and is a meeting place for young people. The life of the Place du Tertre where artists set-up their easels is colorful. The nearby Moulin Rouge, with its shimmering cabaret, where Henri de Toulouse-Lautrec first painted the can-can dancers, reminds one that the hill was once covered with windmills.

The last visit of course is to the two islands in the Seine, reached by the elegant Pont-Neuf. The Notre Dame, Palais de Justice, and entrancing Place Dauphin are on the Ile de la Cité. Those visiting the less frequented Ile St.-Louis will find a place full of charm that they would prefer not to leave. Paris evokes a yearning for it even while you are still there.

Metropolis of cooking

LYON is a stronghold of Nouvelle Cuisine – the old town is a unique architectural gem

BEST TIME
Fall – harvest time but also spring and summer

ACCOMMODATION
La Tour Rose (hotel with a gourmet restaurant). Simple hotel on the edge of the city

GASTRONOMY
Pike fish cakes, sausages, wild boar with slices of truffle, rabbit in mustard sauce, Cervelle de Canut (fresh cheese specialty)

SOUVENIRS
Textiles, antiques, potted delicacies, Bernachon pralines

FESTIVALS
Open Air Festival in the Roman amphitheater (June-September), Festival of Light (around December 8)

SPECIAL TIP
The Fourvière hill offers the best vistas of the city

The Saône flows right through the center of the old town of Lyons just before it joins the Rhône (top)

Grand scale squares like the Place des Cordeliers are popular meeting places. The children's carousel adds some additional atmosphere (bottom left)

The old town has restaurants and sidewalk cafés at every corner like here in the Rue St. Jean

Truffles and cep mushrooms alongside chickens, pigeon, and nuts, together with oysters and pike, accompanied by vegetables, fruit, and sweet-smelling bread: nowhere is better for a first acquaintance with Lyon than the Saint-Antoine market on a Sunday morning. Thousands of promenading citizens throng the stalls, smelling, touching, and tasting the food that is to become their evening meal. Chefs from the restaurants, or their buyers search for the freshest of ingredients.

Lyon is a stronghold of the relish of food and gastronomic center of France. No surprise then that the prince of culinary delights, Paul Bocuse, created the new "light cuisine" in a suburb of Lyon that had such a triumphant response that today he is "still counting his money." And if things become calmer at his famous restaurants and bistros there are the crown princes of Philippe Chavent and Thierry Bonfante ready to take center stage.

How did this city become so famous? Without any doubts its situation played an important part because the second largest French city (1.3 million inhabitants) benefited from the stimulus of the traveling traders on the silk route. Equally the proximity of the vegetable gardens of Provence and the Alps played their part. The legendary poultry of Bresse near at hand helps too and a world famous red wine evolved on the slopes of the nearby Beaujolais.

Riches through silk

Lyon was established as the Roman colony of Lugdunum in 43 AD in one of the valleys formed by the Rhône and Saône rivers. It quickly became the capital of the Gauls and second only in size to Rome. When Caesar Septimus Severus had the city burned to the ground two hundred years later in revenge for an alliance with one of his opponents there were 100,000 people living there.

The former metropolis fell from significance for more than a thousand years until a charter was granted in the fifteenth century to hold a market four times each year led to a renaissance. In the late Middle Ages Lyon became a center for weaving of cloth and silk and the fairs held in the city brought such riches that an entire quarter was built in Renaissance style that is one of today's architectural gems of Lyon. In the nineteenth century the industrial revolution displaced the city's man-

ufacturing. Later Lyon established a new economic base with the chemical industry.

In spite of this upturn and a considerable pioneering spirit – after all cinematography and cinema were invented here – Lyon fell behind other French cities until the 1980s when intensive wooing of tourists brought a change. Suddenly Lyon was attractive again, its gastronomy boomed and Unesco gave a further helping hand in 1998 when it placed the entire 500 hectares of the old town under protection as one of the most extensive sites of its kind. Since then the city has truly shed light on its glory. More than two hundred protected buildings are now lit up until well past midnight. With the banishment of the dark the city has really come alive.

Traboules as rarity

To experience Lyon is to experience pleasure and excitement simultaneously since the old town possesses a true rarity in the Traboules with their partially covered passageways. Hundreds of narrow streets lead from the elegant residential district to the simple streets of the workers' quarter of Croix Rousse that are dark and secretive, opening out to a courtyard or fine portal. In the maze of streets one finds the Bouchons, small businesses selling the genuine Lyonnais cuisine, solid and fuller variants of tripe or pigeon stuffed with truffles.

Once the so-called Mères – wives of the silk weavers – sold their wares here. They also paid for the start of the building of the majestic basilica of Notre Dame de Fourvière in 1871. This is one of the key places in Lyon together with the Opera House, the Saint-Jean cathedral, the town hall, and the Hotel-Dieu. One of the city's special assets is its great assortment of many squares which like the Places des Terreaux and Bellecour contribute to the grand scale of Lyon. In addition to that Lyon boasts a diversity of museums similar to that of Paris.

Finally one might perhaps take a seat at a bouchon and declare over a glass of red wine: "Lyon was created from the flow of three streams: the Rhône, Saône, and Beaujolais."

Love of life à la Nice

The rich and beautiful throng the Promenade des Anglais.
The old town is a strong point of Gastronomy

BEST TIME
Nice has an year-round season but is busiest in July and August

ACCOMMODATION
Hotels Negresco (every room with sea view), West End, Elysée Palace. Many two-star hotels near rail station

EATING AND DRINKING
Salad Niçoise, basted poultry, fish, socca (unleavened bread of chick-pea flour)

SOUVENIRS
Perfumes (from nearby Grasse), Mediterranean delicacies

SPECIAL TIPS
The ice cream parlor at Place Rossetti offers 90 different flavors.
The Fish Market at Place St. Francois

The wind blows the hair of the young couple on the balcony of the Negresco, high above the English bay of Nice as they enjoy the breeze, the sun, and the luxury of the belle-epoque hotel with its pink cupola. Dreamily they lean over the parapet and gaze at a dazzlingly white ship that is setting to sea.

This is a place exclusively for the rich and super rich, the elegant and cool, a town that Friedrich Nietzsche described as outrageously beautiful. Extremely fashionable, it nestles in the English bay, caressed by the sea, fanning itself with palm trees, that with the pastel buildings and soft light resembles the Italian shore. After all Nice had been Italian until 1860 and since then has played the role of French "diva" with considerable grace.

The sheltered bay has been attracting people since the Greeks founded Nice in the fourth century BC as Nikaia (bringer of victory). The Romans followed on around 14 BC with their desire for the natural harbor, and af-ter them the Saracens, Lombards, and Goths before Nice was endowed under the protectorate of the Lords of Savoy. The harbor city of Nice enjoyed almost five hundred years under the rule of Savoy and returned to France following a referendum in 1860. Now known as "Nice" the city quickly became established under its new government, though not so much with the French as those world champion travelers, the British. They came – only in the winter – for in summer there was the social season, and played every type of society game in the healthy air and surroundings of flowers and palm trees that were to make Nice legendary.

Parade of the barouches

It was quite a coup to create a boulevard with English money, which as the Promenades des Anglais became the parade ground for coaches and barouches of queens and cocottes, fortune-hunters, and the genuine aristocracy. Elsewhere the Crimean "champagne" flowed as accompaniment of the rich Russian society and its aristocracy who had also discovered the Côte d'Azur or "blue coast." Nice became a stronghold of idleness, of pleasure, and carefree zest for life, and so it has remained.

Chip millionaire from Moscow

Those who sit themselves down on the Promenade des Anglais with a famous Salade Niçoise in front of them, consisting of tomatoes, pepperoni, beans, radishes, onions, olives garlic, tuna, anchovies, and lots of olive oil, can relax entirely because although the tin-can caravan thunders past on the busy expressway and the "great princes" are "chip" millionaires from Moscow rustling dollar bills, whatever the blend of bygone glory and modern luxury, worldly social life and showing off, elderly married couples and perfect bodies, the great city of Nice, with its 350,000 inhabitants remains the main attraction. The beach-front promenade is five miles

long, which in spite of modern fast-food restaurants still has filigreed resort buildings, an extravagant display of flowers, and nonchalantly arranged chairs in which one can view the entire beach from where you are staying. The sea becomes blurred in the red evening light and the warm wind from the hills of Provence bears a scent of cloves and mimosa.

Many of the principal attractions of Nice can be found along the Promenade, such as the Hotel Negresco, founded in 1913 by the Romanian Henri Negresco as a homeland for splendor, luxury, and abundance, or the Masséna Palace with its enchanting park, that is now a museum.

One must also visit the old town though for the Cours Saleya with its flower and vegetable market to experience its restaurant scene that offers something special even for the discriminating gastronomic tastes of the Côte d'Azur. The Russian Orthodox cathedral is close by with its onion domed towers decorated with stars reminiscent of Czar Nicholas II, who did not wish to see his countrymen without a church when they visited Nice. Best of all though are the many museums in which one can make a journey of discovery, such as the Musée Raoul Dufy, the Matisse Museum, or the Museum of Modern Art. With its hilly hinterland and the mountains pressing right down to the sea, Nice has long been a place of work for painters and today serves as the cultural metropolis of the Côte d'Azur.

Nice's sea front Promenade des Anglais with its palm trees (top)

Flowers and fountains create the splendor of the Place Massena (bottom left)

The sidewalk cafés in the old town around the Place Charles Felix are a popular meeting place at any time of day

The eternal city

Spanish steps, Trevi Fountain and the Vatican add to the legend of **ROME**

ACCOMMODATION
Hassler Villa Medici luxury hotel above the Spanish Steps and Hotel Raphael

MARKET
Campo dei Fiori – the most colorful and opulent Roman market

FESTIVAL
Festa de Noantri in honor of the Madonna del Carmine: a week-long street festival in Trastevere in late July

GASTRONOMY
Spit-roast suckling pig, pasta (e. g. Tonnarelli with oxtail sauce)

SPECIAL TIPS
Audience with the Pope every Wednesday at 10.30. Book two days before

St. Peter's Square and St. Peter's Cathedral – visited by pilgrims from all over the world (top)

Angels guard a fort and a bridge over the Tiber (bottom center)

The Barcaccia fountain at the Spanish Steps attract hordes of tourists (bottom right)

The Coliseum provided space for 50,000 spectators in antiquity

The tourists throng to the Trevi fountain to cool themselves off and with a dreamy glance throw a few coins into this magnificent blend of water and sculpture – because those who do are guaranteed that destiny will bring them back to Rome.

Return to a city that is the metropolis of chaos? Where motorists make such great demands of the pedestrians? Which is brash and noisy, hectic, and full of stray cats? That's as maybe but with a shrug of the shoulders the countless fans ask where else can one find so much magnificence and elegance? Where else can one playfully wander through almost three thousand years of history and also receive a blessing from the Pope? What's more, where else is life so good as in a Roman trattoria? During his Italian travels, Goethe laconically suggested that Rome was beyond our comprehension.

According to legend the sons of the god Mars, Romulus and Remus founded what was to become the great city of Rome in 753 BC. In reality it was farmers who settled along the Tiber together with encroaching Etruscans who with fire and sword but also with astonishing skill with the cultivation and irrigation and an exemplary administration created the Roman empire, with Rome as the glittering center of the world or caput mondi. Under Emperors Augustus, Nero, Trajan, Hadrian, and Marcus Aurelius, the town of the seven hills continued its ascendancy.

Luxury for idle hands
The Coliseum, with space for 50,000 people was built and the Caracalla hot springs with their hot and cold baths, cosmetic salons, libraries, and lecture halls for 1,700 visitors offered a world of beauty and leisure.

A crucial turning point occurred in 391 when Emperor Constantine endorsed Christianity. The Christ-ian Rome came into being and the imperial Rome diminished. There were times when the city became abandoned such as following the departure of the Pope to Avignon in 1309 but every decline was followed by the city regaining prominence and it was a stronghold of the Renaissance and rediscovered its special glory during the Baroque era.

Against the will of the Pope the city was selected as his place of residence by the newly chosen Italian king in 1871 and remained the capital city when the Italians voted for a Republic in 1946. The Vatican City is a sovereign state and has its own rail station, post office, radio station, and its own diminutive army, the Swiss Guard, which legend has it wears uniforms designed by Michelangelo.

Living antiquity
Those who want to get to know the eternal city can best head for the Forum Romanun, where you will be confronted with the elegant world of antiquity that has been assembled together, visit Hadrian's column, and the Pantheon with its arched dome but also the Coliseum, the Catacombs, and the Via Appia Antica. Another tour of the city is worth while for Renaissance Rome and the powerful Baroque face of the city which form a symbiosis of art and way of life that is so right for this city on the Tiber. There is such zest for life at the Piazza Navona with its four teaming fountains, such elegance at the Spanish Steps, and such perfect harmony at the Piazza della Rotonda!

A stroll through Rome is crowned with a visit to the Vatican City, with must see St. Peter's Square by Gian Lorenzo Bernini from which St. Peters rises up in perfect harmony with the Vatican Museum, the Sistine Chapel and its Pietà or ceiling paintings by Michelangelo. Lovers of the art of gardening should wander through the parks and admire the Farnesi gardens to admire the sumptuous water features. After all in the end there is nothing the Romans adore more than flowing water.

Florence
ITALY
Mediterranean

Where the Medicis hoarded their treasure

Ponte Vecchio, Uffizi, and Duomo: **FLORENCE** is a superlative treasury of arts

BEST TIME
Spring and Fall (very hot in summer)

ACCOMMODATION
Luxury hotel Excelsior with dreamy roof gardens, Hotel Villa Medici and small hotels in the old town

GASTRONOMY:
Bistecca all Florentina (thick piece of beef rib grilled on charcoal), Pollo all diavolo (young and spicy chicken fried in olive oil), Zuppa di fagioli (fresh white bean soup)

SOUVENIRS:
Ceramics, shoes, jewelry, olive oil, wine (e. g. Vino Nobile di Montepulciano)

MARKET:
Food market in the S. Lorenzo and Sant' Ambrogio markets

SPECIAL TIP:
The picturesque view of Florence can be enjoyed from the Piazzale Michelangelo. The in place is Café Giubbe Rose

Panoramic view of Florence and the banks of the River Arno with hills of Tuscany in the background. The Duomo can be recognized from far off, rising above a sea of buildings with its arched lantern (top)

Open air museum, Florentine style: sculpture is displayed at the Piazza della Signoria (bottom left)

A night-time view of the Duomo Santa Maria del Fiore. The building designed by Brunelleschi is 500 ft (153 m) long and 380 ft (116 m) to the top of the dome, the fourth largest church of the Occident.

It is a must to climb to the ridiculously enormous lantern of the cathedral (Duomo) in order to come under the spell of Florence's magic. The red tile roofs shine like velvet, the sandstone palaces glow with golden hue, and churches, squares, and bridges are threaded like pearls in a masterly manner to form a masterpiece. But beware of too much euphoria: frail souls like the poet Rainer Maria Rilke found themselves drowning "in the pounding waves of strange splendor" and the novelist Stendahl shed tears in the church of Santa Croce.

The Romans gave the name Florentina to the town on the Arno river, meaning "flowering." The name was an omen since Florence flourished, became rich and powerful, and the seat of an extremely tactically astute City Republic. In the fourteenth century rebellious and penniless wool weavers in Florence started the first workers' uprising and Michelangelo created David as a symbol of the cautious Republicans. Today the original is in the Galleria dell' Accademia and a reproduction stands on the Piazza della Signoria.

But the power of money had been underestimated and the Medicis who became rich as bankers to the Popes became the overlords in the fifteenth century. They ruled Florence with their tyranny for three centuries and created the city of great culture on the Arno with great wealth and passion. The Palazzo Medici with its palace chapel and superb frescoes by Benozzo Gozzoli was created for them, they decorated churches with precious imported art, erected the Uffizi, extended the Palazzo Pitti, and laid out the Boboli gardens.

Patrons second to none

The most individual architectural inheritance is undoubtedly the Vasari Corridor, the almost one kilometer long connection between the Palazzo Vecchio and the Palazzo Pitti that crosses the Arno over the top of the Ponte Vecchio. It is a long art gallery with panoramas in the heart of the city. It houses the Medici collection of artists' self-portraits which are today among the thousands of paintings decorating the

corridor. The Medicis proved themselves to be true patrons at the end of their rule. The last of the dynasty, heiress Anna Maria Ludovica bequeathed the city all the Medici art treasures in 1743 "so that the libraries and collections shall remain in Florence forever." They can be seen in the Uffizi Gallery.

Art treasures at every turn

And so the city is a treasury brimming over with riches in addition to the Medici valuables, like the Baptisty, the Ponte Vecchio – once a fish and vegetable market but from the fifteenth century filled with goldsmith's stalls, many churches including the prominent flower of Florentine Romanesque architecture, the San Miniato al Monte, and of course the Santa Croce with the Capella Bardi where Michelangelo, Galileo Galilei, Macchiavelli, and Rossini are buried. How one is dazzled by these great names. Dante found his muse Beatrice in Florence, Giotto painted here as did Raphael, and Botticello created his Birth of Venus in the city on the Arno. Leonardo da Vinci originated from a nearby village and finally, on a less rarefied note, the writer Carlo Collodi wrote Pinocchio in Florence.

Florence is on a par with Milan and Rome when it comes to shopping. There are shoes for everybody with hand-made creations that adorn the feet of the world. The likes of Rita Hayworth, Audrey Hepburn, Anna Magnani, and Ava Gardner have had their feet measured by Ferragamo. Eventually one sees the city bathed in silver light that is the finest sight in terms of lines and perspectives. Except perhaps when one glances at a beautiful woman!

This mastery of architectural perspective has also given Florence its unique squares: Piazza SS. Annunziata, Piazza della Signoria, and also Piazza Santa Croce. It is calm here in the evenings and the city regains its medieval image. Around the Piazza Santa Croce lies the most primitive part of the city with its small craft businesses, trattorias, and dream-like stores. And close by is the St. Ambrogio market where all the delicacies of Tuscany are sold.

Secretive Venice

Of the Grand Canal with its magnificent palaces, gondolas, and secluded watery alleys

Venice · Adriatic · ITALY · Mediterranean

Dream or reality? Past or present? If you stand on one of Venice's bridges in the evening when the light on the buildings merges with the reflections in the water and a last gondola silently passes by, you will feel yourself transported to another world, imagining you can hear a plague victim gasping for breath, or perhaps even believing you have seen Giàcomo Casanova at a window.

Venice – beguilingly and suspiciously beautiful (Thomas Mann) – keeps its face hidden behind a facade of luxury, casualness, and indifference and masterfully manages to guard its secret. A city resting on uncertain ground that has been proclaimed dead a hundred times yet which remains such a magnet for the entire world that the numbers of admirers have to restricted in summer.

A collection of 118 islands seem to have appeared an ideal place to settle for the first inhabitants from dry land. Venice was founded in 421 and the first Doge was elected in 697 followed quickly by the meteoric rise of the city. The Venetian merchants pulled off a great coup in 828 when they stole the remains of the evangelist Mark from Alexandria, who as patron saint – with the impressive lion as heraldic animal – was clearly a great improvement on the modest predecessor of Saint Theodor.

Center of trade with the Orient

The inauguration of the St. Mark's cathedral was held in 1094 in the presence of Henry IV and when Venice conquered Constantinople a hundred years later during the fourth crusade the way was open for

Venice to play the dominant role in the Mediterranean. Venice became powerful during the thirteenth and fourteenth centuries and with the discovery of the route to India it became a center of trade with the Orient. A cleverly devised system with one Doge, ten city fathers, and 287 noble families controlled the destiny of the city, ensuring the money remained in the hands of the few rich families and transforming Venice through the building of palaces, churches, squares, arcades, and bridges into an architectural wonder. Napoleon ended the city's independence and removed the last Doge in 1797. In 1815 Venice was ceded to Austria and later became part of Italy.

The city is built on ten thousand piles of oak and elm and is cut through by two hundred canals that are spanned by four hundred

bridges. The at least two and a half mile long Grand Canal that overflows slightly is the watery boulevard that is superbly lined with palaces that all show their best sides to the canal. How theatrical are the churches with their defiant domes, the bridges, and the unique Piazetta that is washed with water from the lagoon.

Masterpiece of St. Mark's Square

St. Mark's Square, bounded by the grand town hall, the Basilica di San Marco, and the Doge's Palace is a masterpiece. In masterly Venetian fashion St. Mark's cathedral reveals itself in a confusing manner because the strange-seeming Byzantine interior with gilded walls of the gem-studded Pala d'Or exhibits a Byzantine past which Venice does not possess. In contrast the Doge's Palace tells of victories and intrigues, of murders and magnificent entrances with its rooms overflowing with luxury.

But Venice is alive and so you sit yourself down at Europe's oldest café, the Florian on the Market Square, listening to a violinist, and pay an appalling price for tea and

cakes. Or you wander onwards to where the gondolas are not in the slightest in mourning, even if they are jet black and shiny and rocking on the green-blue water of the lagoon, wholeheartedly vain and with unsurpassed elegance.

Everyone is a little bit theatrical in Venice and the same is true of hotels like the Cipriani and Sanieli dating from the time of the grand entrance. Many of the small squares, that in the main lie in front of one of the hundreds of churches, are delightful with osterie where one can eat outstandingly good morsels of food. Venetian delicacies, and especially for most people Fegato alla Veneziana, are very enticing.

But Venice also tempts one to take excursions because the entire network of islands reveals the wonder of the city. Vaporettos constantly make trips to the cemetery island of Isola di San Michele – and to Murano where glassblowers conjure extremely delicate creations (since the thirteenth century), or to Burano – where the houses are painted in brilliant colors. Or take a trip, dressed in a white summer suit, to the Lido with its muted colors that provides such sought after scenery

for painters and film directors. Then there is the fascinating degenerate Venice, particularly during carnival, which provided the only chance – courtesy of a mask – in the Middle Ages to break free from the oppression of authority, which is perhaps why Napoleon banned it. Carnival was rekindled in the 1970s and has held its own since then as a third season.

Gondolas gently bob on the water at the entrance to the Grand Canal with the vaulted dome of Santa Maria della Salute visible in the background (top left)

The Rialto Bridge spans Venice's busy water thoroughfare, the Grand Canal (top right)

The center of Venice is St. Mark's Square that leads to the Basilica of San Marco with the Doge's Palace next to it (center right)

A gondola trip is the best "theater box" from which to view the drama of Venice. Historical costume is appropriate of course for this opera singer celebrating her appearance

ITALY
Bologna
Mediterranean

Venerable Bologna

Of towers for family honor and arcades stretching for miles

BEST TIME
Early summer and Fall

ACCOMMODATION
Grand Hotel Baglioni, cheaper hotels near the exhibition center

GASTRONOMY
Spaghetti Bolognese, Mortadella, Parma ham, Polenta with fish, Bolito misto (sturdy dish of different types of meat), Porchetta (suckling pig)

SOUVENIRS
Delicacies from Emilia Romagna, haute couture

SPECIAL TIP
Collection of manuscripts at the Biblioteca Communale

The floodlit town hall on the Piazza Maggiore in the center of the city (top)

The young like to meet with their scooters on the superb Via dell' Independenzia (bottom left)

Portico alongside the buildings of the ancient university (bottom right)

The sidewalk cafés on the Piazza ensure a relaxed atmosphere

Bologna la Rosse (the red) reminds one of the tile-clad roofs and the color of the houses but also recalls that venerable Bologna has been governed by the left for more than fifty years. It is known as La Dotta (the cultured) by those impressed by this educated city with its university that was founded in 1088, making it one of the world's oldest. But those who roll their eyes towards heaven and mutter La Grassa (the fat) are thinking of Bolognese sausage – this is where one finds Mortadella – or roast pork, truffles and not least Bolognese sauce made with minced beef – now found in jars throughout the world.

In art defying Upper Italy, Bologna holds a special position since no other city except Venice has so retained its medieval appearance. The Portici are arcades stretching for more than twenty-one miles that were built in the fifteenth century as a kind of immediate solution to housing need. A second row of buildings were constructed in front of the houses with the top section providing accommodation for students and traders and the bottom being used as a footpath.

Founded as Felsina

Bologna, that today is the capital of the Emilia-Romagna province, was founded by the Etruscans in the sixth century bc as Felsina. Four hundred years later the same site became the Roman colony of Bononia which quickly became strategically important because of its position on the great Via Emilia military road. After the Romans the Byzantines and Lombards ruled Bologna which acquired a considerable measure of autonomy following victory over the ruling dynasty at the Battle of

Fossalta in 1249. In 1506 Bologna had to yield up that freedom to the Papal States. Since 1860 the city has formed part of the unified Italy and with its 450,000 inhabitants is best known today for its progressive politics.

Stage set for historical drama

The center of the city is easily recognized since the Piazza Maggiore – that is a hive of activity from early until late – is a grandiose stage for an historical drama. Beside the Palazzo Communale, the Town Hall, the Palazzo Podesto, the Palazzo de Notai, and the Archaeological Museum, stands the Palazzo Re Enzo in which the illegitimate son of Frederic II – King Enzo of Sardinia – was held prisoner following the Battle of Fossalta for twenty-three years.

All Bologna's buildings are shaped by history, such as the twin towers like minarets that rise above the confusion of roofs. At the time Dante was staying in Bologna there were more than a hundred towers proclaiming family rank and status. Today it is worth climbing the Asinelli tower for the unique vista.

Once one has taken in everything there is to see at the Piazza Maggiore the rest of Bologna's architecture has remarkable symmetry. Instead of elongated buildings overwhelming smaller palaces, those of the Strada Maggiore are lined with porticoes. Among the churches the one dedicated to the city's patron saint, the Basilica di San Petronio stands out together with San Domenico and especially San Stefano which is inspired by the holy site in Jerusalem.

The Byzantine Madonna

A special experience can be enjoyed walking up to the foot of the Church of the Madonna di San Luca. An arcade in Bologna climbs mainly upwards for 2.2 miles (3.6 km) to the church with its Madonna originating in Byzantium, and is the longest in the world. The arcaded way was built so that the Madonna can be taken to the city every Ascension Day.

With such magnificent sites is it any wonder that Bologna is also a city of poets and filmmakers? Dante, Boccaccio, Petrarca, Erasmus (from Rotterdam) and more recently Umberto Eco (The Name of the Rose) lived or live here and film

directors like Pasolini, Fellini, Antonioni, and Bertolucci hail from the city or the province of Emilio Romagna. The composer Rossino also chose to live in Bologna because it offers the bon viveur good food as well as a passion for music.

Let us also enter the hustle and bustle of the old town where the finest stores can be found amid the arcades selling hams, salami, cheese, herbs, wine, and liquors. In the evening one finds an osterie somewhere on the Via del Pratello and enjoys their "slow food" created as a counter to fast food with everything served on a plate. Bologna la Grassa precisely!

The queen of the Adriatic

Medieval Ragusa is now known as **DUBROVNIK**

CROATIA

Adriatic   Dubrovnik

Mediterranean

The motto of Dubrovnik declares that "freedom is not for sale for all the money in the world." The city unusually aroused a passion in the renowned cynic George Bernard Shaw who described the city as "a paradise on earth".

Like a fiery flower the "Pearl of the Adriatic" sits in a cerulean sea, protected by massive fortified walls, with beautiful Italianate architecture. There was an outcry throughout the world when the Serbs fired on Dubrovnik during the Balkan War because everyone knew the collective heritage was irreplaceable. Today the war damage has been extensively repaired thanks to the commitment of the local people and international aid, and the city's life has returned to normal.

A settlement known as Epidaurum was established on the mainland by the Greeks. When the Slavs invaded in 614 and conquered the place the inhabitants fled to a rocky island off the coast which today is the site of the old town of Dubrovnik. It speaks volumes for the diplomatic skills of the inhabitants that a couple of centuries later they formed a joint republic with their former enemies the Slavs settled on the mainland under the sovereignty of Byzantium.

Rivals to Venice

By the tenth century Ragusa – as Dubrovnik was then known – was an important maritime trading power that managed to retain much of its freedom through clever tactics and heavy tolls in spite of occasionally coming under Venetian, Turkish, and Hungarian rule. With its powerful fleet, Dubrovnik was a rival for Venice in the fifteenth century when the superb monasteries, churches, and palaces were built that make the city such a work of art. After a short intermezzo under Napoleon the republic came under Austrian rule in 1815 and later became part of the united Yugoslavia. Today Dubrovnik is part of Croatia and is a popular tourist destination.

Where does one start a tour of the city? The classic route is along the city walls because with every step these show off the beauty of the city. With a length of almost 1 $\frac{1}{4}$ miles (2 km) encircling the fortifications they rise up to around 80 feet (25 m) above them and are 13–20 feet (4-6 m) wide. One's eyes are constantly drawn to the view across the expanse of sea and wanders back to with fascination to the jumble of thousands of roofs.

From the fortifications you can also discern the clean lines of the city. Two main entrances, the Pile and Ploc gates lead to a car-free Dubrovnik, the heart of which clearly beats on Stradun also known as the Placa (main street) with its stores. Here where there are elegant middle class "palaces" and colorful stores past which people stroll are also the cafés where you can get a kava – coffee as black as night – where people hold discussions, and gaze at remarkably beautiful girls. It is still apparent today that the Placa was built by filling in the arm of the sea that separated the island from the mainland as it leads dead straight from the old town.

The main sights of the Sponza palace, town hall, and cathedral are close to the harbor basin. The outstanding architectural gem is the Renaissance-style Rector's palace in which the Rector once lived as the senior elected official. The spiritual heart is formed by the St. Blasius cathedral dedicated to the city's patron saint.

Bless St. Blasius

An entirely different sight awaits if you turn off onto one of the numerous side streets with their many steps winding up the hillside. Washing flutters here, women call to children, and the smell of food wafts from open doorways. If you want to get really high then climb the Sergius hill that towers 1,351 feet above the sea. From here one gets the finest view on the Dalmatian coast which also reveals that Dubrovnik has spread inland beyond the city walls with all the functional buildings needed by a city.

Bless St. Blasius people whisper faced with this segregation of the utilitarian from the island and probably hope the patron saint will continue to protect Dubrovnik. In the Middle Ages he is even supposed to have caught a cannonball fired by the enemy and effectively hurled it back. An exceptional city needs an exceptional patron saint.

BEST TIME:
The entire year thanks to a mild climate but September is the best month

ACCOMMODATION:
Hotels in the old town with dreamlike views

GASTRONOMY:
Dalmatian raw ham, sheep's-milk cheese, risotto with mussels and shrimps

SOUVENIRS:
Silver jewelry, leatherware, embroidery

FESTIVALS:
Dubrovnik Summer Festival (July–August)

SPECIAL TIP:
An evening at Marin Drzic's intimate Neo-Renaissance theater

Massive fortified walls still surround historical old town of Dubrovnik, built on its island (left)

The buildings of pale stone form narrow alleys that create an intimate atmosphere (bottom center)

The joy of life expressed by local song and dance: folk dancing is an everyday affair

The majestic Acropolis

ATHENS temple mount is a center of cult worship from Oriental history

TRAVEL
Athens has good international flight connections

BEST TIME
Temperatures can reach 104 °F (40 °C) in the shade in summer. The rainy season starts around mid-October and the weather remains damp and cool until February

ACCOMMODATION
Private hotel nights in Athens are expensive. Pre-booking is advisable. Package holidays are better value.

TIPPING
Restaurants 5-7 %, coffee waiters € 1-1.50, chambermaids € 1.50-3

The Acropolis rises majestically above modern Athens. The diagonal of the Parthenon is clearly apparent with the Erechtheion immediately in front (top)

Old town taverna in the Plaka. Guests are mainly tourists (bottom left)

The front facade of the Parthenon. The enormous temple is the most famous building of the Acropolis

The exuberant and chaotic traffic in the city center hardly touches the people in the crowd. The drone of traffic and car horns has little effect on the people in the countless sidewalk cafés. Even the businessmen who hectically weave through the mass of people seem composed in spite of their haste. The Athenian does not forget to laugh or show their disarming friendliness, or express pride in their city, which continues to grow in this new millennium.

Little remained of Athens when it became capital of Greece in 1834. Only four thousand people lived in the small row of houses on the northern hillside of the Acropolis when King Otto was imported from Bavaria as ruler of the Greeks. Initially the eighteen-year-old son of Ludwig I had to make do with a modest two-storey house while his German architects prepared plans for his palace and a new landscape for Athens.

People returned as the city was rebuilt. In 1921 the Greeks and Turks exchanged their minorities and of the half million Greeks who had to leave Asia Minor half of them poured into Athens. Then those working the land increasingly sought work in the capital and with a building boom in the 1950s the city expanded beyond all previous boundaries. By the 1960s Athens had once again become one of the most interesting metropolises of Europe. With new plans this city of one million people is on its way to becoming a modern world metropolis.

Victory against the Persians

The first blood shed over Athens was 2,500 years ago. Evidence for this are the ruins of the Acropolis, 511 feet (156 m) above the teeming city. This steep hill site attracted people from the Neolithic period for seven thousand years.

The first powerful town was built on the high plateau by Mycenaean settlers around 1400 BC. By the sixth century the Acropolis and the settlement of Athens were synonymous. For the first time people started to build on the hillside.

The golden age began with the defeat of the Persians around 500–479 BC and colonization of the Mediterranean coast by the Greeks. Athens blossomed culturally under Pericles around 450 BC and this led to the construction of the Acropolis.

Athens remained the center of philosophy and intellectualism of the Mediterranean world during Roman rule from 86 BC until well after the division of the Roman Empire. Athens became a mere provincial town in 529 with the closing of its school for philosophy.

In the following nine hundred years the land had constant new rulers and settlers until the Ottomans seized power in 1456 and held it until the War of Independence between 1821 and 1827.

In the temple city

Following independence the new capital had to cope with fourteen revolutions, occupation by German troops, and a gruesome Civil War before becoming the lively city that today attracts visitors from throughout the world.

The Acropolis is certainly the most impressive place from which no visitor can fail to take away an aura of history. Nevertheless only the faded remains are preserved of Pericles' giant and extravagant temple and the massive statues of bronze and marble that were inset with gemstones. The Propylaia, Parthenon, and Athena Nike temple are not all that has survived from the stormy past. Even in the new metro station at Syntagma square in the city center, the outline of walls provide a literally deep impression of past times and the display cases are filled with rescued treasures that the building workers found here.

The Middle Ages also left impressive buildings behind such as the Byzantine Metropolis Church from the twelfth century that was built with the rubble from ancient buildings. They stand in the shadow of the larger Metropolis cathedral in which stones were discovered in the nineteenth century from seventy earlier basilicas.

Both churches are at the edge of the Plaka, the ancient Turkish center of Athens that nestles alongside the picturesque Acropolis hill. This part of the city was all that remained when Athens became the capital city. Even when its streets are filled with tourists this part of the city still radiates its own original atmosphere.

Shining light of the Bosporus

Two thousand years of European and Asian tradition meet in **ISTANBUL**

Black Sea
•**Istanbul**
TURKEY

Mediterranean

TRAVEL
A new earthquake-proof airport came into service in 2001 with flights by all the well known international airlines. Driving in Istanbul is not advised. Car ferry from Venice and Ancona April to October take two days and three nights

BEST TIME
Best time is April-June and September-October with temperatures around 68° F (20° C). In summer often above 86° F (30° C). Rainy season November-February

ACCOMMODATION
Hotels in all price categories. Some former residences of the Sultans have been converted into modern hotels. There are some bed and breakfast places amid Byzantine and Medieval surroundings in the old town

TIPPING
A Service charge is usually included. Where not (taxis with meter, hotels, western-style restaurants) 5-10 %

If there is a city that can claim to be full of contrasts then it is Istanbul, which spans two continents. The Bosporus both separates Europe from Asia and binds them together. Paradoxically while the European way of life has become widely adopted on the Asian side, oriental traditions have been maintained on the tongue of European land known as the Golden Horn.

While women in the western parts of the city, Eyüp and Fatih, cover their heads and faces and their men wear the turban and obey the call to prayer of the muezzins from their age old minarets, smartly-dressed businessmen in gray suits and discreetly made up female students hurry through the stores and offices of the shore opposite the Golden Horn. And youth in the parks of the satellite town of Üsküdar on the other side of the Bosporus do rap dancing and skateboarding. In the brash, narrow streets of old Istanbul which mix diesel fumes with oriental smells and sea air, donkey carts compete with ramshackle trucks and sparkling shiny carriages in a chaotic jumble of traffic in order to move forward. It is this animated but also difficult tension between culture and tradition that creates the atmosphere in this city of eight million people, which has renewed itself constantly for two thousand years.

The city was only razed to the ground once. That was in 196 when the Roman Caesar Septimus Severus took his revenge for Byzantium siding against him in a civil war.

The second Rome of the East
Byzantium had 850 years of history behind it. Legend has it that Byzas, leader of the Greeks from the town of Megara, conquered the peninsula held by Thracians in 657 BC and built Byzantium.

On May 11, 330 AD the Emperor Constantine resolutely chose Byzantium as his "second Rome" but quickly renamed it Constantinople in his own honor. Sixty-five years later Constantinople became the capital of the Eastern Roman Empire.

The city reached its zenith under Emperor Justinian I in the sixth century. Many Christian churches and palaces such as the incomparable Hagia Sophia and the impressive Hippodrome stem from this time.

Constantinople fell to the Ottoman Turks in 1453 when the Ottoman army of Sultan Mehmets II conquered the city and made it capital of his realm. The Ottomans developed the classical architecture of mosques that characterize the city today. Under them the Hagia Sophia acquired its four minarets and became a mosque.

Museum of Sultan's rule
Four hundred and fifty years later the rule of the Sultans came to an end and a new secular Turkish Republic was born in 1923 that separated religion and politics. To emphasize the change the government chose Ankara as the capital and turned Istanbul as the former residence of the Sultan into a museum.

Even the Hagia Sophia lost is religious role and today is a museum although in recent time increasing numbers of Muslims come here to pray. It is certainly the largest example of Byzantine architecture. Caesar Justinia I had it built in 532 in just five years. For centuries it was the largest church of Christianity.

South of the Hagia Sophia are the extensive grounds of the Topkapi Palace. The Sultans and their four thousand servants once lived here in a bewildering complex with apparently infinite numbers of rooms – there were four hundred for the harem alone – enchanting courtyards and generously proportioned gardens. Today the Palace houses a priceless collection of jewels, porcelain, weapons, and relics of the Prophet Mohammed.

The entrance to perhaps the most bizarre attraction of Istanbul is in front of the Hagia Sophia: the Yerebatan Cistern. This was constructed in the sixth century with 336 pillars, the plinths of which are embellished with Medusa heads, that support the vaulted roof of the reservoir that can store 104,636 cubic yards of water. It is the restored part of a complete system, the construction of which was begun by Constantine in the fourth century.

The Hagia Sophia was once the largest church in Christendom. The Ottomans turned it into a mosque and built four minarets. Close by is the Topkapi Palace, former residence of the Sultans (top)

View under the dome of the Hagia Sophia. The former sacred building is now a museum

The Galata bridge crosses the Golden Horn, a small bay that branches off the Bosporus

Capital of Europe

The Grand' Place in **BRUSSELS** is one of the world's finest squares

North Sea

English Channel

Brussels

BELGIUM

BEST TIME
Spring, early summer. Virtually everyone in Brussels is on holiday in August

ACCOMMODATION
Metropole (grand hotel with Belle Epoque charm), Dorint (uniform modernity). Simpler hotels around the Grand' Place

MARKET
The largest Brussels' market is on Sundays at Marollen. Flea market at Place de jeu de Balle. Week-end antique market at Place du Grand Sablon

SOUVENIRS
Pralines from Neuhaus, Brussels' lace, speculaas (spiced biscuits)

SPECIAL TIP
The royal hot houses are cathedral-like masterpieces of glass and steel. Only open for visits between April and mid-May

The traditional guildhalls give the Grand' Place a certain something. The Flower Market is particularly picturesque (top)

The Manneken Pis is a much visited tourist attraction (bottom left)

Chopping and cafés in the Galéries Saint-Hubert (bottom center)

Built for the World Exhibition of 1958, the Atonium is now the symbol of Brussels

Sit yourself down at one of the many cafés of the Grand' Place and you feel like a guest in one of the finest salons of Europe. Festively lit, the Grote Markt glitters pure gold and guildhalls, Maison de Roi, and the town hall form a triad of Gothic, Renaissance, and Baroque. The Grand' Place is one of the finest squares of the world but also a place where history has been made. It was here that the Spanish Duke of Alba had the Lords of Egmont and Hoorn beheaded in 1568 following an uprising and it was the Grote Markt which Louis XIV fired on so mercilessly with his artillery in 1695 that it had to be almost entirely rebuilt, giving it today's unity and distinctive stringency.

Brussels has an extensive history linked to many nations. The city began its career as the metropolis of Europe in the 1950s, carefree and open-minded. Around one-third of its population has a foreign passport and it is not only in the European Parliament that many languages are spoken. With the wisdom of Solomon the choreographer Maurice Béjart wrote of the Belgian metropolis as "being beautiful without possessing beauty."

Richness from colonial past

Brussels was already prosperous in the Middle Ages thanks to the cloth trade but with Burgundian, Austrian, Spanish, French, and Dutch governors having their say which generally was not in favor of any form of independence. Following a performance of an opera celebrating liberty in 1830 the time was ripe for revolution. The Bruxellois drove the Dutch from their country and the first king in Brussels of the newly-formed monarchy was Leopold I of the house of Saxe-Coburg-Gotha.

Under his son, Leopold II, the city was rebuilt with the rule of the extended colony of the Congo financing one of the most modern cities in Europe. The largest Palais de Justice of the continent was built on the site of the gallows hill and fine museums arose on this Mont des Arts or Kunstberg (mountain of art) and an exemplary rail station. Ironically the Stock Exchange (Bourse) was built on the site of a former monastery of a mendicant order. Money and abundance characterized the buildings of the formative years that were soon to impress themselves on city's style.

Soon after this came Brussels' answer to so much pomposity. The Art Nouveau/Jugendstil movement made Brussels its center and the likes of Henry van de Velde and Victor Horta with their diversity of form created a new style of architecture. The Horta House in Rue Americaine and the unique department store Magasins Waucquez in which the Comic Museum is now housed are examples of this era. With the Avenue Brugmann and entire street of villas consists of Art Nouveau and anyone who sips a cocktail in the Hotel Metropol takes a step back to the Belle Epoque.

Floral splendor at the Grote Markt

Elegant Brussels resides in the upper town where the museums with their world-famous collections, the royal palace, but also the leading hotels and stores are to be found. It is fun to go shopping around the Avenue Louise and the Chausée de Waterloo stopping in Pain Quotidien for a second breakfast or to be pleased amid one of the planted areas that the Bruxellois are so obsessed with flowers. Perhaps one goes a little fou (crazy) when you see the Grand' Place for the second year with its floral carpet of 2,224 square yards (1860 square metre), or a fiery goblin that delights the eyes.

Finally all the roads eventually return to the Grand' Place anyway not just the four passages built in 1846 that encourage strollers. The surrounding area is known as the Ilôt Sacré (sacred isle) and actually one gets the impression of being in a parallel world because of sumptuous goods on display as one passes through the narrow alleys. At Grand Sablon one finds a square famous not only for its intimacy but also for its antique market. The Gothic facade of the church of Notre Dame du Sablon looks as if it is draped in Brussels' lace.

Evenings are best on the Sablon when the restaurants are fully occupied and the air is filled with lively conversation. Eating and drinking are special passions of the Belgians and perhaps, or so they whisper behind their hands, Brussels is the capital of Europe because the best French cuisine is not served in Paris but in Brussels.

The old world charm of Bruges

Flanders' Medieval trading center has retained its aura

BEST TIME:
The entire year. Those in the know come in fall and winter

ACCOMMODATION:
Hotel De Swaene, smaller hotels on the canals

GASTRONOMY:
Cheese croquettes, fish, sea-food, beer

SOUVENIRS:
Pralines, truffles, lace

SPECIAL TIP:
A carillon plays melodies by Bach, Mozart, or Verdi a number of times each week and also folk tunes and evergreens

A drop of Christ's blood is responsible for a unique bit of street theater in Bruges. The "jewel of Flanders" turns to is magnificently colorful past for the procession of the Holy Blood on Ascension Day. Elsewhere this would not be the spectacle it is here. Catholic Bruges is dominated by churches and chapels and the city is adorned by no fewer than six hundred small statues of the Madonna.

The finest of them was purchased for a very huge sum of money in the Middle Ages because the marble Madonna and Child was the only work of Michelangelo to leave Italy while he was alive, and since then it has struck a wistful note in the Church of Our Lady with its filigree towers. Bruges is referred to rapturously by its natives as Brugge die scone or "the beautiful Bruges," and certainly the collection of Gothic and Baroque buildings in so little space, the streets and squares are marveled at by a million visitors each year.

Blessed by storm and flood

Like swarms of bees the tourists throng the Markt with its enormous town hall, with bells chiming from its belfry, enjoy the balustrades during a fascinating tour of the city and country, admire the town hall with its Gothic facade and then visit the Heilig Blut Kapelle (chapel of the Holy blood) with its priceless relic. Above all the richness of Bruges is created by its museums. The best of these are the Groeninge Museum with its astonishing wealth of Flemish paintings, the Memling Museum in the St. Jan's Hospital and the Gruuthuse Museum with its sculpture, lace, and decorated faience pottery assembled in the finest preserved of the Gothic houses.

Bruges' grandeur results from clever calculation and diplomacy with the help of a couple of favorable strokes of fate. A breakthrough by the sea that flooded the land in the twelfth century brought Bruges close to the sea enabling large vessels to reach the town by means of an arm of the sea and a canal. Bruges became the most important trading center in the world at that time with its trade in wine and cloth and the business of exchange

proved to be so successful that today's Bourse is still an important name and the financiers of the Middle Ages can be found back among the families of the present day members. The Dukes of Burgundy with their marked interest in the esthetic also chose much-praised Bruges as their principal place of residence when they acquired the Lordship of Flanders in 1384.

Bruges basked in the brilliance of Burgundian life for at least a century before having to quit the stage. Antwerp took an increasing lead in trade and when the outlet to the sea silted up the city fell back on its faded glory. That Bruges lacked money for renovation for centuries is its greatest luck today because such a collection of buildings in the city has been preserved that attracts art lovers but also gourmets and those who frequent the bars.

Beer and beet go well together in the city, and with its superb palaces Bruges is also a stronghold of bars and discreet restaurants. Tourist can experience Bruges from the water by taking a trip to watch

the elegant frontages of houses glide by but the true enthusiast explores on foot and thereby discovers the everyday sight of the celebrated diva, the small streets beneath the walls, or the Beguinage which is best visited in the evening. For it is then this thirteenth century Medieval residence for devout women – today it is a Benedictine monastery – has a peace that transmits itself to its visitors.

Preference for winter

The route continues to the Fish Market with its halls dating from 1820 with their decorative pillars and all the delicacies of the nearby sea available. Housewives cast critical eyes and small dishes are steamily prepared in iron pans by traders before your very eyes.

The Fish Market is best during the cooler times of the year and Bruges is an ideal winter destination. Not only are you then spoiled with the golden light of evening, stews, and flickering fireplaces, you also get to speak to the people who are recovering from the great hordes. Not only can we drink a

glass with them to the return of the tourists in the spring, we can enjoy the daffodils in the Beguinage.

The old town of Bruges is built alongside canals such as the Rozenhoedkai that offers a variety of views (top)

The center of the old town is the lively Grote Markt with its many cafés and restaurants

Merchants' splendor in Flanders

ANTWERP'S fame is based on maritime trade and Flemish painting

BEST TIME
The entire year. Plenty of conviviality too in winter

ACCOMMODATION
Hotels in every category

SOUVENIRS
Diamonds, avant-garde fashion, books about art

GATRONOMY
Waterzooi (stew of chicken pieces), Frikadelle (sausage) with beer, mussels, cheese croquettes

SPECIAL TIP
Picturesque maritime museum in the old Het Steen fort by the harbor

A château for the arts? One scales the inviting flight of steps of the Royal Museum for Fine Arts in Antwerp as if for a royal reception and step with absolute reverence through the portal that is framed by massive pillars. Inside the steps merge into a hall filled with the splendor of the paintings of early Flemish masters and a solemnity to match any cathedral. Art in Antwerp is rather like a declaration of trade. The city on the Schelde coexists with art in perfect harmony.

As the "Manhattan of the Middle Ages" Antwerp was wealthier in the sixteenth century than any other European city and a major center of the western world with its 125,000 inhabitants. It was at this time that the buildings were built which today create Antwerp's scenery like the town hall, guildhalls, churches, and palaces, not forgetting the cathedral that took 269 years to complete. Besides this Antwerp's fame was also furthered by its local artists such as Anthony van Dyck, Jacob Jordaens, Frans Snyders, and above all Peter Paul Rubens and Jan Breughel whose pictures astonished the world.

Riches through its port

The brightness of its art was some consolation when Antwerp underwent a decline in the seventeenth and eighteenth centuries. The re-emergence of its port – today Antwerp is the second largest port in Europe – in the late nineteenth century ensured the city on the Schelde once again became a cultural metropolis. The railway station was built like a truly overwhelming reception hall that with its superb cupola and Neo-Baroque walls creates just as much a readiness to depart as the wide tree-lined avenues, Neo-Classical palaces, and Art Nouveau mansions. Progressive Antwerp though demanded the avant garde and hence the city became a center in the last century for experimental art. In the 1950s the Middelheim Park became an open air museum of modern sculpture without equal in Europe. In recent decades Antwerp has become a stronghold of fashion bringing a fresh spind of wit, fantasy, and elegance to haute couture. It provides shopping of the utmost quality.

It is no coincidence that the mood in the center of the city is created by the main shopping streets, and Keysersley, Leystraat, and Meir (with its former royal palace) link the grand boulevards running to the station with the Grote Markt. If you wish to spend some time in this lively part of town then you will find the population in the many bars and cafés extremely well-paid but respectful. Mockers insist the people of Antwerp have added an eleventh commandment to the ten: "Thou shall enjoy."

Lively bar scene

The Grote Markt with its 220 foot (67 m) long Town Hall that is framed by superb guildhalls with gilded statues is so close to the heart of the Flemish hedonists because they sit inside the informal restaurants eating fried shrimp when it is snowing or raining or enjoying a Trappist beer outside in the fresh air on a summer evening. The bar scene is also lively in the narrow streets surrounding the extraordinary elegance of the cathedral of Our Lady with its 403 foot (123 m) high spire (a second spire is unfinished).

One gets a glimpse of an entirely different world in the area around Pelikaanstraat close to the main station. There is the sparkle of thousands of diamonds in well-secured windows, with kosher bakers and butchers offering their wares, and men wearing broad-rimmed fur hats on their heads hurrying along the streets. Antwerp has the largest orthodox Jewish community in Europe and is also the center of the diamond trade.

Since Sephardic Jews found a new home in open-to-all-comers Antwerp following their flight 450 years ago from Spain and Portugal they have traded so successfully in cut stones that today seventy percent of the world's trade in diamonds passes through this city on the Schelde. Antwerp simply sparkles everywhere.

Town hall and guildhalls of the sixteenth century with their magnificent facades on the Grote Markt. The city's emblem of Brabos is seen on the left. Legend has it that the Roman Brabos slew a giant that hampered shipping in the Schelde (top)

Today there is a maritime museum in Het Steen, and old fort defending the harbor. It is the city's oldest remaining building.

The Leystraat and Meir are a shopping paradise and place for the people of Antwerp to stroll

Gabled houses on the canals

AMSTERDAM takes care of its heritage – from fine houses on the waterfront to houseboats in the center of the city

North Sea

Amsterdam

THE NETHERLANDS

BEST TIME
The entire year. Main season April–June

ACCOMMODATION
An hotel with a view of a gracht is a must

GASTRONOMY
Outstanding Indonesian and Vietnamese restaurants

MARKET
Flower market on the Singel

SPECIAL TIP
Concerts in the Concertgebouw of 1888 with its world-famous orchestra

If you look out of your hotel window across the sluggishly flowing water of the Herengracht in which the elegant facades of the houses, trees, and bridges are reflected then you have arrived in Amsterdam. You can also spend a couple of hours in a "brown café" and find yourself in the "liveliest city of the world." The walls are almost black with cigarette smoke, the polished beer tap is in constant use and the clacking of billiard balls sounds above the roar of laughter. There are some five hundred of these brown cafés in Amsterdam and they are all filled with people, serving as living room, information exchange, and favorite local bar.

Amsterdam vibrates with life but can also be surprisingly calm and rooted, revolutionary and insistent, exotic and tolerant. The

changing seasons on their own provide constant variety and seem more marked here. For instance when its seems all of Amsterdam are enjoying themselves skating on the frozen canals in the cold of winter, when the gabled houses are lit up by the early evening light and bridges span the canals like golden arches, then one understands why Dutch artists have painted these scenes time and again. Amsterdam is a Breughel set, even while the city pulsates with modern life.

Standing still is unknown to the principal Dutch city and boundless curiosity led to Amsterdammers pursuing the sea. They controlled the trade with the East Indies with their ships and brought spices from East Asia in the early seventeenth century to all of Europe. In the

"Golden Century" Amsterdam was the most important trading power of the world and today this city astounds people not least because it is founded on five million spruce piles.

Oddballs and artists

It was seen how well water and architecture combine on the Singel, the first of the ring of grachten that encircles this historic city and so a further three circular canals were formed with almost mathematical precision – Herengracht, Keizersgracht, and Prinsengracht – on which the fine but narrow merchants' houses were built. Simpler folk were also thought of with a place of their own which the Huguenot settlers called the Jardin but eventually became De Jordaan in Dutch. Today this is a part of the

city with houses and little courtyards peopled by oddballs and artists, with small stores and galleries. It is a village within the city with the most individualist appearance of Europe.

Cycles everywhere

Innovation and not fitting in is a trade mark of this Dutch metropolis that is not the seat of government, a role played by The Hague. But Amsterdam sets the scene though and this started a revolution in the 1960s that caused unrest throughout Europe. The Provos fought against the values by which society felt driven to grow and created a revolution with humor, bare backsides, and the challenging proposal of giving everybody a cycle to prevent traffic gridlock.

Cycling is the most popular method of getting about without government edict and cycles are also found picturesquely parked on bridges forming a method of decoration. Those with a passion for photography are spoiled for choice in Amsterdam, with more than the canals and the photogenic houseboats, the street organs, the royal

palace, the fine churches, and the "skinny bridge" or Magere brug. There are also the wide streets such as the Damrak, where people sit on terraces and watch people strolling past, and the parks such as the Vondelpark and the eccentric medieval beguinage of the Begijnhof with its cloistered calm that makes visitors feel at home.

Next to the royal palace on the Dam the museums display the riches of the city with some five hundred Rembrandt paintings in the Rijksmuseum (including The Nightwatch), the Van Gogh Museum with the world's largest collection of Dutch paintings, and the most important museum of Judaic history outside Israel.

Amsterdam has a great diversity of experiences and this includes

making new discoveries while shopping. The flea markets are famous, particularly the one on the Waterlooplein but one can also rummage in the small stores or winkeltjes that are extremely tempting while the imaginative Amsterdammers have the shrillest, most colorful, and craziest stores in Europe.

The colors of fall on the Prinsengracht close to the Noorder Markts (northern markets). Houseboats are part of the scenery of Amsterdam (top left)

The Dam Square with the royal palace is the center of the city (top right)

Without drawbridges shipping would be unable to move in Amsterdam. The "Magere Brug" or "skinny bridge" crosses the Amstel and is one of the best-maintained historical monuments

A new luster for Berlin

The old German capital benefits from the political changes in Europe

ACCOMMODATION
Forum Hotel on the Alexanderplatz with rooms on 20 floors. Cheaper bed and breakfast around the Kurfürstendamm

FESTIVALS
International Film Festival in February, Love Parade in July

GASTRONOMIC
Knuckle of pork and sauerkraut, smoked loin of pork, rissoles, curry sausage

SECRET TIP:
The Nikolai Quarter, perfect village in the center of the city

Berlin's showpiece avenue, Unter den Lindens is a Prussian creation. A mounted figure statue in front of the Humboldt University is a memorial to Frederick the Great (top)

The Potsdamer Platz that was destroyed in World War II is today a popular shopping center (bottom center)

The new cupola of the Riechtag building is accessible to visitors (bottom right)

One city has re-invented itself. No metropolis on earth has undergone such radical change as Germany's oldest and newest capital. What was gray before the wall came down is now colorful and strident, and what was chic is now totally out of fashion. Berlin now buzzes as people celebrate the tough 1920s and nasally cry out to waiters in the Hotel Adlon: "Herr Ober, Champagne."

Berlin was residence for the Electors of Brandenburg-Prussia by the seventeenth century but the new Berlin arose under the Prussian king, Friedrich Wilhelm I after 1701 and his son Frederick the Great had much built too. In 1800 Berlin's population was 172,000 and it developed increasingly as a place in which "a person could find intellect," according to Heinrich Heine. The Berlin under Wilhem basked in appearances of the Kaiser but it was also this city on the River Spree that Hitler made center of government for the Nazis.

After severe disruption through war Berlin was divided in 1945 in accordance with the Potsdam Agreement. The western part was controlled by the Allies and later by the German Federal Republic while the eastern part was controlled by the Soviet Union and in 1949 became capital of the German Democratic Republic or East Germany under Communist rule. With the erection of the wall in 1961 partition in the most literal sense became concrete and Berlin was not re-united until the bloodless revolution of November 1989. In 1999 the German Bundestag or parliament met once more in the city on the Spree.

Pearl necklace of architecture

The Unter den Linden was Berlin's magnificent boulevard and place to show off for three centuries and here one finds buildings created by

architectural geniuses such as the Alte Bibliothek (old library), Neue Wache (new guard post), the Zeughaus (armory), State Opera House, palace of the Crown Prince and the Gendarmemarkt (police market) that is a little to one side of the grand avenue. The Brandenburg Gate marks the end of Unter den Linden like a final chord. Its chariot drawn by four horses so fascinated Napoleon that after his war with Prussia he had them copied in Paris.

Central Berlin cultivates stucco

The young gravitated to the area around Den Linden and the Alexanderplatz following re-unification. Here in the quiet streets a Theodor Fontane or a Kurt Tucholsky could find fantasia and affordable accommodation with stucco, and heating by stoves.

The former Jewish quarter too around the Oranienburger Strasse and the Hackesen Höfe were rediscovered, especially when the Oriental-Moorish synagogue destroyed during the war was reopened in 1995. Today more than 12,000 Jews live in Berlin once more and are part of an energetic scene.

People see the new Berlin as a work of magic and an almost endless stream of visitors swarm all over Sir Norman Foster's rebuilt and converted Reichstag building and beneath its glass cupola. The Friedrichstrasse is once more an elegant shopping street and the Potsdamer Platz is now a new artistic Babylon with enormous buildings. Almost as intimate on the other hand as in the days of Marlene Dietrich is the Pariser Platz which the avenue of Unter den Linden shields and keeps exclusive from the government offices and contributes to the city's image with new offices for a bank by Frank O. Gehry. In the Hotel Adlon diners are accompanied by *As time goes by* as they peruse their newspapers and converse.

Parisian charm in West

The Strasse des 17 Juni also runs dead straight from the Pariser Platz to the Tiergarten, Berlin's largest park, passing victory columns and from there to Berlin's former upper class neighborhood – with Kurfürtsendamm, the Remembrance church, and Europa Center, the counterpart for the booming center. The most colorful blend in the western part of the city is Charlottenburg with its charm reminiscent of Paris, the dreamy gardens, and the cheerful

fort. The landscape of Havel towards Potsdam provides an abundance of fine mansions and temples which visitors from throughout the world regard as "Prussian arcades."

But it is the art that take first place bearing in mind three opera houses, and an extremely lively theater and cabaret scene with more than one hundred museums filling the role of prima donna. With its collection of museums recreated from old temple-like buildings including the Alten Museum (museum of the ancients), Bauhaus Archiv (archive of Bauhaus style), the National Gallery, and the Museum of the Present Day in the "Hamburger Bahnhof" Berlin is one of the world's most important centers for art.

The gallery scene in particular has exploded. Anyone not in Berlin for a few weeks will find new galleries opened up, surprising experiments, and strident happenings and new locations. The city has a hunger for life. And no day is the same as the next.

ACCOMMODATION
Traditional family hotels on the banks of the Trave and also modern luxury hotels

FESTIVALS
Schleswig-Holstein Music Festival June-August, FriendSHIP party in August, Christmas market close to the Marienkirche

GASTRONOMY
Labscous beef stew with potato, onion, beet, and gherkins, Plettenpudding, fish

SOUVENIRS
Marzipan from Niedereggger Haus in Breiten Strasse, ties of the type worn by Thomas Mann (from the Buddenbrook house), bottled Holstein delicacies such as Sauerfleisch (braised beef marinated in vinegar) and Rode Grütze (red fruit pudding)

SPECIAL TIP
Young Lübeck is found in Hüxstrasse with its many small stores and restaurants

Lübeck - queen of the Hanseatic League

Thomas Mann's Buddenbrooks survives amid the treasures of the seven towers

While other cities scratch around for a writer to associate with their town Lübeck came up trumps with a Nobel prize winner. In his family saga, *Buddenbrooks*, the author Thomas Mann, born in the Hanseatic town in 1875, made his home town come to life in the novel so well that they know what the traditional merchant town looks like in faraway Japan.

This is how it was: the Senator's family sat at table eating hearty dishes from solid silver tableware. The mighty spires of the Maria church soared outside their window and the clip-clop of horses rang out like distant music. Today one gets a sensation of hiding away and being protected in the narrow streets from the seven Gothic towers and their modest yet skillful architecture.

Lübeck first appears in history fairly late with first mentions for its success in 1159 in finally establishing itself after fires and devastation as the town of Liubice (Die Liebliche or "the pleasing"). Rebuilt in brick from now on it avoided conflagration and developed as a model of town planning for the entire Baltic region and likewise the Marienkirche under its twin spires and the twin tower cathedral. The city fathers also created a masterpiece with their town hall, with its Gothic pediment, Renaissance staircase, and elegant colonnades, that delineate the market place. In order to protect the crossing of the River Trave the Holstentor was erected between 1469 and 1478. Its inscription "Eintracht im Innern, Frieden draussen," (harmony within, peace without) promotes the city fathers' diplomacy. The salt store a few hundred yards away is a relic of the age when those possessing supplies of salt – the white gold of the Middle Ages – could become filthy rich.

The Hanseatic League of trading towns

Lübeck's wealth was derived from trade and the merchants sent their ships loaded with salt from nearby Lüneburg throughout the Baltic and as far afield as Reval and Novgorod. On the return voyage the captains brought iron, copper, fur, and amber to the Trave and with them nautical knowledge and sophistication that made Lübeck ever more successful.

In order to further their interests the merchants established a trading union and out of this arose the powerful Hanseatic League union of towns in the fourteenth century with Lübeck undisputedly as the "Hanseatic Queen" taking the leading role. After Cologne, Lübeck was at that time the next largest German town with 30,000 inhabitants. Charles V spoke respectfully to the city fathers when he visited as "You gentlemen of Lübeck."

The Hanseatic luster lasted for two hundred years before other ports developed and pushed Lübeck into the second rank. The city was severely damaged by an air raid in 1942. Following spirited rebuilding it is now such a gem that Unesco has listed it as one of the World Cultural Heritage sites. With one thousand buildings given protection as historic monuments Lübeck is the best preserved Medieval city of the Baltic region.

Culture and delicacies

Lübeck is also a modern city with great vitality beneath its red-tiled roofs. Thanks to a number of colleges, various theaters, and lively shopping scene one can enjoy modern comforts in a traditional manner. Music in particular has a prominent position in this town in which Heinrich Buxtehude first worked as an organist.

The people of Lübeck know how to live stylishly and with relish. Traditional restaurants like the Schiffersgesellschaft in the 470 year old guildhall serve dishes that entirely forget about calorie counting. And of course one drinks a robust oak-matured Bordeaux red wine.

Lübeck's fame has also increased through the konditorei business of Johann Georg Niederegger, a migrant from southern Germany, who brought his world-famous marzipan to the Trave, making Lübeck into an imaginary land of idleness and luxury. Today around a hundred varieties using his secret recipe of sugar and almonds are sold from the Niederegger Haus in Breiten Strasse and is at least as highly regarded by tourists as the stern beauty of the cathedral.

The Buddenbrook house in Mengstrasse dedicated to the writings of Nobel prize winning author Thomas Mann

The formidable Holstentor in front of the Marienkirche and the historic salt stores. (top)

This symbol of the city was built for defense between 1469 and 1478

The von Höveln Gang is a narrow street with simple old houses (left)

The ancient Markt or market is in front of the town hall with its elegant Renaissance staircase.
The Marienkirche is in the background

Hanseatic trading splendor

HAMBURG'S greatness can be seen around the Alster

BEST TIME
Spring, summer, fall

ACCOMMODATION
Grand hotels like the
Atlantic or cheaper ones
near the main station

SOUVENIRS
Ships in bottles,
sea-going sweaters,
English gentleman's
clothing, haute couture

GASTRONOMY
Pannfisch, Labskaus
(beef stew with
potatoes, onions,
gherkins, and beet)

FESTIVAL
Port anniversary (May)
and the Christmas
market

The town hall has more rooms than Buckingham Palace and the city has more bridges than Venice. The Hamburg merchants were clearly a self-confident lot who appear not to have been greatly troubled.

The city is cool, not just because of the prevailing west wind but also because of architecture that pushes everything aside that stands in the way of progress. Though the sober reckoning of the Hanseatic merchants was right for no other German city today is and elegant or aesthetic.

A fundamental part of the townscape are the malls now spread throughout the city. In 1980 the Hansa district was opened as the longest shopping mall in Europe, bringing an area under a glass atrium that had previously consisted of individual sites. By combining traditional bricks with glass and marble the splendor of Hanseatic architecture was so effectively captured that this style has also become a characteristic of the city. Today more than fifteen of these "galleries" provide for relaxed shopping that provides an alternative for a stroll to the traditional Jungfernstieg boulevard.

One of these Passagen, as the Germans call them, exits to the Inner Alster, that expanse of water in the city in which the surrounding tall office blocks, Hotel Vier Jahreszeiten, and delightful cafés are reflected. The aquamarine blue of this city landscape is partly formed by the adjoining Outer Alster with its surface of 405 acres (164 ha) making it possible to sail after work.

The Alster provides fun but the wealth is created on the Elbe. Once mainsails piloted their way across this broad expanse of water but today container ships with gigantic cargoes dock here. The port accounts for a considerable proportion of the city and is still the most important source of work in the city.

Joining the Hanseatic League
The good people of Hamburg needed a little coaching in the twelfth century when their charter from King Barbarossa (Frederick I) vanished and they replaced it with an improved forgery since this guaranteed ships passage to the mouth of the Elbe, the right to catch fish, and freedom from liege to the local ruler which were the basis for the city's economic development. The

joining of the Hanseatic League in 1342 gave such excellent trade relations that Hamburg quickly outstripped Lübeck.

The nineteenth century brought a golden age with passenger sea travel between North and South America largely developing through the port of Hamburg. Even the mighty Chancellor Bismarck had to yield to the mighty Hamburg when he entered a customs agreement in 1888 when Hamburg was granted free port status.

Today the cathedral-like warehouses still dominate the view in the storage area of the port in which goods are held duty free. In World War II the city was severely damaged but the economic miracle quickly restored it to one of Europe's wealthiest cities and a popular tourist destination for people from all over the world.

The Reeperbahn originally attended to the yearnings of sailors after long voyages and although the big ships now berth for unloading in the modern outer docks there is still the legendary mixture of jet-

ties, ship's masts and hooters, and screeching seagulls.

The Fischmarkt and the Reeperbahn are also legendary. The latter is the most famous pleasure district of the world which each evening summons a gaudily colored procession and offers the inexpensive and brilliance but also human company and exotic pleasures. Recently the Reeperbahn has also attracted people to its theaters like the Schmidt's Tivoli and the temple of music that is the Opera House.

Where the Beatles played

It is not far from St. Pauli to the Elbchaussee with its mansions, parks, and gardens, that runs towards the former fishing village of Blankenese – the "Naples of the north" – that can be explored up and down its many steps. Back in the city one can devote oneself to art since the area around the main station has five distinguished museums that are just as attractive as the diversity of galleries in the select Harvestehude quarter and Pöseldorf.

But Hamburg also has nooks

and crannies and in parts of the city such as the Karoline quarter the image is quite different. Here one finds stores meeting a diverse assortment of sub-cultures, brash cafés, amid the multi-cultural neighborhood in which people from many nations live. The city in which the Beatles kick-started their career in the 1960s still fanatically cultivates a traditional openness towards the world.

Panoramic view of Hamburg across the Inner Alster to the jetties at Jungfernstieg (top left)

The cathedral-like warehouses of the storage area of the port are famous (bottom right)

The Grosse Freiheit (great freedom) is home to the infamous night clubs of the red light district of St. Pauli. Salambo has been famous for decades.

Bavaria's star glitters

MUNICH has the right setting for everyone with its old royal brewery, produce market and English garden

BEST TIME
Summer for the Englischen Gartens, winter for the cultural offerings

ACCOMMODATION
Hotel Vier Jahreszeiten is Munich's fin-de-siècle stronghold, Bayerische Hof is a superior hotel. Cheaper hotels in Schwabing

FESTIVAL
February carnival (Fasching), Oktoberfest (mid September), Christmas market (Christkindlmarkt) in December

GASTRONOMY
Weisswürste (veal sausage), pretzels, beer, dumplings, and sauerkraut

SPECIAL TIP
The Städtische Galerie in Lensbachhaus contains many works by the Expressionists

Leopoldstrasse and the Church of Our Lady in the center of Munich with backdrop of the Alps (top)

Unrestrained Bavarian zest for life in the beer tents of the Munich Beer Festival (Oktoberfest) (bottom left)

The Baroque Schloss Nymphenburg is surrounded by extensive gardens

The Bavarian Crown Prince promised a great deal when he announced: "I want to make Munich a city that Germany shall honor, the like of which has not been seen in Germany or in Munich." As King Ludwig I from 1825 he had the Königsplatz and Odeonplatz, Ludwigstrasse, Pinakotheken, Feldherrnhalle, Siegestor, Ruhmeshalle, and quite a lot of churches built, and converted his residence, putting his words into action so that he bears the title of Germany's biggest commissioner of art. In addition he moved the University of Landshut to Munich and fully pursued his love of beautiful women.

That Munich sparkles today – which given the bright domes is quite true – is not entirely due to Ludwig alone since the Elector of Wittelsbach first introduced a wealth of Baroque to Munich in the seventeenth century. Bavaria first became a kingdom in 1806. Thanks to outstanding architects the Nymphenburger Schloss arose as a Baroque marvel and the Theatiner church was a glorious act of gratitude for the birth of a crown prince.

The architects introduced Rococo decoration as the highest expression of their art to produce masterpieces like the Asam church, the St. Annen church, the ornate chambers, and the indisputable stronghold of Rococo that the Amilienburg is in Munich. Although the Cuvillies Theater was destroyed during the war its interior fittings were safely stored and it is once again a dream of red and gold that nowhere else in Munich can equal.

Favored place to live

The city has more single people than any other German town and beer gardens so huge that they could accommodate entire small towns. Zest for life is a characteristic of Munich and enjoyment and pleasure are the most sought after qualities. The attractive siting of the city undoubtedly stands the Münchner in good stead since the city has a very sociable relationship with the River Isar. The river winds like a snake for almost 9 miles (14 km) through the green parts of Munich and shows due respect to the Englischen Garten (English garden). The popularity of Munich as a place to live owes much to the valuing of time off and it is precisely the Englischen Garten with its two-hundred-year-old trees, the Monopterus "sun temple", and the extensive areas of grass that make a vacation possible right in the center of the city. Shopping too is great with the Produce market and Italian market with magnificent Bavarian sausage, fragrant bread, and large white radishes more then three feet (one metre) in length, all typical of Munich. The former artists' neighborhood of Schwabing is an attractive part of town with its bars and small stores that dress not just students but also the glitterati.

Of all Munich's grand streets the Maximilianstrasse serves most as fashion catwalk. Both Pinakotheken create their own world and are the prima donna among the city's fifty museums. Those who enjoy theater are also well served since Munich has more performance venues than any comparable German city.

There are still other stars that glisten. The Bavarian capital is held in high regard for its cooking yet while you eat Italian food along the Isar – and this is the true home of the Münchner for a third of the inhabitants were born here – it is during an afternoon in the beer garden that one really experiences freshness. Seated with simple dishes you can enjoy the shadow play of the chestnut trees, drink your beer and truly delight in what goes on at the neighboring tables. Many beer gardens allow you to bring your own snacks because this is a long-held tradition in Munich.

The visitor quickly notes tradition is an immutable law in this provincial capital. At any rate there are still tailors making bespoke lederhosen – the Bavarian costume – the Hofbrauhaus or former royal state brewery and the volumes they shift, oompah bands and dirndl clothing for Sundays. And last but not least people come from all over the world to celebrate the popular Oktoberfest here.

"Florence" on the banks of the Elbe

DRESDEN'S Brühl's Terraces, the "Zwinger", and Semper Opera House are legendary

BEST TIME
Spring, summer and fall. Rich cultural offerings in winter

SOUVENIRS
Meissen Porcelain

FESTIVALS AND MARKET
International Dixieland Festival, Elbhang festival on the slopes overlooking the Elbe between Pillnitz and Dresden, Christmas Market

FOOD AND DRINK
Saxon sauerbraten (beef marinated in vinegar), pickled egg with bacon sauce. Dresdner Christstollen (special Christmas cake), Radeburger beer, wine from the slopes of the Elbe

SPECIAL TIP
Paddle-steamer trips on the Elbe, Pfundt's Molkerie (dairy) with the dairy story told in thousands of Jugendstil tiles

The old town bank of the Elbe with the cathedral, August bridge and Semper Opera House in the background (top)

The Semper Opera House with square in front of it (bottom left)

The Baroque buildings of the Zwinger personify the unity of architecture and garden design

More than 350 children were said to have witness horseshoes being bent with bare hands. Friedrich August II (1670–1733) Elector of Saxony and king of Poland after 1697 was so blessed with bodily strength that he was also known as "The Strong." The ruler with the muscular biceps also had other gifts: he was determined to create a "Venice of the north" from his residence on the Elbe, wanted to outdo the court in Berlin – in which he succeeded – and to bring the luster of Versailles to the Elbe.

Since his son, Friedrich August III (1696–1763) was also an enthusiast for the arts, the wonder of Dresden came into being but the nickname "Venice of the north" eluded him. The German philosopher Johann Gottfried Herder had effusively named it "Elbflorenz" (Florence of the Elbe) and this name got wider acclaim as the "most beautiful town of Germany" when it was reduced to rubble and ashes on February 13, 1945 by Allied bombing.

Protestant "St. Peter's" cathedral

Today Dresden is rebuilding, hewing and sawing sandstone and even repairing the destroyed Frauenkirche (Church of Our Lady), the Protestant's "St. Peter's" cathedral as a symbol of peace and a new beginning. The Dresden-born author Erich Kästner wrote: "History, art and nature hang over city and valley like a chord bewitched of its harmony," adding: "A marvelous city and not a museum that happens to be occupied by Dresdeners."

Indeed Dresden is not a museum, although art and town life coexist alongside one another. From the Brühl's Terraces one can promenade in royal gardens and palace, royal church, and Augustus bridge that seem mere backdrops for the river slowly flowing by.

Europe's finest square

There is a broader harmony on the Theaterplatz, for around this square – one of Europe's finest – dance the galleries of paintings, the Semper Opera, the guardhouse by the architect Schinkel, and the Taschenberg palace that has been resurrected as a luxury hotel. Courtly elegance also oozes from the Zwinger fortress built between 1710 and 1728. It is a perfect symbiosis of architecture and garden design and such a perfect open air party place that August the Strong celebrated the marriage of his son to the Austrian emperor's daughter here. No fewer than 60,000 candles lit the enormous feast.

Things started modestly alongside the Elbe and the settlement is first-mentioned in 1206 simply named "Drezdzany" after the original Slavic inhabitants. Dresden soon acquired its first courtly gloss in the thirteenth century, leading in 1300 to the founding of the Kreuz school. The city was then rebuilt in the sixteenth century as principal residence with pompous palace buildings in Renaissance style and later masterfully extended by August the Strong in Baroque fashion. The discovery of European porcelain contributed greatly to the rise of Saxony. Today such porcelain is

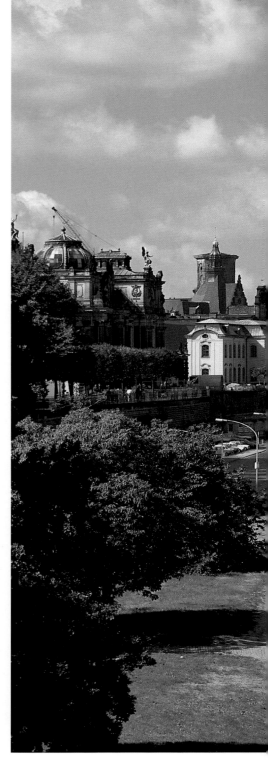

still crafted around Meissen of the type of genuine Meissen favored for their tables by emperors and kings. The Stadtpavillon houses the world's largest collection of porcelain and in the prince's palace the eight hundred year history of Saxony is depicted on 25,000 Meissen tiles.

City of music and art

Dresden is particularly an art and music city of the highest reputation. Not just that the city has built a perfect collection over hundreds of years beneath its "green arches": Raphael's Sistine Madonna can be admired in the Gemäldgalerie (gallery of paintings) and the formation of Die Brücke (the bridge) group of artists in 1905 led to a rich expressionist inheritance. In addition the city sings and swings. The Kreuz choir with its seven hundred years of tradition, the Semper Opera with the State Orchestra and

Philharmonie ensure the boom of musical tourism.

But there are also more profane pleasures. Sauerbraten (marinated beef), Quarkkeulchen (curd cheese drumsticks), and crispy duck do not taste as good elsewhere as in one of the many beer gardens with a cooling breeze from the Elbe. Many traditional bars and restaurants are found in the "new town" or Neustadt that was built over three hundred years ago. Together with the elegant boutiques of the Königstrasse and small theaters and restaurants they give a buzz to the city. From the right bank of the Elbe Canaletto painted his famous view of the city which was an illusion hovering before the eyes of all lovers of Dresden following the city's destruction. Today the city is almost totally back in force.

BEST TIME
The entire year but Lake Zurich gives the city a special charm in summer

ACCOMMODATION
Luxurious hotels like Dolder and Baur au Lac. Hotel Zum Storchen offers old-world Zurich flair. There are comfortable guest houses overlooking the lake

FESTIVAL
Mardi Gras (Tuesday before Lent), Sechseläuten (Six Bells) Festival with colorful procession of the guilds in April

SOUVENIRS
Folk art, clocks, jewelry

GASTRONOMY
Zurich schnitzels with Rösti (thinly sliced fried potato), fondue, fish from the lake

SPECIAL TIP
Pure nostalgia: the fire-engine red Polybahn cable cars have been running from the central station to the Technical University ETH since 1899

The well-mannered Swiss

Kings, diplomats, bohemians, and the financial aristocracy choose **ZURICH** as their meeting point

If you approach Zurich by ship you will get an impressive view of the soft silhouette of the city and the green promenades on the shore. If you later stroll along the Limmat that divides Zurich in two like a smaller version of the Grand Canal or see the towering large minster, when you are up and down steps in the old town, or gazing at the jumble of roofs then you will understand why the author Gerhart Hauptmann enthused about the "unique spirit of Swiss bourgeois."

Zurich it is said is a large-sized small town or a small-sized city and indeed when you consider the huge amounts of money that are handled in the world's biggest store of money and through the veritable International airport of Kloten...yet Switzerland's largest city of 350,000 people quickly shrinks back to a comfortable size. Much to the pleasure of its inhabitants who feel pretty good under the lime and chestnut trees and very proud that it is possible to take a swim in the lake during their lunchbreak.

The location tempted the Romans who built a castle to defend themselves on the banks of the Limmat. Following the occupation of Roman territory by the Alemannians from the fifth century of the former Turicum the town slowly flourished and was formed into a free city state in 1218. In 1351 the city joined the Swiss Confederation and after bitter struggles finally gained a leading role. Nevertheless Berne rather than Zurich was chosen as the capital when the Swiss Republic was formed in 1848. Zurich remains the largest Swiss city and has developed into one of the world's leading financial centers.

Destination for educational travelers

Right from the beginning of the eighteenth century the Swiss Confederation was a destination for those traveling to educate themselves and from the mid nineteenth century it was regarded as the height of chic to pay the city on the Limmat a visit. The Hotel Baur au Lac was built in classical style in 1844 and became a home for queens, diplomats, the aristocracy, and Bohemians. They lived idyllically alongside the blue lake, with

luxury, with just the boats of the big houses, with just the ponderous chiming of bells from the old town. But artists and writers were also drawn to Zurich and it became the capital of the Dadaists with the forming of the Cabaret Voltaire in the Spiegelgasse. Later the Café Odeon was where the exiled writers could be found. No other theater in Europe had the abundance of intellectual talent at their command as the Zurich Schauspielhaus with those who fled here between 1933 and 1945.

Trade and finance

Zurich already enjoyed an economic boom with industrialization and when the rail station was opened in 1871 the city's international trade flourished. Following the example of the Parisian boulevards the road from the station towards the lake (Bahnhofstrasse) was stylishly planted with lime trees. This street is still the nation's showcase and one of the most elegant shopping streets of the world. The big fashion names and fur couturiers have their establishments here and cafés offer hot Schoggi (hot chocolate) and it is still a pleasure to stroll along the Bahnhofstrasse when the limes are in blossom. Just a few steps remove you from the dominance of the large buildings of the big banks.

One quickly notices that tradition is rigidly upheld in Zurich and the same is true of their architectural inheritance. The Meisen town hall and guildhall, the church of St. Peter, the Zurich town hall with the finest Baroque hall in Switzerland, the Grossmünster (large minster church), and the Fraumünster (noble women's church) with window by Chagall, the Wasserkirche ("water" church), and the Neo-Baroque Opera House represent the same kind of continuity as the Kronenhalle restaurant in which you can enjoy food surrounded by original pieces of modern art. Art is highly regarded in Zurich and the collection in the Kunsthaus form one of the highlights of the European museum scene.

Zurich is also a stronghold of youth culture. The sub culture constantly seeks out new places and young people remain non conformist where other quasi revolutionaries long ago became leaders.

The Grossmünster dominates the old town, the Limmat, and Lake Zurich. Ulrich Zwingli who led the Reformation in Switzerland preached at this church (top)

Bahnhofstrasse was built along the lines of Parisian boulevards. It is now the world's most elegant shopping street (left)

Sidewalk cafés and restaurants invite one to linger in the narrow streets of the old town

City work of art of the Swiss Confederation

BERNE unites the modern awareness of life with that of the Middle Ages

"Berne is Berne like God is God," goes the saying but they also say that the city always bears a smile on its face. The Swiss capital is an institution with is palatial Federal Parliament building in which the country is governed while by comparison the people of the Aare appreciate an easy manner. Casonova spoiled himself in the baths here, the daughter of the Russian Czar, Anna Feodorovna laid out a romantic garden in Berne, and Lenin industriously wrote his philosophical books.

That is all in the past say the students. They are more interested in the fact that one can so easily swim in the river – in the Europe's earliest river bathing lido. The River Aare with its crystal clear glacial water flows through Berne in a large sweep making it ideal to view the city from the water.

A town was established on a spur of rock high above the Aare in 1191 that was granted rich privileges by Friedrich von Hohenstaufen. The town lived from foreign trade and also the income from markets dues levied. The Bernese were not enthusiastic salesman, rather good administrators and later also excellent politicians. Above all they were talented town planners. The Markstrasse was built 78 feet (24 m) wide in the Middle Ages, in line with today's freeways.

Colonnades and arcades

When a fire destroyed almost the entire town in 1405 Berne was rebuilt in its present layout. A hundred years later the buildings rose anew in sandstone and huge colonnades spanned the wide streets to form arcades under which one can stroll with dry feet. Berne built almost four miles of covered walkways in the Middle Ages while most metropolises first created galleries in the nineteenth century: a rain and heat defying and extremely communicative shopping paradise.

Berne was further enhanced in the sixteenth century with a clock tower with a superb astronomical clock as a striking centerpiece of the town. Fountains were also created to beautify the city with masterful wooden watering places including the Zähringer and Simson

fountains. The ideas and spirit of the French Revolution reached Berne where people met in coffee houses and directed their attention afresh to the city's development. The facades were altered to acquire French style and the interiors were furnished with fine carpets and fabrics.

But France did not just contribute such a fine way of life. Napoleonic troops occupied Berne for five years and even carried off the city's treasures to Paris. The demand for Berne to be the Swiss metropolis did the city no harm and in 1848 it officially became the Federal capital with the Federal Parliament building being built fifty years later. The country's affairs are regulated in the plenary chamber beneath a huge painting of the Alps.

Brown bears as symbol

Like New York, Berne's Medieval grid of streets and the market are so laid out that it is easy to find your way. The market is the most opulent broad and wide weekly market. Berne's finest street is the Märitsgasse with a building line that is so unifying one can recognize what the city architect had in mind for the collective impression. In the surrounding area there is much worth seeing including Einstein's house (the Theory of Relativity dates from the eight years Einstein stayed in Berne), the town hall, the corn exchange, the clock tower, and not least the church of St. Vinzenz that is the finest late Gothic basilica in Switzerland.

A distinctive feature is the former tanner's district of Matte that teems with small cafés and avantgarde theaters. Berne is famous for its Kellertheater but even more famous for its bears. Brown bears in a wide moat have been the emblem of the town since 1441 and the entire city celebrates on Easter Monday when their offspring are shown off.

Berne is also passionate about art. Paul Klee spent his boyhood and youth here and Berne was also the first place where the Romanian artist Christo wrapped up a building when he wrapped the Kunsthalle in the early 1970s. Don't let anyone suggest the Bernese are behind the times.

BEST TIME
The entire year

ACCOMMODATION
Grand Hotel Bellevue Palace. Cheaper hotels in the old town and surrounding area

SOUVENIRS
Swiss hand crafts, antiques, chocolate, Bernese gingerbread

GASTRONOMY
Bernese Rösti (thinly sliced fried potato), Bernese plate (sauerkraut with sausage, meat and ham), liver marinated in vinegar, meringues

FESTIVAL
Gassenfasnacht (carnival in February), International Bernese Dance Days (August-September), Onion Market (last Monday in November)

The spire of St. Vinzenz soars majestically above the city that sits in a wide bend in the River Aare (top)

The clock tower on Marktgasse dates from the sixteenth century. The Zähringer fountain can be seen in the foreground (bottom left)

The Federal Parliament has been the center of Swiss democracy since 1900

Vienna keeps the waltz step

Austria's capital still bears signs of a glorious past

BEST TIME
The entire year but the city blossoms in spring. The high season for culture is winter

ACCOMMODATION
Luxury hotels like the Bristol, Imperial, and Sacher but also less expensive hotels

MARKET
Naschmarket for everything that makes a gourmet's heart beat faster. Art and antique market along the Danube Canal

SOUVENIRS
Recordings of the famous New Year's Day concerts, Austrian wine

GASTRONOMY
Wiener Schnitzel with potato and gherkin salad, fried chicken in breadcrumbs, pastries, Bohemian and Hungarian specialties

World famous "temples of culture" lie around the Ring, that encircles the city center, such as the Opera House, the Hofburg (with Schauspiel theater), and shown here left the Museum of Art History (Kunsthistorische Museum) with its sophisticated fountain

What exaggeration, what magnificence! The entrance to the Spanish Riding School in the royal palace in Vienna was created by the genius architect Fischer von Erlach in 1730 with galleries and enormous chandeliers as though it was the throne room. If you see Lipizzaner stallions pirouette and enthuse about the harmony between horse and rider then you have arrived in Vienna. You could also order a Kleinen Braunen in a coffee house, peruse the newspaper, and after a thorough bout of ill temper establish that there is absolutely nothing in the paper.

Of European cities, Vienna is the most confusing and with a quickly spun waltz one can completely lose their sense of direction. Snide humor and delicacies or suddenly high art, the sound of opera and Beethoven's symphonies, Sissi's misfortune and the lightness of being in the Prater: Vienna remains Vienna. But the city of 1,650,000 people and almost half its area covered with greenery first needs to be made sense of. That is something hardly anybody manages to do.

Bulwark against the Turks

Vienna first appears in history when the Austrian governor, originating from Franconia, moved his residence to the town in 1156. His court soon became a center of good company and famous minnesingers (German lyric poets and singers) such as Walther von der Vogelweide drew a colorful crowd of carefree courtiers. After the Babenberger line came to an end in 1246 the Habsburgs appeared on the scene and they considerably extended the domain of the Danube monarchy from Vienna – in particular as a bulwark against the Ottoman Turks. The monarchy survived until the emperor abdicated in 1918 and Austria became a republic.

Of the Austrian emperors the one who stands out is Maximilian I who was the first to use the politically astute marriage with his alliance with Maria of Burgundy. (Tu, felix Austria, nube). And Maria Theresa of course who defended her empire against half of Europe despite the

consequences of the loss of Silesia. At the end there was Franz Joseph I, a monarch with power who ruled for almost seventy years, who had a lasting effect on Vienna. The gray emperor, who always wore uniform, still dominates the city today, with greetings from bags to T-shirts and even cuts a fine figure molded in marzipan.

It is the imperial Vienna that dazzles and creates the impression that everything here moves in waltz time. The Hofburg palace is listed by Unesco as a site of world cultural heritage. It has 2,600 rooms, in-

cluding the showpiece hall of the National Library and the crypt with emperors' sarcophaguses that is just as impressive a relic of the Habsburgs as the highly historic Heldenplatz. The superb Belvedere Palace and Schloss Schonbrunn also have a story to tell of Vienna's glittering past. The Ring with is grand buildings has offerings like the Burg Theater, opened in 1888 and the Opera House. Under sponsorship of the imperial court many churches were built, including the outstanding St. Stephen's cathedral. The horse-drawn carriages wait at

the cathedral to take you at a light trot through the elegant streets on a journey back in time.

The coffee house as heritage

The other side to Vienna is not less exciting though. This is the city of the artist and architect who with the Viennese Secession movement held exhibitions in their Jugendstil building that were shrouded in scandal and ensured excitement. The literary figures have left the coffee house behind as their heritage and the theaters too at which famous writers such as Arthur Schnitzler, Ödon von Horvath, and Thomas Bernhard have worked in Vienna. Most of all though Vienna was the European metropolis of music with Haydn, Mozart, Beethoven, Schubert, Brahms, and Mahler all having composed masterpieces in Vienna. At the Opera House and in the Goldenen Saal of the Musikverein this musical inheritance is stylishly upheld.

But there is also the light-hearted Vienna that can be found at the Prater and at the Naschmarkt, in the informal bars known as Beisl, at the Heuriger inns serving new harvest wine and food, on sausage stalls, and increasingly frequently also in the colorful parts of the suburbs in which today an increasingly lively night-club scene has developed.

One is tempted further and further away from the "golden Vienna" and ought to be present, at least as onlooker, when the ladies (not in trousers suits, always in evening dress) and the gentlemen of the society (in tails) drive up to a court ball, a soft murmur of "Wien, Wien, nur du allein..." seems to hang over the roofs and domes of the city.

Viennese literati made the coffee house their place of work. The Café Central is still a legendary institution (top right)

The Hofburg is the center of imperial Vienna. A glimpse of the entrance shows the size of the building.

A symbol of Baroque

SALZBURG'S position as a city of culture gains new impetus from the Festival

BEST TIME
The entire year. The town is overrun in summer

ACCOMMODATION
Grand Hotel Österreichischer Hof and cheaper hotels in the suburbs

FESTIVALS
Mozart Week (January), Easter Festival, Salzburg Festival (late July–end of August)

GASTRONOMY
Salzburg Nockerln (dumpling soufflés), Krautspatzen (blobs of cabbage), pastries such as plum and poppy

SOUVENIRS
Mozart "balls" from Konditorei Fürst, artistic hand-crafted items, traditional costume

SPECIAL TIP
The Salzburg Marionette Theater with performances of operas

The fortress of Hohensalzburg is like a huge sentinel above the town. Beneath the domes of the Baroque churches determine the panorama (top)

Mozart's music is omnipresent. Even street musicians are occasionally virtuosos (bottom left)

The Mirabel Gardens are among Salzburg's finest. In the background are the dome and twin towers of the cathedral

On a warm summer evening and with the backdrop of the Salzburg cathedral a gigantic theatrical feast is provided. People drink and yell in the company of the wealthy Mr. Jedermann (Everyman), God, and the world, who faces up to life but without realizing his time was over long ago.

Performances of Hugo von Hofmannsthal's Jedermann (Everyman) seem absolutely right for this city with its eighty fountains, thirty-six churches and five monasteries and convents that could be a smaller Rome. The city wavers between yesterday and today and is used as a setting for the world famous Festival that Alexander von Humboldt once counted as the world's finest. The theatrical genius of Max Reinhardt recognized the stage-like qualities of the town with his expert's eye and the Festival was born. The cries of Everyman first echoed across the cathedral square on August 22, 1920 and since then the work has formed part of the otherwise varied and star-studded repertoire.

More than two hundred productions are offered annually these days at ten performance venues and the high level of musical and theatrical presentation makes Salzburg one of the most important world festivals – with glittering first performances but also as a meeting place for prominent persons.

The music of Mozart dominates the festival – the genius of a composer was born in Salzburg, discovered here, developed his art and his own individual "musical footprint" and then resigned from service to the Prince-Archbishop. Mozart shrugged this off, maintaining that Salzburg "is not the place for my genius."

All is forgiven today and Mozart is everywhere. The house in which he was born and his later home can be visited and his likeness goes all over the world as the famous chocolate ball known as Mozartkugeln.

Wealth founded on salt

The people of Salzburg quickly gained a reputation as efficient businessmen and the first wealth of this region was founded on salt that was excavated between 900 and 40 BC. This "white gold" was also the reason for a settlement to be founded on the banks of the Salzach river in 7 AD that made a living from trading salt and marble. At the same time the foundation by Bishop Rupert of Worms of a monastery here set the foundations for Salzburg's importance as a spiritual and cultural center. In the

thirteenth century the archbishop of the region also extended his power to becoming its ruler and he enlarged the fortifications of Hohersalzburg which have since served as a symbol high above the town. The era of Baroque and Rococo architecture led to the creation of buildings that make Salzburg so unique.

Under Prince-Archbishop Wolf Dietrich von Rateneau the cathedral was dedicated in 1628 as the first Baroque building north of the Alps. Eighty years later, with the Kollegienkirche (Collegiate church) of Johann Bernhard Fischer von Erlach, a further magnificent edifice was created that with the Residence, fountains, and castles makes a work of art of the city.

Then, like many other towns in the modern age Salzburg became somewhat sleepy. Following the dissolution of the principalities and the accession to Austria in the nineteenth century Salzburg slumbered only to awake when the Festival cast its eyes on the view alongside the Salzach river.

Nature and art united

Salzburg is confined between the Mönchsberg and Kapuzinerberg. The best vistas of town and valley are from the vantage point of the Kapuzinerberg where you will appreciate, as the composer Franz Schubert did when he praised them, the gardens, the castles, the quality, the river, and also the Alps towering like sentinels. This feeling of nature uniting with art is equally felt in the parks and gardens such as Schloss Hellbrunn with its opulent waterworks or in the park of Schloss Mirabell with its superb gardens including the dwarfs garden with Baroque statuettes that seems created for a small minuet.

Music and the art of living come together well in Salzburg. Salzburg dumpling soufflés known as Nockerln are created from candyfloss and are objects of great temptation for the palate, like apricot dumplings and nut horns. This elegant city on the other hand shows its indigenous face with krautspatzen (blobs of cabbage), sour sausage, and dumplings. Finally you can enjoy unforgettable hours in coffee houses with their Thonet chairs, newspapers, excellent speciality coffees, and truly special talents. The most elegant of them are Tomaselli and Bazar. Here during Festival one can be Everyman without the need for greasepaint. With a cup of Milchkaffee or milky coffee of course.

North Sea

Prague
CZECH REPUBLIC

Moldau murmurs for golden Prague

The Czech capital is a glittering metropolis in Central Europe once more

ACCOMMODATION
Grand Hotel Pařiž near the state reception hall. Cheaper small hotels in the old town

SOUVENIRS
Hand blown glass, glass crystal, garnet jewelry, Becherovka "herbal liqueur"

GASTRONOMY
Dumplings, cabbage, roast pork, roast beef lights (lung), Prague ham, pastries

FESTIVALS
Prague Spring, International Music Festival mid May–early June

SPECIAL TIP
Bertramka Mozart Museum in the summer home of the Dušek family where Mozart was often a guest

The Charles' Bridge with its statues of the saints is the most popular thoroughfare of Prague. The road passes through the ancient city gate to the Staré Město (Old Town) (right)

View of the old town (Staré Město) with the town hall tower and Týn church (bottom right)

The light of evening catches the roofs of the historic city center and truly makes Prague a golden city

Mozart fell in love with Prague as if it were a lover. For Franz Kafka who was born close to the ring of Old Town on the other hand it was a tenacious little old lady who grabbed hold with her talons and never more let you go. For most people the city of a hundred spires though is more a miracle than reality. No comparable city in Europe possesses such a unified preserved Medieval heart as golden Prague. With the Hradčany it also has unique castle grounds. The Charles bridge is listed by Unesco as an outstanding example of secular Gothic architecture.

If you visit Prague you can do no better than pay a visit first to the Charles bridge, for this offers the most outstanding view of the city and the Hradčany. Here too much of Prague's history has been played out and it is where kings and emperors entered. It is also where the priest Nepomuk was thrown in the river when he refused to reveal the secret confession of his queen. A bronze high above the river now embodies the unyielding people of Prague which has also produced the likes of the Reformer Jan Hus.

In the ninth century Prague consisted of forty fortified courtyards. It developed into a lively settlement between the Hradčany and Vyšehrad forts and Malá Strana (Lesser Town), and acquired a town charter in 1257. It flourished culturally for the first time when Emperor Charles IV chose it as his residence and gave a signal with the founding of a university in 1348.

Rudolf II, the only Habsburg to reside in Prague, polished the golden luster and added a distinctive Renaissance structure to the Hradčany. Prague was hit hard by the Thirty Years War and the city only flourished again when the separate local authorities of Staré Město (Old Town), Malá Strana (Lesser Town), and Nové Město (New Town) combined together with the Josefov (Josefstadt).

In 1918 Prague became the capital of Czechoslovakia and after World War II came under Soviet control. The world looked on in 1968 as troops from the Warsaw Pact forcibly brought the "Prague Spring" to an end. In 1991 Prague became capital of the new Czech Republic that is governed from Hradčany.

Art Nouveau on Wenceslas Square

Many ways lead across Prague and many eras have left behind their traces. Next to the Charles Bridge is the ring road of the old town where Prague's heart beats – strongly and loud in the traveling months and subdued and quiet in the winter. Around the market place with the Týn church, St. Nicholas, the Jan Hus memorial, town hall, and astronomical clock one can dive into a secretive jumble of streets where there are small theaters but also stores for glass, garnet jewelry, and marionettes. Prague is a theatrical city and becomes so wrapped up in its drama that students are dressed in historical costumes to advertise

opera performances. Don Giovanni strolls across Wencelas Square alongside the Queen of the Night and bows gallantly for tourist from Wales and Bavaria.

Hemmed in by Art Nouveau buildings, Wencelas Square is very closely tied to Prague's history. It was here that the Republic was declared and where the Prague Spring was ended in blood and the revolution twenty-one years later was peacefully achieved. A hundred thousand demonstrated here then and so helped to bring an end to Communist rule.

In the Hradčany

For those for whom the Art Nouveau of Wenceslas Square is not enough there are other places of great interest too such as the fine building used for state receptions, or the Parisian street in the Josefov. This part of town is where Jews have lived since the twelfth century The six synagogues, Jewish town hall, and Jewish cemetery remain as impressive evidence of the past.

Malá Strana or Lesser Town on the opposite bank of the Vltava (Moldau) is the most lively part of the city, juxtaposed with the palace and the cobblestone streets. One climbs up through the 750 year old part of the city to the Hradčany and loses oneself in the largest inhabited castle of the world with the residence of the Czech President alongside the St.Vitus cathedral and basilica of St. George. The golden streets in which goldsmiths once lived are popular with tourists for their densely-packed houses yet hardly anywhere is better for rummaging around in amusing stores as here.

And finally we return to the Charles' Bridge and dream of the waters of the Vltava with a violin solo by a young musician, which the composer Smetana made famous throughout the world.

The Bohemian spa resort

KARLSBAD became a legendary Spa through royal patronage

North Sea

Karlsbad

CZECH REPUBLIC

BEST TIME
Early summer and fall

ACCOMMODATION
Grand Hotel Pupp and cheaper hotels like Promenada in the resort center

GASTRONOMY
Roast pork with dumplings, cabbage, peas, and Becherovka (herbal liqueur)

SOUVENIRS
Moser glass crystal, Karlsbad wafers

FESTIVALS
International Jazz Day (May), International Film Festival (July), Karlsbad Fall Festival (September)

Where else would an aesthetic such as Goethe happily live than Weimar and Rome? In the Bohemian Karlsbad (now Karlovy Vary) of course where he stayed at the health resort for three years in all. He traveled by coach over poor roads sixteen times to reach the magnificent Spa town where he was surrounded by the superb courtly buildings of the Bad.

But Goethe is by no means the star among the visitors. Czar Peter the Great came here, as did Casanova and Prince von Metternich, and virtually all the prominent musical people did the honor, including Beethoven, Wagner, Mozart, Chopin, Liszt, Grieg, and Brahms. That Count Wallenstein was once borne through the town in a sedan chair, racked with pain and plagued with gout and then later rode away rejuvenated on a horse is the best bit of advertising for the world's most famous health resort.

What kind of town is this established on the banks of the small River Tepla that in no sense humbly nestles between the wooded hills? There is not the space for expansive buildings but the facades are imposing like palaces with the promenades running alongside the cooling waters and with bubbling fountains. No other spa resort in the world is so insistent in its uniqueness and although it has some irritating inheritances from the Communist era, with its bath houses, villas, and grand hotels, Karlsbad is still "a brilliant in an emerald setting" as Alexander von Humboldt once enthused over his delight.

According to legend Emperor Charles IV who resided in Prague discovered the health-giving spring while hunting deer. In reality a town was built here in 1350 at the confluence of the Eger and Tepla rivers because of the hot springs and was generously blessed with privileges.

Healthy springs

From the Middle Ages until the sixteenth century the health therapy was restricted to the baths but in 1522 a Leipzig doctor, Wenzel Payer, recognized the health-giving properties of the springs and recommended drinking the mineral rich Karlsbad spring water as medicine. In the seventeenth century the town developed into a spa resort for the nobility of Russia, Poland, and Saxony and also the darling of the Austrian monarchy. Famous guests were greeted with fanfares from the castle turrets.

In 1759 the resort almost entirely burned to the ground and arose again in an impressive manner. The confectioner Johann Georg Pupp opened his legendary hotel in 1775

that was soon regarded as one of the world's most elegant. Around the turn of that century Karlsbad gained a new face with important buildings in the style of Art Nouveau, Neo-Classicism, Empire, and Rococo.

On entering the resort you first encounter the Antonin Dvorak Park, at the edge of which the Sadova Colonnade was built in 1881 as a masterpiece of wrought ironwork with eccentric filigree detail. People once wandered here in hooped skirts and today they still drink the water from the fountains in the park. Only a philistine uses a normal glass for the health-giving drink. Drinking beakers with special spouts have been a specialty of Karlsbad since 1800 and hundreds of different designs are still in use today.

Magnificent colonnades

The famous Karlsbad water originates from twelve springs and the power of the water is obvious at a fountain that rises more than 45 feet (14 m) into the air at a temperature of 164.3 °F (73.5 °C) sometimes referred to as the "big fizzy drink".

The Mill Colonnade has five springs available within its 124 columns and length of 433 feet (132 m). At the heart of the city, it is embellished with allegorical figures and also provides a stylish venue for concerts. The number III bath is also captivating with its classical facade but the finest is the emperor's bath that was erected for Franz Joseph I.

Enthusiasts for fashionable hotel ambiance have much to admire because from the promenade along the river bank there are a succession of banqueting halls in which the light of chandeliers of Bohemian glass is reflected. The sociable center of the Spa resort is the Hotel

Pupp of course. With its Roman bath, magnificent concert hall, and colonnaded banqueting hall, it offers a combination pregnant with history and a carefree present. This is just what people have sought from a Spa resort for centuries and especially in Karlsbad where it always seems to be Sunday.

Karlsbad's Promenade with the River Tepla in the center of the city. In the background one wing of the Hotel Pupp (top left)

The St. Peter and St. Paul Russian Orthodox church was built close to the Russian consulate (top right)

Hotel Pupp is an extensive complex founded in 1775 by the confectioner Georg Pupp

The beauty on the Danube

BRATISLAVA is the Europe's newest capital.
The Slovakian city has a moving past

The many wine bars in the old town prove that Bratislava may well be Europe's newest capital but the gates of this city have seen a long history and also produces first rate wine. Close to this "beauty of the Danube" a fossilized wine grape has been found that is 150 million years old.

The fertile Danube valley was inhabited early and after the Celts and Romans, present-day Bratislava was settled in the sixth century by the Slavs. At the beginning of the eleventh century King Stephan I of Hungary founded a border fortress for his kingdom and in 1030 coins were minted with the inscription Breslava civitas (city of Bratislava).

The great hour of the city was when the Hungarian king made the city his residence in 1526 following a defeat at the hands of the Ottoman Turks which lost him his government seat at Buda. The city became the royal town of Pressburg under the Hungarian Habsburgs and all the rulers were crowned up to 1830 in the cathedral of St. Martin. After 1848 and during the dual Austro-Hungarian monarchy, the province of Slovakia was governed from Budapest. Although Bratislava (Pressburg) was central to Slovakia from the mid nineteenth century it did not become the capital of a free and independent Slovakia until after the partition of the former Czechoslovakia in 1993.

Long nights, short skirts

Only a little over thirty-seven miles from Vienna, Bratislava today gleams once more with its fine buildings. The city was favored as a place to live for the aristocracy and famous for its glittering balls. The former Pressburg is flourishing once more and the industrial area is also expanding so that the old town is like a real gem. There is friendly rivalry with Vienna but those in the know maintain that the nights are longer here and the skirts shorter than in the Austrian capital.

The character of the former royal city can be discovered at the market place where the cafés are constantly besieged. The old town hall that was created in the fifteenth century for a number of houses does without a dominating grand facade. But the former home of the city's founder Jakob gives an impression of grandeur and spacious mansion with its colonnade and imposing tower. In the Apponyi Palace close by there is a museum dedicated to the wine-growing of the region. And the Rococo Mirbach Palace and classical Primate's palace are magnificent buildings with great heritage. The Peace of Pressburg was signed in the hall of mirrors in the Primate's Palace on December 26, 1805 following the Battle of Austerlitz when Napoleon overcame the Austrians and Russians and Europe's frontiers were redrawn.

The Jesuits and Franciscans combined to build the cathedral of St. Martin and the many other churches bear witness to the devout religious nature of the Slovaks. Within the shadow of the cathedral is the Holocaust Memorial that remembers 60,000 Slovakian Jews who lost their lives in the pogroms. The quarter of the city in which they lived no longer exists, all demolished together with the synagogue in the early 1970s to build a freeway.

The most important street in the city is the Michaelertorgasse (St. Michael's Lane) that is almost sentimentally adored by the inhabitants as an elegant place to go for a stroll. Its finest building is the St. Michael's Gate with its massive tower through which Hungarian kings passed to their coronations. The present head of state remains faithful to the style because the Grassalkovic Palace that houses the Slovakian president is like a royal residence.

How the Danube waltz began

Before climbing up to the castle one should not overlook the House of the Good Shepherd. Small and charming like a dancer, it is one of the finest Rococo buildings of central Europe. The castle itself was constantly rebuilt, turning into a Baroque residence under Maria Theresa before being destroyed by fire in 1811. Today it has been restored to its condition in the seventeenth century and with its four towers it is a widely visible landmark.

There is a wide vista of the Danube valley from here. The river was the city's lifeline and at the sight of the dancing waves Johann Strauss is supposed to have composed the first bar of his famous waltz. The city in which Johann Nepomuk Hummel was born is certainly regarded as a stronghold of music where music is widely performed. But there is also a lively coffee house culture, for example in the legendary Café Mayer. Finally the diplomats are back and their appearances are just the same whether the city is ruled by emperor or a president.

BEST TIME
Early summer, summer, particularly beautiful in fall

ACCOMMODATION
Grand Hotel Carlton (Radisson SAS) one of the most famous hotels of central Europe in the 1920-1930s, and the floating Botel Fairway

GASTRONOMY
Cream of chicken vol-au-vents, cabbage soup with cep mushrooms, pancake with sweet filling (of poppy seeds, nougat, and hazelnuts), steamed dumplings, Wuzin noodles (potato in batter with poppy seeds and sugar), game, wine

SOUVENIRS
Wooden toys, linen tablecloths, clocks (clock-making tradition since the 15th century)

FESTIVAL
Bratislava Music Festival (September–October), Christmas market in the main square

SPECIAL TIP
Bystrica Café with great view 278 feet (85 m) up on a pylon of the new bridge

The main landmark of Bratislava: the castle with its towers from which the old German name of Pressburg was derived (top left)

The sidewalk cafés in Bratislava like these in the main square are competitors for the traditional coffee houses (bottom left)

The Grassalkovic Palace with a large fountain the foreground is today the residence of the Slovakian president

The zest for life of the Magyars

BUDAPEST celebrates its spa culture and spicy goulash

People travel to this city on the Danube with set ideas of gypsy music, spicy food, czardas, and golden Tokay wine and are not disenchanted: the gypsy musicians really exist, the women are among the most temperamental and most beautiful of Europe, and the food is so spicy that it can burn the throat.

The Magyars were nomadic horsemen that were neither Slavic or Germanic but related to the Finns, who around 900 AD came from Asia Minor with a language that brings beads of perspiration to the forehead of every foreigner. They made it as far as Italy but following a major defeat at the hands of Otto they settled on the lowland plain of the Danube at the mercy of east and west. Then in the fourteenth and fifteenth centuries there was a magnificent epoch for the Hungarian kingdom yet in 1541 they came under Ottoman Turk rule. When freed in 1686 the Hungarians fell under strong influence of Austria, In 1867 the Ausgleich officially brought equality to the relationship in the dual monarchy of Austria-Hungary that lasted until 1918.

The independent towns of Buda and Pest both lay on the banks of the Danube river and were united into a common city with Obuda in 1872. The finest buildings and structures were now constructed at breath-taking tempo including the rail station, museums, and bridges. A circular road following the example of Vienna was also constructed. The parliament building is really gigantic at 879 feet (268 m) long and with almost seven hundred rooms, making it one of Europe's biggest seats of government. With the laying out of the Heroes' Square (Hösök tere) the Hungarians celebrate themselves. An imposing column is encircled by columns and the entire monument is dedicated to a thousand years of Hungarian history.

There could just as easily have been a two thousand year monument since the Romans enjoyed a good lifestyle on the site of present-day Budapest as evidenced by the Roman remains of their amphitheaters and thermal baths. The Ottoman Turks left a special inheritance after their 150 year rule ended in 1886 with three fine bathhouses dating back to their time.

The most distinctive legacy apparent in today's cityscape is from the union with Austria when there was a close relationship with Vienna during the dual monarchy. The coffee house culture is also derived from Vienna with the Café New York in particular being a fin-de-siècle legend.

The city's pulse beats in the Café New York, especially when one can indulge in the favorite activities of the Vaci Utca after a strong Mocha coffee, seeing and being seen, and admiring the elegant store windows. In fine weather people also stroll along the promenade beside the Danube to the chain bridge and back which links Pest with Buda.

Buda has its own special charms because the castle that was extensively modified under Emperor Franz Joseph I sits high above the Baroque and Classical buildings. The principal attraction of Buda though is the Neo-Romanesque Fisherman's Bastion with its Moorish looking towers that create a romantic impression.

From bubbling springs

The Hotel Gellert is a Mecca for all lovers of Art Nouveau/Jugendstil with its pillar-adorned swimming hall that is a superb temple of Budapest's legendary love affair with their hot springs.

It is quite some phenomena that the city sits on ground that as it were bubbles. One hundred and twenty-three springs spew more than 18,494,000 gallons (70 millions litre) every day at temperatures of 78.8–168.8 °F (26–76 °C). The healing properties vary so that each bath has its different purpose. The King's, Raitzen, and Rudas baths also recall Roman or more accurately Turkish times while the Szechenyi Bath is fashioned in Neo-Classical style.

Putting on productions between Buda and Pest is popular and the 1,500 seat opera performances are just as worthy of a visit as the Vigado concert hall. It is not just Franz Lehar the king of operetta and Emmerich Kalman that originate from this musical country but also the composers Bela Bartok and Franz Liszt. The virtuoso whirl of Liszt's Hungarian Rhapsody is best appreciated when visiting Budapest from where the Puszta is not far off.

ACCOMMODATION
Grand Hotel Gellert, Atrium Hyatt, smaller hotels in Pest

BEST TIME
Spring and fall

GASTRONOMY
Goulash, stuffed goose liver, sweet pancake (filled with nut cream), chestnut purée

SOUVENIRS
Fashion, porcelain, embroidered tablecloths, silverware, apricot brandy, Tokay wine

The Danube flows through the center of Budapest. View across the chain bridge to the parliament buildings (left)

Meeting place for the people of the city: sidewalk cafe in the Vari Utca (bottom left)

Open-air spa baths. The Neo-Classical Szechenyi Thermal Baths

The Paris of the east

WARSAW'S townscape is formed by a combination of statues of St. Mary and other saints and elegant stores

BEST TIME
The entire year. Best in May and September

ACCOMMODATION
Bristol and Europejski as expensive traditional hotels, Marriott near the central rail station with every comfort

MARKET
Stadium market in suburb of Praga. Traders from the east offer junk and better. Kolo Sunday market in district of Wola for antiques and jumble

FESTIVAL
August 1 - commemoration of the Warsaw Uprising of 1944. Festival of Classical and Contemporary Music

GASTRONOMY
Pancakes with marinated forest mushrooms, stuffed eggs, sour soup with small vol-au-vents

SPECIALLY RECOMMENDED
A concert is held every Sunday from May to September by the Chopin Monument in Lazienki Park

A 100 ft high column on the palace square recalls King Zygmunt III who made Warsaw the Polish capital in 1596

The Barbican with its turrets was built in 1548 as part of the city's defenses

The old town market (Rynek Starego Miasta) is a popular meeting place for young and old

Music by Chopin of course, and in the palace in which the Polish kings once feasted. In the interval of a summer piano concert one should not be at all surprised to see a younger man greet an older woman with a kiss on the hand.

The Polish capital is a city full of astonishment, and that old Warsaw is newer than the pre-war Warsaw is due to the determination of the people of Warsaw. Those who remember that eighty-five per cent of all buildings were destroyed in 1944 by demolition squads of the German army following the suppression of the Warsaw rebellion will look in disbelief through the streets in which the royal palace, the Sigismund column, the University library with its glockenspiel, the university itself, but also the many fine buildings and churches have been recreated in high Baroque or the clean lines of Classicism.

Warsaw rose again from the hands of the people, who after World War II gave an incredible number of hours of their time in order to rebuild their city. The faithful reproduction of the old city though is courtesy of an Italian named Canaletto who had been dead for 150 years when his fifty-seven city views were used as architectural drawings. The collection of architecture of the re-created city has been named as a world cultural heritage site by Unesco.

Ex Occidente Luxus

Present-day Warsaw is fast and somewhat hectic but above all modern and its people cast an interesting gaze towards the west. Ex Oriente Lux, ex Occidente Luxus (from the east enlightenment, from the occident excess) is the aphorism of Stanislav Jerzy Lec. This is also true of the architecture because of the many architects from Italy, France, and Germany who worked in Warsaw following its elevation to royal residence in 1596 and in cooperation with Polish architects created a forward-looking town.

The market place of the old town was always central and its square lined with middle-class houses today also has cafés, and is where in Montmartre style you can have your portrait done or take a tour in the waiting carriages. In the square in front of the palace you will find the Sigismund column that is a worldly memorial that sets a cosmopolitan note amid the statues of St. Mary and other saints

and the royal palace itself with its marble rooms took a leading place when Poland as second country in the world adopted a democratic constitution in 1791 immediately after that of the Americans.

The University and Opera House should be visited and especially the Ostrogski Palace with its Chopin memorial. The heart of the composer who died in Paris was brought to Warsaw in 1850 and now rests in a column in the church of the Holy Cross.

Chopin a national hero

The greatest Polish composer was born about twenty-miles away in Zelazowa Wola and he lived for a long time in Warsaw before moving to Paris. There is a towering Chopin Memorial in the Lazienki Park and these courtly gardens with the lake, theater and palace are just one of many parks in which one can enjoy undisturbed summer pleasure as also in the Saxon Garden or around the Belvedere. The memorial to the Ghetto Uprising for the many Jews killed is a place of quiet reflection. At least one third of the population of pre-war Warsaw were Jewish. In the suburb of Praga, that once stood in the shadow of the old town, one finds an entirely different Warsaw that was left undisturbed after the war and today is a crumbling idyll but also a dynamic part of the city. This is where the big market is. In the Communist era they also had restaurants serving the best Polish plain cooking. The best views of the old town of Warsaw are also from Praga.

Finally we turn back to the bridge over the Vistula and also to the bubbling Warsaw with its elegant shopping streets like Nowy Swiat, with fine hotels like the legendary Bristol and an arts scene attracting exciting galleries. In Nowy Swiat there is the legendary Café Blickle in which the beautiful Elizabeth Taylor enjoyed the delicacy of fritters. It is not just fritters one finds in Café Blickle, albeit they are a symbol, for in Warsaw they maintain the old while being passionate about the new.

BEST TIME
May to October, rich
cultural offering in
winter

ACCOMMODATION
Grand Hotels in
keeping with the
historic city like
Francuski, Hotel pod
Roza, or Europejski.
Cheaper hotels in the
old town

SOUVENIRS
Small stalls in the Cloth
Hall sell from more or
less kitsch to
outstanding works of
art, leatherware, and
embroidery

EATING AND DRINKING
Bigos, a dish of
sauerkraut and white
cabbage with three
different types of meat,
mushrooms, and spicy
sausages. Blinis, caviar,
Krakow biscuits. Polish
vodka is particularly
smooth

**FESTIVALS AND FEAST
DAYS**
Lajkonik Feast with
colorful procession to
remember the
expulsion of the
Tartars. Concerts with
international artists
amid the architecture
of the old town.
Christmas crib
competition in the
City's Museum

Krakow, the old royal residence

A masterpiece of Renaissance architecture that retains its flair

Every hour on the hour a shrilly blown trumpet tune is sounded from the tower of the church of St. Mary that stops suddenly. Full of pride, the waitress with a black veil in her hair – in the Rynek Glowny Café on the market place in the city center – explains that this Hejnal alarm trumpet call commemorates a trumpeter who attempted to warn of an attack by Tartars in 1241. He was abruptly silenced by an arrow through his heart.

Krakow is not only the "town of the speaking stones" but also the city of legends. There are still hundreds of churches and cloisters, nuns as beautiful as a Madonna, and young men who unselfconsciously pray in front of a monument to the St. Stanislav.

Growth through cloth trade

By the year 900 Krakow was already a vibrant trading town and was elevated a century later to the dignity of bishopric and in 1038 became the place of residence for the royal dynasty of the Piasts. From the Wawel, the chalk rocks that rise steeply from the Vistula, they built a castle and succeeded in holding the town when the Tartars came close to taking it in 1241–1242. Krakow flourished again in particular under King Boleslaw and his successor Casimir II and acquired its chessboard like town layout and a market place that at 656 feet by 656 feet (200 by 200 m) might at the time have been considered ridiculously big.

The University in which Copernicus taught for a time was founded in 1364 and in 1430 the city joined the Hanseatic League. The city was so sought after as a trans-shipment place for fabrics that a Gothic Cloth Hall was created as a cathedral of trade. The streets were planned with great artistic flair that today is astounding with the uniformity of the elegant town center buildings. A lot of money was spent on the furnishings for churches including two

hundred gilded figures carved by Veit Stoss from lime wood on the Neckar for the biggest Gothic altar in Europe. Italian architects and painters created courtly magnificence when they produced the Renaissance masterpiece of the "altar of the golden age" in Krakow.

Location for Schindler's List

The dignity of capital city was over in 1596 when King Zygmunt III chose Warsaw as his capital. Krakow was somewhat lost for what to do before it thought of making itself a cultural metropolis. The Jews had a considerable share in this having been freely admitted to Krakow from the Middle Ages and settling in their own quarter at the end of the fifteenth century. The largest Jewish community of Europe lived in the Kasimierz until the Nazis deported 65,000 Jews from Krakow and then killed the majority of them in Auschwitz-Birkenau. Jew-

ish culture is returning only hesitantly years after this barbarity and the Kasimierz quarter in which the film director Steven Spielberg shot Schindler's List once again is a part of town in which Klezmer music sounds each evening.

If you want to experience Krakow turn off here somewhere and lose yourself in thoughts. The chances are you will follow the old royal route from the Florian gate through the exclusive Florianska district with its select fashion stores, silversmiths, and stores selling delicacies and to the Rynek Glowny lined with sidewalk cafés. At the memorial to the national poet Adam Mickiewicz the youth congregate on the flat steps, and at the flower market in front of it women offer roses, stocks, and lilies while musicians in colorful traditional costume play melodies from far and wide. Through the Grodzka, Krakow's second boulevard, the way leads to the Wawel Hill where the

castle, cathedral, and neighboring buildings rise up to form their own town above the roofs.

Why does all this magnificence not become wearisome? There is a certain lively atmosphere in Krakow that surely stems from the nearby expanses of the Tatra mountains or simply from the people who are really the southerners of Eastern Europe. Fifty thousand students get things moving even in an old city and the long time during which Poland's god of theater, Tadeusz Kantor, tried out his experimental theater has left its traces. But what need is there for a great stage when there are the streets? Music is made everywhere, mime artists enchant with their bizarre faces, and even the smallest flute is sufficient for a cheerful minuet. At night-time one dives into one of the many vaulted cellars in which jazz rings outs, where there is cabaret or simply discussion.

The Church of the Virgin Mary with its different towers dominates the Rynek Glowny main market place in the center of the old town (left)

Impressive Medieval cannons in front of the cathedral on Wawel Hill (top)

Within the colonnades of the Cloth Hall one can buy local arts and crafts

The rebirth of Gdansk

The historic center is rebuilt by Polish restorers

Baltic

Gdansk

POLAND

GETTING THERE
Ferry links with Germany and Sweden. Rail connections and internal Polish flights

ACCOMMODATION
Good mid-range and some luxury hotels

BEST TIME
Spring to fall

TIPPING
General rule of thumb: the more luxurious the hotel or restaurant the bigger the expected tip. Bills are appropriately rounded up

EXCURSIONS
Half-day excursions to Oliva and Gdingen. Whole day trips to Marienburg and Elbing

A stroll across the "Long Market" on a hot summer's day has been one of the finest forms of pleasure for centuries for the people of Gdansk on the Baltic. Fine patrician houses line the stroll between the ochre-colored Town Hall and the "Green Gate" and the oxblood red trellis. Souvenir stores beckon with amber necklaces and attractive embroidery. The Neptune fountain burbles and raspberry ice cream is sold in front of the three-storey high windows of Arthur's Court. What a scene!

This was all an expanse of rubble in 1945. Instead of fine Baroque and Renaissance frontages only well-built fireplaces and burnt out church towers still rose from the ruins. No-one could image the much acclaimed beauty of the former Danzig ever returning. It appeared as if the age-old struggle between Germans and Poles over the city had been literally rendered invalid through the inferno of World War II.

Initially it was fishermen who settled in the neighborhood of the later "Long Market" in the tenth century. From this village in the valley of the Vistula (Weichsel) river grew the harbor and trading town of Danzig with mainly German but also some Polish inhabitants. In the ever-changing history of the town it was under rule of a German order for a time and then under protection of the Polish king before falling to the Prussians and remained in German hands until the end of World War I. Between the wars Danzig was a Free City within Polish territory under the protection of the League of Nations and separated from Germany by a strip of Poland known as the "Danzig corridor."

World War II started here

The armored cruiser Schleswig-Holstein fired on Polish military positions on the Westerplatte, a fortified peninsula off the coast from Danzig on September 1, 1939. This action, ordered by Adolf Hitler, started World War II during the course of which the Hanseatic town became part of Germany once more but following its destruction in 1945 finally became Polish, with virtually all its German population either fleeing or being expelled.

That the "Long Market" and the rest of the historic center once more have the appearance of the former Danzig's glory days of two to three hundred years ago is deemed a miracle but is the result of hard work. Supported by leadership that in addition to its Communist ideology also wanted to build along traditional lines, preservers of historical monuments and craftsmen started faithfully rebuilding the city according to its original form. The result supports the claim of Polish restorers to be the best in their field.

Of the 450,000 inhabitants of present-day Gdansk only a diminishing minority are of German origin. Germans though are in the first rank when it comes to foreign visitors. In common with other towns that were taken over by Poland, the Germans have good neighborly relations with their former enemies in the town where the anti-Communist Solidarity movement began in 1980.

Crane as landmark

There are tourist groups everywhere throughout the rebuilt old section of the city. There is much to see, "Long Street" and "Woman's Street" with their gabled rows of houses, the Main Gate with its Polish and Prussian arms of the city, and the Renaissance triumphal arch of the "Long Street Gate." The town hall is also worth a visit with its 269 foot (82 m) high tower from which there is a good all-round view across the historic center and of the churches, including the enormous Church of the Virgin Mary close by and below with room for at least 25,000 people.

Gdansk's old landmark is found on the former river port. It is the wooden Crane Gate constructed in 1444. Its hoist was solely powered by prisoners who had to move a treadmill with all their strength. The oldest bit of industrial archaeology of the city is a corn mill from 1350. It operated with eighteen mill wheels, which were finally replaced by turbines in 1945.

The newest attractions are three giant crosses welded from ship's steel. They stand on Solidarity Square in front of the former Lenin wharf and are dedicated to the twenty-eight martyrs who were shot by the police in December 1970 during a major strike by the longshoremen.

The inner harbor area with the Crane Gate of 1444 on the banks of the Mottlawa river (top)

After World War II the city was faithfully rebuilt. The "Long Street" with its attractive gables (bottom left)

The Neptune fountain in the "Long Market"

In the track of the Hanse

Estonia's capital **TALLINN** is a blossoming trade center on the Baltic

GETTING THERE
Frequent flights from Scandinavia and Russia and flights from Western Europe and the USA. Many ferry links across the Baltic

BEST TIME
Hottest months are July and August with maximum of 86 °F (30 °C). Long periods of frost in winter

ACCOMMODATION
Many Western hotel chains have built new hotels or converted restored historic buildings. Pre-booking is advisable

TIPPING
Not normal. Bills are generally rounded up though

The cathedral mound of Tallinn has been a visible landmark for seafarers for centuries. In clear weather it is possible to see across the Gulf of Finland to Helsinki. There are about twenty ferries daily across the Baltic from the Finnish capital, bringing Finns to take advantage of lower Tallinn's cheaper prices and to spend a few hours experiencing the Medieval mystic of the centuries old town.

Buildings that have been carefully restored stand alongside each other representing 700 years of continuous architectural history. The square in front of the town hall from the thirteenth century and the town dispensary founded in 1422 are at the heart of Tallinn. Hordes of laughing, friendly people sit at the tables of the numerous cafés and restaurants that spread across the entire square, unconstrained by the Gothic buildings of the early fifteenth century.

Animated life also rules in the narrow streets in which small stores, fashion boutiques, bars, nightclubs, and restaurants line the way as far as the Toompea hill.

Town history since 1050
There was already an established settlement on the steep hill in the first century BC. In 1050 the first stone fortifications were built to protect the 150 year old merchant settlement of Kolywani. The reputation of the town grew so fast after this that the Arabic cartographer al-Idrisi included it in his world map of 1154.

In 1219 Waldemar II from Denmark conquered the trading settlement and named it Reval and founded the Church of St. Mary the Virgin (Dome Church) which was built on the Toompea Hill between 1229 and 1233.

He did not succeed in dominating the ethnic people, who had settled here together with the Finns between 3000 and 2000 BC. More importantly, Reval had a key position for the west in trade with the east and flourished increasingly in the shadows of the fortifications. All the same the Estonians did not gain much from it since they remained vassals of foreign powers until late into the twentieth century.

Reval became an early member of the newly-formed Hanseatic League in 1285. In 1346 the knights of a German order purchased the town but as the order slowly dissolved two hundred years later Reval became Swedish and gained the monopoly on trade with the east in the fifteenth century.

The Russians followed the Swedes in 1710 when Peter I conquered Reval. From then until 1918 the town became Russian.

Under Russian rule
When Alexander III ascended to the throne in 1881 the "Russianization" of Estonia began with everything non-Russian and ethnic Estonian being banned. As a sign of their power over the German upper class which administered the Baltic provinces of Estonia, Livonia, and Courland the Russian had the cathedral built by Alexander Nevski on the Toompea Hill.

The Germans occupied Estonia during World War I and then with the war lost to the Germans but the Russians occupied with their Revolution the hour had come for a state to be formed on an ethnic basis with Tallinn as capital. This was only for twenty-two years though until German troops marched into Tallinn in 1940. When they withdrew defeated in 1944 they left behind piles of rubble.

The Germans were replaced once more by the Russians who made Estonia part of the Soviet Socialist Republic and began a new process of Russianization. It was not until the Soviet Union started to fall apart in the 1980s that Estonia became independent with Tallinn as its capital.

Upper town and Lower town
Today the government uses the ancient space in the castle that was carefully restored after its destruction in World War II. Embassies now occupy many of the old houses in the Upper town. The oldest remaining Estonian church, the Lutheran cathedral of St. Mary the Virgin, radiates a renewed magnificence just like the less popular Orthodox basilica of St. Nicholas.

In the Lower town the enormous white-walled Niguliste church close to the market place is extremely worth a visit. Today the former church is a museum for ethnic arts and crafts displaying an impressive collection of Medieval objects from the city such as altars from the fifteenth and sixteenth century and a fragment of Dance Macabre by

Bernd Notke from the fifteenth century. Contemporary art of Tallinn is displayed in the upper-floor of the three-storey Kiek-in-de-Kok (peek in the kitchen) watchtower.

Outside the city walls one can stroll in the Catharine Park and admire its well-cared for appearance. It is a popular meeting place for lovers. Czar Peter the Great had the gardens laid out for the citizens of Tallinn. Right in its heart is the massive Baroque palace that was built between 1718 and 1836 by the Italian architect Niccolo Michetti as a summer palace. Today it is the presidential palace of the President of the Republic of Estonia.

View from the St. Nicholas Church across the old town to the modern port (top)

The town hall square in the center with its sidewalk cafés is a popular meeting place in summer (bottom left)

A group of children in ethnic dress rehearse a folk dance. The cathedral by Alexander Nevski is in the background

Russia's gateway to the West

Peter the Great built legendary **ST. PETERSBURG** in the marshes of the Neva delta

The western city in the north of Russia quickly became something special and not at all Russian, for Czar Peter the Great intended his window to the west to be European in style, with a bit of Prague, a pinch of Vienna, and at its core Amsterdam.

Hence this city with its wide avenues, parks, waterside promenades, and countless bridges sparkles with its open-minded yet reserved Nordic atmosphere. There is a constant bustle on the Nevski Prospect – the best-known of the handsome boulevards – but not a hectic tumult. One magnificent grand palace is resplendent alongside another. Superb town houses, merchant's houses, and churches of many denominations line up alongside one another: the Lutheran St. Peter's, Roman Catholic St. Catherine's, and the Russian Orthodox Kazan cathedral. Countless cafés and restaurants entice one to linger and be lost in admiration, but also the literary café once known as Wolff & Béranger that was a second home to Alexander Puschkin.

St. Petersburg is a clear product of a drawing board, created on impracticable, mosquito-infested marshland at risk of flooding at high tide between the numerous tributaries in the Neva delta. But this was the only spot where Russia had access to a Western European sea and could acquire Western European culture.

Victory against the Swedish
Russian settlers lived in Ingermanland (Ingria) at the tip of the Gulf of Finland from the eighth century. Alexander of Novgorod drove off the Swedish in 1240 who ruled this thinly settled area, but in 1617 they once more annexed the territory, building fortifications along the River Neva to Lake Ladoga.

The great opportunity came for Czar Peter the Great with the start of the Northern War (1700–1721). One night he came with boats across Lake Ladoga, conquered the Noteburg fortifications at the point at which the Neva flows from the lake – today's Petrokrepost – and shortly after this took Nyenschanz on the lower reaches of the river. Peter did not delay in laying the foundation stone for the Peter and Paul fortress on the Sajatski Island in the mouth of the Neva.

In the following year work began on the admiralty wharf diagonally opposite. The settlement, fortress, and wharf were quickly constructed. The new town was built on wooden piles using Amsterdam as an example. The grueling work was carried out by forced labor and many lost their lives. They say St. Petersburg is built on men's bones.

Although initially the marsh area was only populated by small wooden houses Peter moved his capital here from Moscow in 1712. The Czar compelled both aristocracy and citizens to resettle on the Baltic from deep inside Russia. The first masonry building, which is still standing, was constructed in 1710 for Prince Alexander Danilovski Menskikov, the first governor.

Following the Peace of Nystad in 1721 architects came from throughout Europe to create a unique and extensive collection of fine buildings: Baroque and Rococo in the eighteenth century and Classical in the nineteenth century.

Only ruins remained of the many magnificent buildings of the inner city when troops besieged and bombarded the then Leningrad between 1941 and 1944 for 900 days. After the war the Soviets undertook tremendous efforts to rebuild the Czar's city and give it back its former sparkle. By 1960 the city once more radiated its full beauty.

Winter Palace and Hermitage
Surely the finest building – the Winter Palace – was built to orders of Czarina Elizabeth, daughter of Peter the Great. The Italianate Baroque structure is white and green and Catherine the Great extended it in Classical style for her Hermitage in 1764 and purchased art treasures throughout Europe. Today this collection with at least three million pieces of art is the world's largest art museum.

One of the largest churches in Europe is the St. Isaac cathedral. At 328 foot (100 m) high it dominates the skyline of St. Petersburg. Its interior is a veritable symphony of marble, precious and semi-precious stones of every color and it has space for 14,000 worshippers. The golden cupola is gilded with more than forty-five pounds in weight of pure gold. From the top there is a breathtaking view of the finest square of the old city.

Cascades of pure Classicism. Steps and fountains in front of Peter the Great's palace where the Czars once lived (left)

The Baroque Winter Palace contains the Hermitage with the world's largest collection of art. Catherine the Great established the collection in the magnificent building (top right)

The Gribojedov canal with the Church of the Resurrection in the background. Cafés alongside and boats bobbing in the water are part of the scenery

Unchanging Moscow

The Russian capital has survived the storms of history and radiates a new sparkle

Moscow • RUSSIA

GETTING THERE
Sheremetyevo 2 airport has world-wide flights. European rail links via Warsaw and Berlin

BEST TIME
Best time is high summer with many hot days and in snowy winter with a crisp hard frost

ACCOMMODATION
Luxury and mid-range hotels. Very expensive for independent travelers but reasonable price for package holidays. Pre-booking necessary

TIPPING
Not more then 10 %. Agree taxi fares in advance. Pay for journeys to and from Sheremetyevo 2 airport in US$

Moscow's Red Square and the walls of the Kremlin at the center of the Russian state. Also on view the Spasski Towers opposite the white facade of the Gum department store. St. Basil's cathedral is in the background (top)

In the glass-covered shopping arcade of Gum (bottom right)

View of Moscow at night with the Moskva river, the huge cathedral, and the walls of the Kremlin

The enormous city appears improvised and without any planning. Everything in Moscow is bigger than anywhere else. The buildings, the cathedrals, and the streets. Yet this gargantuan approach does not overpower the countless valuable century's old gems in which the pulsating Russian capital is so rich.

About 12,500,000 people live within the catchment area of Moscow. But there is no such thing as a typical Muscovite. A broad mix of as many as one hundred European and Asian ethnic origins mold the city's atmosphere.

The great readiness to help and warmth of hospitality are very agreeable whether you meet them in the throng of a shopping precinct or the modern business area of the new Arbat. The old Arbat was formerly the center of art and literature but today is a more colorful and lively junk market while you will find restaurants of every region of Russia in the new Arbat.

Moscow has grown explosively in the past two hundred years, like London and Paris. Four ring roads document the history of this growth. At the city's rim an expressway rings the city through areas of apartment blocks and new industrial areas. The tracks of a circular rail line mark the original boundary of the eighteenth century. The Garden Ring follows the line of old fortifications, and the ring of boulevards surrounds the rectangular Kitai Gorod or old town at the center of which is the triangular Kremlin. Simple earth banks and ditches were built in 1156 on the high point of land between the Moscow and Neglinnaya rivers – the latter a tributary that is now built over.

First signs of life

The date given for the city's foundation is April 4, 1147. An early document records that on this day Prince Yuri Vladimirovitch Dolgorukay feasted with his ally the Prince of Novgorod-Severskay in "Moscow."

There were soon troublesome times though. The town had to be defended constantly against the Mongols, often without success. Although the fortifications were constantly improved it was not until 1408 that conquerors became a thing of the past. From now on the rise of Moscow as an international trading center could not be halted by fire, famine, or battles with Mongols and Tartars. Even Czar Peter the Great furthered the eco-

nomic development despite him moving his seat of government in 1712 to the westward-looking St. Petersburg at the mouth of the Neva river to the Baltic.

Why Napoleon failed

Moscow nevertheless remained the economic center of the country and also the military target for Russia's enemies. When Napoleon marched into Moscow in the fall of 1812 he thought Russian resistance had been broken. But he found the city deserted and three-quarters of the buildings burnt to the ground leaving his troops without shelter or food. In October he made his disastrous retreat through the freezing cold Russian winter.

Hardly had his soldiers retreated before the Muscovites were planning in 1813 the rebuilding of their city in order to take care of the steady stream of people. Many buildings from this era still remain. Under Stalin the city was systematically renewed in the 1930s and from 1980 new satellite towns have been built on both sides of the ring expressway.

There are still superb surviving examples of Classical Moscow even amid the sea of buildings outside the Garden Ring, with its many industrial buildings and apartment blocks from the early and mid twenties that determine the cityscape. These include fortified cloisters and countless churches from the sixteenth century.

The main monument for sightseers in Moscow is the Kremlin. The red brick walls with their twenty towers were constructed by Italian architects who Ivan III invited in the fifteenth century. With its countless churches and palaces the Kremlin is easily the most imposing collection of different architectural styles.

In the old city around the Kremlin and Red Square are precious historical monuments of the fifteenth century side-by-side with functional buildings of the twentieth century. These latter wedding-cake style structures are of the late Stalinist era and glass-concrete skyscrapers from the 1960s. World-famous and well-visited theaters like the Bolshoi and magnificent museums are impressive evidence of the depth of the people's cultural roots.

Why Dublin is a place of pilgrimage

The Irish capital is famous for its pubs, whiskey, beer, street musicians, and writers

The O'Connel bridge spans the River Liffey in the center of Dublin (top)

View inside the Old Library of Trinity College (bottom center)

Open poetry reading on Bloom's Day in front of a pub (bottom right)

Folk music in O'Connor's Pub with accordion and violins

Half the world – or at least the literary half – knows what a certainty Leopold Bloom had in Dublin on June 16, 1904. Because the author James Joyce accompanied his hero on his bewildering expedition through the city for more than a thousand pages in such accurate detail that one could rebuild old Dublin from Joyce's novel. Joyce himself did not stay in the city on the River Liffey because at the turn of the nineteenth and twentieth centuries he settled in continental Europe, following the motto of his colleague George Edward Moore who wrote: "An Irishman must flea from Ireland because he will not want to leave."

These are strong words which are easily understandable if you visit Dublin. Dublin is youthful and colorful and above all one hundred per cent individual. Seven hundred pubs and no two the same, surely as many musicians as inhabitants, and with Grafton street a shopping area that is up to the minute with international fashion. What else is there? A glass of stout of course, brewed by Guinness, the world's biggest exporting brewery. The company, which brews the Irish national drink, has been a patron for more than one hundred years, making the renovation of St. Patrick's cathedral possible, and also the creation of several parks. The Dubliner sighs that God provides the result from hops and malt.

It was Vikings who settled where present-day Dublin stands in the ninth century and were evidently so happy that it was not until the twelfth century before they could be expelled. The Anglo-Normans then made Dublin the center of their English colony, built a castle, and the Christ Church cathedral. A further milestone in the development of Dublin was the foundation of Trinity College in 1591 financed by Queen Elizabeth I as a bulwark against the Catholic church. The library has a copy of the illustrated Gospel in manuscript from the ninth century known as the Book of Kells.

The way to the poorhouse

The city was blessed with architectural greatness thanks to flourishing trade during the seventeenth and eighteenth centuries but the Act of Union brought an end to independence in 1801. Ireland was united within the British Isles and as had happened before, cut off from its trade connections. The country and its capital sank into poverty and Ireland became a poorhouse which Friedrich Engels contemptuously referred to as "a wasteland." Most of Ireland became a free state in 1921 but the island of Ireland remains divided with the majority being the independent republic of Eire while the north-east still forms part of Great Britain.

Anyone who knows Dublin from Irish films in which it buckets down with rain and the streets are dark and narrow will be surprised by its glorious magnificence. The Castle with its opulent interior, the National Museum with its columns and colonnades, the Main Post Office in O'Connell Street, the St. Mary's Pro-Cathedral, and the former building of the Irish parliament with its Classical facade all recall Dublin's great heritage. The cathedral of St. Patrick is in the Protestant mold and is where Jonathan Swift who created Gulliver's Travels was Dean for thirty years.

At home in a pub

Poets are to Dublin what the emperor is to Vienna. Three Nobel prize winners were born in Dublin: William Butler Yeats, George Bernard Shaw, and Samuel Beckett, who with Oscar Wilde, James Joyce, Patrick Kavanagh, Flann O'Brien, and Brendan Behan are names that make every literary heart beat. That they all had their second home in a pub

is ideal for today's tourist since a pub crawl with appropriate readings leads to literary retreats such as Davy Byrne's, Mulligan's, and the Palace Bar. There is also a museum dedicated to their fine words: the Writers' Museum displayed personal mementos of the Irish poets.

But who needs a book in Dublin when the streets themselves are poetic. The people love to chat, even with foreigners, the weather is often surprisingly good, and a trip along the coast to Bray is just as picturesque as a drive along the Corniche at Marseilles. The most popular tourist area of the inner city is Temple Bars, a former Huguenot quarter, where stores, bistros, restaurants, and cafés can be found next to one another and also theaters and galleries that all give one an entirely new impression. Here too the stout tastes good and music is made every evening with fiddle and banjo that bring pilgrims to Irish pubs from throughout the world.

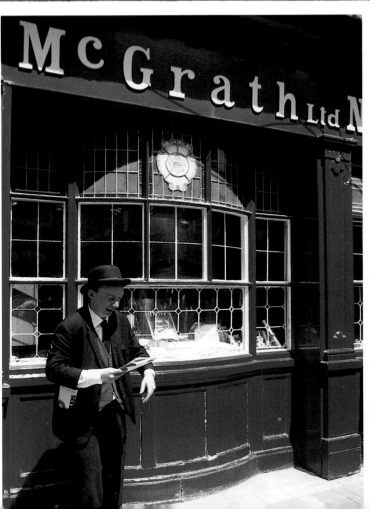

London hides many worlds

The British capital is a European monument

What would London be without its royalty? What would London be without its tradition? No other city in the world makes such a picturesque scene from its traditions as London around Buckingham Palace and many an onlooker sighs in relief and admiration with a comment such as: "This monarchy is certainly not on its way out," as they watch the colorful Changing of the Guard. Black bearskin hats gleam above bright red tunics, the Queen smiles graciously, and the Gothic facade dominates the stage.

London is molded by its thousand year-old monarchy but the city also gave birth to the miniskirt, is the hall of fame of the Beatles, the birthplace of Punk, and stronghold of "fab" fashion. London is unrestrainedly creative yet nevertheless so careful about ritual that the Queen still has to seek permission to enter the City of London.

A certain arrogance on the part of Londoners can be explained by their history, since the Romans made Londinium the capital of the British Isles. After the decline of the Roman Empire the Angles and Saxons invaded Britain and also settled alongside the River Thames. England became Christian in the sixth century and London acquired its first church with the first St. Paul's Cathedral. William the Conqueror determined however to use the newer Westminster Abbey for his coronation in 1066 and established a new tradition. Every English king or queen from then on was crowned in Westminster Abbey.

The bowler hat is a rarity

Under Henry VIII and his daughter, Elizabeth I, the city experienced its most golden age in the sixteenth century and this was certainly not hampered by separation from Rome and formation of the Church of England. By the late eighteenth century London was the world's largest city and later became the center of the Commonwealth and its mother city. The end of the British Empire and the decline of the port of London in the middle of the twentieth century were significant economic set-backs yet London managed to carve out for itself a leading role as financial center and money market. Today about 550,000 people work "in the City" but the image of the bowler hatted banker is now rarely seen with well-groomed hair increasingly on view and a new casual manner and appearance taking its place.

The "fab" London today attracts the world's young people who have made the area around Covent Garden their center but also the contrasting areas of the East End, the Portobello Road Market, and Clerkenwell. Even Americans see London as the "coolest" city with its avant-garde art, long queues outside the wildest discos, and its leading comedy scene that all ensure excitement.

There is such a cultural mix with the superb colors of the Indian sub-continent, with Caribbean rhythms, and African blues, with Asian temple dances brought together. Every eccentricity has its place here and if you want to relax then there are the parks with deck chairs and lakes that are real city center oases.

Stronghold of democracy

Political London is just as apparent and dominates a significant part of the center of the city. In Whitehall, the quarter of government, one finds the main government departments and ministries, the banqueting house, and the Houses of Parliament rise up like a stronghold of democracy and home to the English parliament since 1547. At its northern end is Big Ben that with the

striking of its thirteen ton bells rings out the sweetest melody to the world. The Prime Minister lives at Number 10 Downing Street but this is not open to visitors.

Royal London has become more accessible to tourists since the Queen decided to open parts of Buckingham Palace to visitors. The Tower of London is also on the sightseeing trail where you can see the Crown Jewels that are guarded by Yeomen in Medieval costume. The magnificence of Westminster Abbey is best displayed during a service with views of the bewildering array of pillars.

Eventually every London visit inevitably ends up amid the bustle of Piccadilly Circus, Nelson's Column in Trafalgar Square, and shopping in the upmarket department store of Harrods after a ride on a double-decker bus. The Tate and National Galleries should be visited and for something "very British", take High Tea in one of the Grand hotels such as The Savoy. The British heal all their sorrows with a cup of tea but also celebrate their unique city with it. That is provided they aren't happier holding a pint of bitter in one of their pubs.

BEST TIME
The entire year. Spring is particularly recommended

ACCOMMODATION
Grand hotels such as the Savoy or Claridges but more reasonably priced hotels around Victoria station

SHOPPING
Shoes, "fab" fashion, picnic sets, china, Stilton cheese

GASTRONOMY
Roast lamb with mint sauce, turkey, Plum pudding (Christmas pudding), mince pies, English breakfast, fish and chips

FESTIVAL
New Year's Day Parade (January 1) from Parliament Square to Berkeley Square, Trooping the Colour (official birthday parade of the Queen in mid June), Notting Hill Carnival (Europe's biggest street party, last week in August)

SPECIAL RECOMMENDATION
Madame Tussaud's Waxworks Museum, 100 years in the same place on Marylebone Road. Hugh Grant is one of the dummies

Two symbols of London: red double-decker buses and Big Ben, the clock and bell tower alongside the Houses of Parliament (left)

Buckingham Palace is surrounded by huge parks but is right in the heart of the city (top right)

Piccadilly Circus with its neon advertising signs is recognized by every visitor. The fountain in the middle of the Circus is a meeting place for young people from throughout the world

In the world of colleges

Academic traditions dominate OXFORD

The scenery of Oxford, with its battlements, spires, domes, and columns and extensive sections of Medieval city wall is world-renowned. The crime novels of Colin Dexter in which the author has his Inspector Morse solve secretive murders in ivy-entwined Oxford also enjoy fame world wide. It is a scenery just right for human involvement and magic.

Oxford, whose university along with those of Bologna, Salamanca, Paris, and Padua is one of the world's oldest, possesses an almost hypnotic beauty. Sixty-five churches and colleges rise up in the city that is surrounded by hills. The colleges followed on from previous "high schools" in the late twelfth century within cloistered buildings whose architecture is quite impressive.

The gateway to the student world

Today there are thirty-nine colleges and many British politicians, academics, and writers studied here or in Cambridge, referred to collectively as "Oxbridge." No other university approached them in the nineteenth century. The students and their professors contribute to the picturesque street scene and can often be seen wearing gown and "mortar board" academic hat in their college colors.

The colleges are undisputedly the overwhelming attraction of the city, each with its own appearance. One enters through a gateway to an inner courtyard known as the quadrangle or simply as the quad around which the college chapel, great hall, bedrooms and studies are arranged leaving space for gardens, stone benches, sundials, and ancient trees. Since each college is an independent organization it has its own rules and often has considerable real estate from donations and bequests made long ago at its disposal.

The colleges are also blessed with art treasures with Christ Church College for instance possessing its own gallery of paintings by Titian, Leonardo da Vinci, and Rubens. Other notable college possessions include the Renaissance Library of Merton, the altarpiece attributed to Rubens at Corpus Christi, and a reproduction Venetian bridge linking the old and new wings of Hertford College since 1903. Most colleges can be visited in the afternoon providing real time travel back into history.

How much architecture has influenced teaching and research in Oxford can be seen at the Bodleian Library in Catte Street close to the Radcliff Camera (that is also a library). The bequest of 256 manuscripts to the city by Humphrey, Duke of Gloucester led to the building of a library in the seventeenth century intended to acquire world renown that was financed by Sir Thomas Bodley. Since then the library has become a sort of academic Mecca housing more than six million books in addition to precious manuscripts and books printed before 1501.

You will discover that Oxford is also young and dynamic in the many bars and pubs filled with boisterous chatter. The city really comes alive during late May with an enormous rowing regatta on the Thames in which victory or defeat are passionately fought for. The Thames is also the sociable companion for Oxford and there are many romantic spots to drink a beer and watch the babbling water. The picturesque city is an ideal place for a flirtation since most Oxford colleges now accept women students.

Under Gothic arches

Oxford's main street is the High Street and within a short distance of it are the most important attractions like Christ Church College, the cathedral, the university church of St. Mary the Virgin, Queen's College, the Museum of Oxford, and the Sheldonian Theater in which Oxford's major academic occasions are held. The best overview of the city though can be had from the Carfax Tower, dating from the fourteenth century at the foot of which the city extends with its gossamer-like Gothic arches and higgledy-piggledy roofs like a masterpiece of Medieval town planning.

BEST TIME
Spring and summer

ACCOMMODATION
The Randolph, a luxury hotel dating from 1864. One can lodge inexpensively in many of the colleges during the vacations

MARKET
Gloucester Green vegetable and antique market

GASTRONOMY
Good solid food from the pubs e.g. The King's Arms near the Bodleian Library

SPECIAL RECOMMENDATION
Inspector Morse tours on Sundays

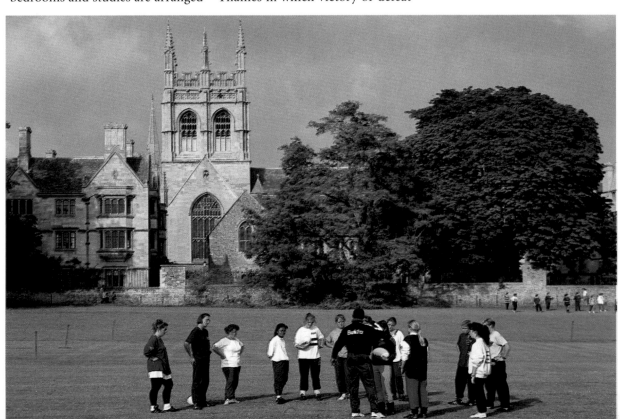

View from two "cathedrals" of research: from the tower of the Radcliff Camera library and legendary All Souls College (top left)

The Carfax Tower in the city center, surrounded by historic buildings (bottom left)

Sport is also on the College agenda. Here on the land known as Christ Church Meadows

The heart of Scotland

Scottish and English history comes together in **EDINBURGH**

Mountain and loch, sheer rocks, and a sky create a drama that scarcely can be beaten. Edinburgh born writer Robert Louis Stephenson could not understand why this abundance of eccentrics was not a theatrical scene but an everyday view of his city.

Edinburgh, world cultural heritage, and festival city masterfully sets the scene and surprises not only the poet with its sense of the theatrical. The castle alone in its imposing position on black basalt rocks with its St. Margaret's Chapel built in 1090 seems shrouded in mystery and today houses the Scottish Crown Jewels, that includes a crown made with gold mined in Scotland. In a tiny room in the castle the Scottish Queen Mary Stuart bore her son James VI who ruled Scotland and following the death of Queen Elizabeth also over England. With his move to London he also sealed the fate of the Scottish monarchy.

The castle on its rock outcrop was residence of the Scottish monarchs from the end of the eleventh century and hotly contested for centuries and remained as a symbol when Scotland eventually fell under the English monarchy with the Treaty of Union in 1707. The dispute between the Catholic and Protestant churches particularly dominated matters in Edinburgh and the reign of terror of Oliver Cromwell from 1650 was very traumatic for the city.

The Royal Mile

Edinburgh experienced a renewed upturn as the Scottish capital in the eighteenth and nineteenth centuries in the so-called golden age of culture and trade with the building of a new town that created a sign that could be seen from miles around. The strong symmetry of its Georgian architecture in this part of Edinburgh, with its monumentally decorated parks makes it a grand counterpart for the idyllic old Edinburgh and the Royal Mile.

The Royal Mile begins at Edinburgh Castle and with Castle Hill, Lawnmarket, High Street, and Canongate it forms the historical backbone of the city. These streets join the castle and the other royal palace and along them are many places worth a visit including the Scotch Whisky Heritage Center dedicated to the Scottish national drink, the slightly more distant Lady Stair's House with its reminiscences of Scottish writers Stephenson, Scott, and Burns, and the High Kirk (church) of St. Giles with its spire

supported by eight flying buttresses that floats above the city like a silver-gray bridal tiara.

In the final section of the Royal Mile the former residences of the nobility impress including Huntly House that is now the City's Museum. Finally the Royal Mile at its end honors its name as it leads inexorably to a second royal residence, built in the early sixteenth century in Renaissance style. The Holyrood Palace today is the official Scottish residence of the British Queen.

Bagpipe festival

What makes the Royal Mile so attractive for sightseeing is its vitality and bustle, the colorful stores, kilt makers, and many inviting cafés and pubs. It is quite different than a walk through the classical New Town that has won Edinburgh the title of "the Athens of the north."

But what would Edinburgh be today without its Festival started in 1947? More than two million visitors come to the city between mid-August and early September for the biggest cultural event in the world with its definite high point being the Military Tattoo with its Last Post played on the Scottish bagpipes. An-

other specialty is "The Fringe", an alternative festival with both organized and spontaneous performances in the street, in parks, and small theaters in cellars by creative people from throughout the world.

The festival has also changed the culinary scene because for some time now one can eat better in the university and port city of Edinburgh than virtually anywhere else in this island kingdom. It is certainly so that the pubs are still as sociable as they have always been with a guarantee of the Scottish sense of tradition.

BEST TIME
Late spring, summer and fall

ACCOMMODATION
The Balmoral Hotel is an Edinburgh landmark with Victorian atmosphere (five stars), bed & breakfast as a cheaper alternative

FESTIVALS
Edinburgh International Festival (August-September)

GASTRONOMY
Haggis (the Scottish national dish consisting of offal within a sheep's stomach, cabbage and seasoning)

SOUVENIRS
Cashmere sweaters, tweed jackets, shortbread, and Scotch whisky without an "e"

The shopping and business area of Princes Street in Edinburgh (left)

A pipe band assembled in front of Edinburgh Castle (top right)

Holyrood Palace is the official Scottish residence of the British Queen

Oslo's friendly atmosphere

The Norwegian capital retains great cultural heritage

Oslo has blossomed in recent years like no other city in Europe. The places in the inner city stay open until late at night. Bars, cafés, and restaurants along the Karl Johan Gate (a street) and in the futuristic Aker Brygge are filled with people at all hours and the theaters play to full houses. Despite this the city – that is the most expensive in Europe – has not lowered its standards. As high as those living standards are, the city has retained much of its cool Nordic provincial yet friendly charm.

Compact but not too small to be a metropolis, Oslo is a city for a stroll or serious walk. The countless museums worth visiting, architectural monuments, and parks are mainly within the inner city and easily reached on foot. At the most perhaps one might take one of the ferries that in ten minutes take you from the main rail station to the island museum of Bygdøy.

The Akershus Festning is a castle that was built on a strip of land south of the station built to orders of Håkon V in 1300. He wanted to halt the Swedish and transferred his seat of government from Bergen to here. At that time Oslo was just a small Hanseatic settlement that had been found 150 years earlier by King Harald Hardråde.

Half the population was killed by the Plague in 1348. Fifty years later in 1397 Copenhagen became the capital and Oslo fell into a slumber for more than two centuries. It finally gained royal attention once more of the Danish-Norwegian king Christian IV when the city was entirely destroyed by fire in 1624. He had the city completely rebuilt and gave it his own name of Christiana.

Viking marine heritage

The growth of the population and economy was slow though. This was speeded-up by the union between Norway and Sweden in 1814 until the two states parted once more in 1905. During this era imposing state buildings arose such as the royal palace, the national theater, and national gallery. In 1925 the city returned to its former name of Oslo.

Long before the first settlement on the northern bank of the Oslo fiord there were Norse living here who as Vikings knew all the seas around Europe, traded with Asia, and brought fear and terror for a time to the shores of the northern Atlantic.

In the "Viking ship house" on the Bygdøy museum peninsula there is the seventy foot long Oseberg ship to marvel at. It was built in 850 and was excavated from the Oslo fiord at Oseberg in 1904. The "dragon" ship was the tomb of a queen. In its wooden poop on the deck all manner of household objects and items of clothing were found with the remains of the queen and her handmaiden. Four sleds and a heavy wagon made of oak were to ease the journey to the hereafter. Such open boats powered by oars, introduced in the seventh century, were the fastest, most maneuverable, and most sea worthy craft in use of their day.

Adventure at sea of more recent times is documented in the Framhuset museum featuring Kon-Tiki and Ra-II. Fridtjof Nansen explored the Arctic between 1893 and 1896 in the Fram, and Roald Amundsen used her for his expedition to the South Pole in 1911. Thor Heyerdal showed on the balsa wood raft Kon-Tiki that before the first millennium people could have traveled from South America towards the west to settle Tahiti.

From Munch to Vigeland

The sea and those long dark winter nights also provoke thoughts of Oslo's best-known work of art. Norway's most famous Expressionist artist, Edvard Munch, who was one of the most important modernist painters, left his work to his home city of Oslo. The Edvard Munch Museum built to house his work contains 1,100 of his paintings, 4,500 drawings, 18,000 pieces of graphic art, and six sculptures.

No less impressive are the 192 realistic-sensitive granite, bronze, and iron sculptures of Gustav Vigeland in Frogner Park. The most important is a fifty-five foot high monolith from a single block of granite. With filigree finesse Vigeland hewed a Life cycle of Man here between 1928 and 1942, from birth to death at old age to say goodbye to his grandchildren before his own death.

GETTING THERE
Good flight connections within Europe and to North America. Comfortable ferry connections with Sweden, Denmark, Germany, and the United Kingdom

BEST TIME
Summers are relatively warm at 71.6 °F (22 °C). Snow is certain in the winter sports season when temperatures remain below freezing

ACCOMMODATION
Oslo's hotels are among the most expensive in Europe. All categories are available. Walking cabins are an alternative. Pre booking is necessary

TIPPING
Not usual. Bills are rounded up

The enormous red-brick town hall by the harbor is an Oslo landmark since its construction in 1950 (left)

The work of sculptor Gustav Vigeland can be seen in the Frogner Park. His monolith is in the center (top right)

The Osberg ship dating from the ninth century can be seen on the island museum of Bygdøy. It shows the great shipbuilding capability of Viking carpenters

In tolerant Copenhagen

The fine buildings of Denmark's capital recall that this country was a great power

DENMARK
Copenhagen
Baltic
North Sea

GETTING THERE
International flights to/from Kastrup Airport. By rail or car from Hamburg as the crow flies.

BEST TIME
Typical island climate with rapid changes of weather. Best time is June-August

ACCOMMODATION
All categories of hotel available. Most are near the main station and the Tivoli. Prices are higher than central Europe

TIPPING
Not customary

In spite of its great traditions Denmark's capital city is defiant, youthful, and free and easy. Copenhagen is more than a flourishing center of famous museums, theaters, galleries, and modern Danish design, for alternative culture and cabaret thrives here too.

At every step one encounters an atmosphere of individualism and tolerance. On what is probably the world's longest good-time strip – Strøget, a pedestrian area of more than a mile (almost 2 km) – there is the usual bustle of business as in any other city but the people here also appear noticeably frequently to have friendly smiles on their faces. The atmosphere of the Ny Havn (New Harbor) – which is actually the oldest – is almost Mediterranean. Tourists flock to Copenhagen in summer to occupy the tables and chairs of the restaurants, bars, and other hostelries immediately on the waterfront.

The amenable, colorful, gabled buildings and the small harbor basin originate from the eighteenth and nineteenth centuries when worthy merchants lived here before the quay became the red light area for seamen for a time.

The origins of Copenhagen are just a few steps away on Slotsholmen, the island with a castle, in which the Danish government now resides. In 1026 there was a fishing village there with the appropriate name of Havn or harbor still present in today's Danish name. When Bishop Absalom of Roskilde decided that this settlement was of strategic importance he had a small castle built at the village.

This remained for two centuries but after the building was destroyed by northern German plunderers in 1369 a new and stronger castle was built. In 1416 the Danish king moved in to the rebuilt castle and in 1443 Copenhagen became the Danish capital. In the late sixteenth century trade flourished so that the city became rich and gradually outgrew its original boundaries.

Building boom under Christian IV

The first cultural blossoming of Copenhagen happened in the seventeenth century. Under the auspices of the art-loving king, Christian IV, the finest buildings surviving today were built, such as the Observatorium Rundetårn (observatory), the exchange with its strange dragon tail decoration, and Rosenborg tower and castle in Dutch Renaissance style that today houses the Museum of Royal Treasures.

The fine years of the building

boom were followed by a catastrophic set-back though. Almost the entire population died of the Plague in 1711 and the city was destroyed by fire in 1728 and 1795, and then fired on by the British in 1807 but was immediately rebuilt.

When the Danes had recovered from these strokes of fate the city underwent a cultural revolution that was a golden age. The philosopher Søren Kirkegaard, the writer Hans Christian Andersen, and the founder of the Danish school of art, Christoffer Wilhelm Eckersberg changed attitudes with their work. In 1849 Denmark became a democracy and in 1856 the defensive wall was demolished.

The old bastions on the shore in Christianshavn that were built between 1662 and 1665 are now covered in greenery and new occupants have created imaginative homes. In 1971 the military terrain of Christiana was mainly occupied by hippies who proclaimed their own free state there. Hotly disputed but eventually tolerated, the settlement is now a rent free, leaderless, and car-free enclave in which a colorful mixture of bohemians, artists, and Yuppies live. From

the spiral tower of the Vor Frelsers church next to the "Free State" there is a spectacular view across the inner harbor and central Copenhagen. In the center the 347 foot high spire of the town hall towers over the broad expanse of the Raadhuspladsen or town hall square. It is surrounded by lively streets in which the pulse of Copenhagen beats.

Art at the Tivoli Gardens

This amusement park was opened in 1834 and is a Danish institution that attracts visitors now solely because of its giant Ferris wheel, carousels, and roller-coaster. There are also displays of folk dancing and international orchestras and ballet troupes perform in its large concert hall.

Immediately alongside the Tivoli the Carlsberg beer magnate Carl Jacobsen built his Ny Carlsberg Glyptothek in the late nineteenth century. This possesses what is probably the largest collection of Etruscan arts and crafts outside Italy but also features French and Danish art of the nineteenth century and an impressive collection of works by the French Expressionists.

One can delve into Danish history way back to the Paleolithic era in the National Museum, situated between the Glyptothek and Slotsholmen. You can admire a more than 3,500 years old chariot and bronze tools from 3,000 years ago or ancient coins and medallions.

The harbor is Copenhagen's popular meeting place (top left)

City center at the town hall square (top right)

Copenhagen's famous statue of a Mermaid

Stockholm - a city of many islands

The Swedish capital is the Venice of the north

Stockholm consists of fourteen islands between Lake Malaren and the Baltic, making it a symphony of water and light. In summer when the blazing northern sun is mirrored in the broad expanses of water of Sweden's capital, the city takes on an almost Mediterranean character but is peaceful and relaxed. At this time the population throngs the countless sidewalk cafés, squares, and parks that beckon one to linger, to play and listen to music.

Originally Stockholm was just the now well preserved and idyllic Gamla Stan or old town on a single island, with its narrow, enchanting streets with small cafés, restaurants, galleries, and boutique-lined squares.

On these rocks between sweet and salt water the Swedish ruler Birger Jarl began extending Stockholm to form a city in 1252. The city expanded extraordinarily rapidly because Birger established close ties with Lübeck with duty free rights given to merchants and the right to settle here in great numbers. The church of St. Gertrud in the old town – which is the most interesting German church from the sixteenth century – stands testimony to this day of the close relationship with the German Hanseatic town.

An approachable castle

The massive Baroque royal castle crowns the northern end of the island alongside the smaller islet on which the Swedish parliament is situated. It is the only royal castle that was open in those days to the public. It was built Between 1697 and 1704 on the foundations of a smaller castle that burnt down and was extended in 1754.

When city purification was introduced in 1859 and then sewage disposal in 1861 the city center was largely reshaped at the same time. Many older buildings were restored but also many new streets and parks were created. Many of the present-day schools, museums, libraries, and hospitals stem from this time.

Because Sweden has not been to war for 150 years Stockholm has been able to develop into one of the finest, most modern, and culturally most colorful metropolises in the world. The theater, exhibition, and museum culture has become an example far outside Scandinavia. A

visit to an exhibition or museum here is a special experience – even for children.

On the island of Djurgården it is possible to view Sweden's cultural heritage within a small area at the Nordiska museum at Skansen. It was established in 1891 as the first ever open air museum in the world and today it has 150 buildings from every part of Sweden from the Middle Ages to the nineteenth century. From the highest point within the museum on Skansen hill there is the best panoramic view of Stockholm.

Close by and housed within a futuristic wooden building is the Vasa, an old wooden Swedish warship that was once the pride of the Swedish navy although it never set to sea. It foundered on its maiden voyage with all hands and sixty-four cannon within the harbor basin. The Vasa lay well preserved in the Stockholm waters for 333 years before she was lifted from her 114 feet (35 m) deep resting place in 1961.

Art from skerries

Passing by the Grand Hotel where Nobel prize winners and state guests stay within sight of the king, continuing on beyond the mooring places of the steam skerries and the National Museum, one comes to berth of the four-master Af Chapman on Skeppshomen – the island of art. Art objects within large areas of grass point the way. Here alongside the Museum of Modern Art and the Academy of Art and Architecture are also many studios. The longest art gallery in the world though is underground – it is the underground railway. About one hundred stations hewn out of deep rock have been in part formed by world-renowned artists.

At Sergelstor, surrounded by modern office blocks and shopping centers of Norrmalm between the main rail station and the castle park of Kungsträgården is a cultural center the architecture and size of which is a match for the surrounding banks and department stores. Three large galleries exhibit changing shows of art, photography, fashion, and design, or multimedia events. From here you can observe the colorful bustle around the famous fountain.

Ridderholmen, an old town island on Lake Malaren with typical Hanseatic restraint (top)

It is hard to choose between the many convivial restaurants in the old town (bottom left)

Crown in front of the royal palace

White nights in Helsinki

Famous architects dominate the scene of the Finnish capital, with its Nordic atmosphere

FINLAND

Helsinki

Gulf of Bothnia

GETTING THERE
Good flight connections with all major cities. Ferry links with all important Baltic towns

BEST TIME
Best time is June-August. It does not really get dark in June. Mid July-mid August it is often 82.4 °F (28 °C) and hotter.

ACCOMMODATION
Hotels in every category and several youth hostels in which grown-ups can also stay (mainly close to the city center)

TIPPING
Not customary. Bar bills may be rounded up. The exceptions are porters and caretakers

The center of Helsinki viewed from the southern harbor. The white cathedral majestically crowns the city (top)

Jean Sibelius (1865-1957) was one of the most important composers of the twentieth century. Helsinki remembers the Finnish composer with an impressive memorial to his distinctive music (bottom left)

Market day at the harbor. Traders sell their wares from boats

When one thinks of sun, sea, and convivial entertainment, Helsinki is not the first place that springs to mind. Yet these are precisely the characteristics that make up the delight of the Finnish capital, together with the slightly Russian style of its townscape and the overwhelming friendliness of the city's inhabitants.

In summer when the days are hot and the nights are clear the life spills out onto the streets, in courtyards, on the water, and in the many extensive parks. Then music of every genre drifts through the air whether by day on the esplanade – where people take a stroll by the harbor – and in front of cultural centers surrounded by greenery, or by night amid the canyons of the sleeping office blocks. Hordes of young people sun themselves on the steps of the cathedral mixed in with tourists enjoying the panorama of the city and its harbor. The atmosphere is almost Mediterranean, especially on the colorful market place alongside the waters of the southern harbor in front of the residences of the mayor and Finland's president.

Helsinki is a young city. Its present-day large-scale townscape and the majority of the Neo-Classical public buildings stem from the beginning of the nineteenth century, uniformly planned by the German architect Carl Ludwig Engel. This is because when Russian troops occupied Finland in 1808 the city's wooden buildings were all destroyed by fire.

Helsinki was founded by the Swedish king, Gustav Wasa in 1550 to compete with Reval (present-day Tallinn) on the other side of the Gulf of Finland. At first he built the town slightly further north on the mouth of the River Vaanta. The move to the present site was made in 1640 for better access to the sea.

Defensive fortifications against the Russians

The Russians made repeated attempts to seize Helsinki in the early eighteenth century. For this reason the Swedish king, Gustav III, had the Sveaborg (Swedish castle) built on rocks at the entrance to the harbor in 1748. Many of the old military buildings such as the old powder store are today occupied as homes and restaurants. At the time of the independence in 1919 it was known as Suomenenlinna (Finnish castle).

The territory became Russian in 1808 and in 1812 the Czar moved the residence of the Grand Dukedom of Finland from Åbo to Helsinki. The city began to flourish when it was rebuilt after its destruction by fire into its present day role as the trading, industrial, and cultural center of Finland.

Early rail travelers were received in monumental fashion. The impressive station building is the major work of the Finnish architect Eliel Saarinen and it was constructed of pink granite in the Art Deco style between 1910 and 1914. Those arriving by ship on the other hand were greeted from afar by the glistening white Lutheran cathedral and the red Uspenskay cathedral.

St. Petersburg classicism

The mighty dome of the great cathedral with its impressive white pillars was built between 1830 and 1852. Its modest Lutheran interior provides an echo of the Senate Place in the city center. The entire square is a unified composition by Carl Ludwig Engel in the style of St. Peterburg's classicism. On one side stands the main building of the university – outshining its neighbors with its beauty – opposite the Government building (formerly the Senate).

The Uspenskay cathedral to the north-east of the harbor also brings a strong note of Russia to the Finnish capital. Architect Alexander Gornostachev build the Orthodox church in old Russian style in 1868 using red bricks with a golden dome. Within its sumptuous icon-decorated interior giant granite pillars bear the richly decorated dome.

Surely the most striking church though is the Temppeliaukio rock church that is one of the most impressive examples of modern Finnish architecture. Rock was hewn to the design of architects Timo and Tuomo Suomalainen to rise almost 40 feet (12 m) in the center of a residential area. The broad and largely uniform rotunda, enclosed by plain hewn rocks, is spanned by a giant copper and glass dome. From outside this is the only part of the building to be seen. The church is also used as a concert hall because of its dramatic acoustics resulting from the rock formation.

There are also concerts by no fewer than three city symphony orchestras in the famous Finlandia Hall on the large Töölonlathi lake within the city. The concert and congress building of white marble with a design reminiscent of the Bauhaus school is a masterpiece of the architect Alvar Alto and it was completed in 1975.

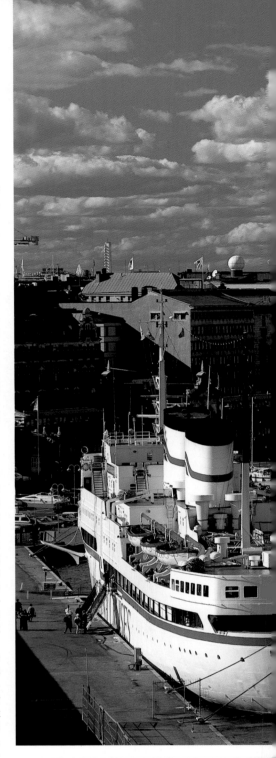

The hub of the universe

NEW YORK has been gateway to the land of unlimited opportunity since the nineteenth century

New York ●
USA
Pacific Ocean
Atlantic Ocean

GETTING THERE
International flights from the entire world to JFK airport or Newark International in the neighboring state of New Jersey. First class domestic flight links

BEST TIME
April, May, September, and October have the most pleasant temperatures

ACCOMMODATION
The city has hotel rooms in every price category

TIPPING
15 %. Taxis 15 % plus change

New York is the quintessence of America. Capital, plentiful cheap labor, raw materials, shipping routes, and rail links made the city the business hub of the world. For all this New York does not accurately reflect the rest of the USA. Nowhere else do so many different peoples live together in such confined space, nowhere else has such a fascinating awareness of life, molded by some two hundred different ethnic backgrounds, nowhere else is so multicultural yet with its own expression, and nowhere else has so many skyscrapers towering above the streets.

Manhattan never sleeps

Between them by day in the glass and concrete canyons of the financial district smart-suited men and fashionably-clad women rush past one another like ants. New Yorkers and tourists party well into the night on Broadway. Thousands of cars creep like broad-fronted glaciers of steel through the miles of avenues and streets, with the constant urgency of police and ambulance sirens. New York never sleeps. It is the city of dreams: of the quick buck, of great success but also of great disappointment.

The Italian seafarer Giovanni da Verrazzano called this place – with its perfect natural harbor at the mouth of the Hudson River – Santa Margarita when he anchored here in 1524. In 1626 Peter Minnewit in the service of the Dutch bought Manhattan Island from the Manhatto native Americans for $24 and named it New Amsterdam. The native American trail that crossed the island is still New York's principal artery: Broadway. Ten years later a second village was established opposite on Long Is-

land, called Breukelen that is today's Brooklyn.

The settlements at the mouth of the Hudson River were a gathering place for people from many different countries right from the early days. The monk Isaak Joques counted eighteen different languages in New Amsterdam in 1643. Nothing altered in this cosmopolitan nature when the British took possession in 1664 and renamed the settlement New York.

Million population in 1870

The first great wave of migrants from Europe rolled into New York in 1836. House building could not keep pace with demand and the first slums came into being. After the end of the Civil War in 1865 former slaves fled here from the hostility in the south and the million inhabitants mark was passed. The five ad-

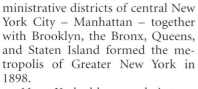

After the World Trade Center was victim of 11 September 2001 the most impressive view of Manhattan's canyon-like streets is once again from the Empire State Building (top left)

The Brooklyn Bridge crosses the Hudson River and links Brooklyn and Manhattan (top right)

Times Square is the center of Manhattan – night-time meeting point for New Yorkers and tourists from all over the world

ministrative districts of central New York City – Manhattan – together with Brooklyn, the Bronx, Queens, and Staten Island formed the metropolis of Greater New York in 1898.

New York blossomed into a world-class city after World War I when the first skyscrapers thrust their way into the sky above Manhattan.

One of the landmarks of that era is the Empire State Building. The view from its visitor facility remains one of the finest vistas of Manhattan. The building, with its elegant Art Deco facade, was built in 1931 on the site of the equally famous Waldorf-Astoria Hotel that until then had accommodated the rich, beautiful, and famous in its 1,401 luxury rooms within a fine Art Deco building close to Grand Central Station.

Lower Eastside is discovered

The old must constantly make way for the new. This is the character of New York. This is how Greenwich Village, founded in 1792, changed from the leading part of the city of the eighteenth and nineteenth cen-

turies to a paradise for free spirits and Bohemians in the twentieth century. But they were drawn more and more over the years to the East Village. This part of the city, in which former migrants from Germany, Poland, Russia, and Puerto Rico settled, became the center for the hippies. Today increasing numbers of well-paid people live in luxuriously rehabilitated apartments above the art galleries. Artists and students now head for the more southerly and once deserted Lower Eastside that is developing into one of the liveliest parts of town. The Latinos have also settled here and

Chinatown, once the Jewish quarter and long ago more than a match for Little Italy, extends its tentacles further eastwards.

Immediately opposite in Brooklyn Heights a charm awaits the like of which is nowhere else in New York. Behind small front gardens are lines of sandstone and brick town houses along cobbled streets and avenues that unexpectedly radiate a peaceful tranquillity. Lower down on the Brooklyn Promenade the gaze drifts across the East River to the island of skyscrapers that from here have the appearance of a grandiose backdrop for an improbable drama.

Washington D.C.

From the Capitol past the White House to the Lincoln Memorial, the Mall is more than a famous avenue

Washington DC
USA

Pacific Ocean

Atlantic Ocean

GETTING THERE
Flights into
Baltimore-Washington
or Washington-Dulles
airports. Good Amtrak
rail connections along
east coast as far as
Boston

BEST TIME
The best times are
March-May and
September-November

ACCOMMODATION
All categories available
but expensive

**SPECIAL
RECOMMENDATION**
Pre-booking of entry
tickets avoids waits of
hours to many places
of interest during the
tourist season

TIPPING
15 %. Taxis 15 % plus
change

The capital city of the USA is a microcosm of a country of great ideals and ugly realities. The inner city of Washington was neglectful for some years of the poor and negative towards them out of the fear of violent crimes that once nullified chances of a relaxed approach to life. For this reason the prosperous residential areas of the government employees are in the outlying districts.

Since the 1980s Washington has done much to improve the quality of living in the center of this government metropolis and to protect its historical heritage. The handsome tree-lined avenues, the monuments, the Mall, and many fine buildings from the nineteenth century generate an astonishing warm and even convivial atmosphere. Once again they reflect the tranquil life style of the southern states rather than the business-like north.

Today many parts of the city are lively centers of multicultural life, like the zest for life of Adams Morgan, heart of the Latino community with its colorful market, or the old Foggy Bottom on the banks of the Potomac River, once home to Irish, Germans, and Afro-Americans with its John F. Kennedy Center for the Performing Arts.

When the young American nation, full of hope, searched for a center of government in the late eighteenth century the Congress chose an area by the Potomac River, centrally-situated between the northern and southern states. This was an ideal choice too for George Washington, who lived on the opposite bank of the Potomac.

Parisian example

In 1791 the states of Maryland and Virginia provided 100 square miles (260 squared km) of land for the District of Columbia. For the citizens the city was Washington and this name stuck.

The French engineer Pierre Charles l'Enfant was given the task of planning the entire town. His example was the Baroque architecture and landscape of Paris and Versailles. The ground plan cleverly took into account the natural lie of the land.

Although l'Enfant quickly fell out with the politicians and was discharged, building work began in 1792 on the Capitol. Yet it was hardly completed when British troops set fire to it in 1812. Although Congress soon wanted to drop the entire notion of building a capital city they did eventually decide to rebuild the Capitol. Continual arguments led to a regular stream of new architects being sought for the government buildings leading to an unusual mixture of different styles. The Senate and House of Representatives wings were added in 1857 and the massive iron dome in 1863 with the eastern elevation added in 1950. Meanwhile the building was twice as large as originally planned. Nevertheless it gave the citizens of the USA the reassuring feeling that their government rested on solid and substantial foundations.

The Mall too, that wide avenue, grand in scale, running from the Capitol to the White House by way of the Potomac was also different to l'Enfant's design. His was based on the Champs-Élysées but ever new plans for buildings completely changed the symmetry of the Mall.

The idea of l'Enfant that every open square in Washington should be embellished with a statue or monument was carried out though. Hence today Washington's squares have three hundred monuments to admire from the elegant Lincoln and Jefferson Memorials to Doric temples.

The artistic movements in America up to World War II passed Washington by completely. The imposing Congress library with surely the largest collection of books, newspapers, magazines, maps, and manu- scripts simply enjoyed a special calling. The famous Smithsonian Institute in its red brick "palace" on the Mall became a serious recognized museum but for a long time was contemptuously known as "the nation's junk room."

Yet this changed after 1941. The demand for art and culture in the capital became a state and federal challenge. Thirteen impressive museums were added to the worthy Smithsonian, creating a Mecca for art lovers of every style.

Temple of modern architecture

CHICAGO'S skyline is one of the world's architectural wonders –
the city on Lake Michigan is gateway to the Mid-West

Chicago • USA

Pacific Ocean

Atlantic Ocean

GETTING THERE
Chicago is the travel-hub of the USA. There are flights from 300 cities in the world daily. Chicago is also the center for both Amtrak rail and Greyhound Buses

BEST TIME
Best time is May to September. This is also the most active period for cultural events. High summer can be very hot (up to 89.6 °F/32 °C)

ACCOMMODATION
All categories available but quite expensive. During festivals e.g. Blues, Gospel, Jazz, Taste of Chicago booking is recommended

TIPPING
15 % or more in restaurants and better hotels. Taxi drivers, waiters, and hairdressers expect similar tips

The jagged skyline of skyscrapers on the southern shore of the enormous Lake Michigan is the proud expression of a city in which everything is possible. Chicago's often audacious, fantastic towering buildings are text book examples of the very best of American architecture. They do not overwhelm you. Everywhere plenty of space is left for broad avenues with prominent sidewalks, for parks, and places with sculpture by famous artists. In between there are numerous churches, low-rise apartment blocks, and even two to three storey town houses.

In the city center as indeed in every other part of town everything people need for their homes, living, working, and their free time is close at hand. People of every color fill the city with a pulsating, multicultural atmosphere. World famous museums, theaters, orchestras, and above all the omnipresent rhythm and blues and jazz have found fertile ground here.

A fur-trader of French-African descent, Jean Baptiste Point du Sab-le from Santo Domingo built the first permanent settlement on the marshy mouth of the Chicago River in 1779. In 1833 the place became known as Chicago and increased in size to more than 4,000 inhabitants by 1837.

The significance of Chicago as a well-situated transshipment center for passengers and goods to and from the West increased in 1848 with the opening of the Illinois–Michigan canal and the first length of railroad that reached Chicago in 1850.

After the great fire

With the sensational downtown improvements of 1855 the needs of the rapidly-growing population were met. Because the streets were often muddy from the wet low-lying ground the outer walls of the buildings were raised 4-15 feet (1.2-4.5 m) and set back at the same time to make room for wider streets.

After the great fire of 8 October, 1871 the second Chicago arose completely new in a few years. This provided an opportunity to introduce modern technology. In 1887 the first nationwide telephone system went into operation and only two years after the invention of the electric lamp in 1879 the new lighting system lit up the streets. The cable car system adopted in San Francisco arrived in Chicago in 1881.

The building boom after the fire made Chicago a Mecca for architects and these included Frank Lloyd Wright who came to the town in 1889. The steady influx of people who found work in the grain silos, slaughter houses, and heavy industry soon demanded new town planning measures because the population rose above one million in 1890. The solution for the increasing volume of traffic was the elevated railroad around the central business areas, built in 1897 and known simply as the "El".

The first skyscraper

By the turn of the century between the nineteenth and twentieth centuries all the technology required for steel-frame construction was available and the age of the skyscraper began. For the first time in architectural history the division between appearance and structure disappeared. This was an achievement of the "Chicago school" of architecture for the new steel-frame construction united both load-bearing function and the appearance of the building.

The finest examples of the impetus given by Chicago's architecture are in the downtown area. Within the Loop district – inside the elevated railroad – one finds the Neo-Romanesque auditorium and the Art Deco Chamber of Commerce. The other high-rise part of the city is River North on the northern bank of the Chicago River. Here between the high-rise buildings there is a lively business center of imposing water towers that provide the city's drinking water.

Along the "Magnificent Mile" section of Michigan Avenue there is a shopper's paradise in the midst of which the Tribune building soars up. This Neo-Gothic masterpiece of 1925 is home to the editorial staff of the famous daily newspaper, Chicago Tribune.

The 1,450 foot (442 m) high Sears Tower became the world's tallest building in 1996 with its 110 floors. From the viewing platform on the 103rd floor the eye wanders across the skyline to Lake Michigan and the wide-open prairies of the Mid-West.

Wide avenues between the high-rise buildings ensure a relaxed atmosphere for strolling. This is State Street by the Chicago Theater (bottom left)

High-rise towers were a challenge for architects. The view at dusk from the Hancock Tower across the city (top right)

Seen from the water the facades of the skyscrapers appear to have filigree-fine detail in spite of their massive scale

GETTING THERE
International flight connections via Atlanta or Newark; train connections with Miami, Los Angeles, Chicago, and New York

BEST TIME
Best times are April–May and October–November. Tropical temperatures above 86 °F (30 °C) in summer with high humidity

ACCOMMODATION
All categories. During special occasions (Mardi Gras and New Orleans Jazz Heritage Festival) booking is necessary

TIPPING
15 %. Servants and porters an all-in $1

The capital of Jazz

NEW ORLEANS has retained its French aura

The most un-American city of the USA refuses all fads and fancies and daily renews its rich and unique traditions. The rubbish from last night is scarcely cleaned-up in the Vieux Carré or French quarter before the joints becomes busy again around noon. And from Bourbon Street the first sounds of the street musicians can be heard.

As the day grows older the greater too is the accompaniment of jazz, Zydeco, Cajun, rhythm and blues, and gospel sounds through the streets and across the places of the old town. The bringing together of black African musical culture with the European traditions of the French Creoles gave birth in New Orleans around 1880 to jazz.

French founded the city

But all the other countless ethnic origins of the people who came to this city across the ages have contributed to the unique synthesis of different cultures. The bubbling zest for life of the city's people can be seen unbridled annually during Mardi Gras.

The first Europeans were the monks Pierre Le Moyne and Jean-Baptist Le Moyne de Bienville in 1699 who came to reconnoiter the Mississippi. At that time the area was solely inhabited by nomadic tribes of native Americans.

About twenty years later de Bienville returned and founded Nouvelle Orléans in the marshes between Lake Pontchartrain and the Mississippi. The first settlers followed from France, Canada, and Germany, with the French importing thousands of African slaves. Because of the harsh conditions of life in the tropical swamp few other settlers were attracted and the economy did not flourish.

Louisiana soon became a burden for the French state. In 1762 they got rid of the worthless territory to the Spanish who also quickly tired of their new possession. When Napoleon offered to take it back in 1800 the territory once more became French. In 1803 he sold the territory to the fledgling American state so that it would not fall into British hands. The resident Creoles were not really enthusiastic. They regarded American culture as vulgar and feared their Protestant beliefs and British-influenced legislation.

By 1840 New Orleans had become the fourth largest town in the USA and ten years later became the center of the slave trade. When the slave-owning states were separating from the Union in the run-up to the Civil War, three-quarters of those in New Orleans with a vote vainly voted at any rate to remain in the Union and to abolish slavery.

Old quarter on the river

Since the civil war and the liberation of the slaves New Orleans has become a flourishing industrial city and developed the second-largest sea port of the USA. Nevertheless the old parts of the city by the Mississippi on either side of Canal Street remain the liveliest heart of town.

Upstream in the French quarter in contrast with expectations the architecture is predominantly Spanish, making its fascinating contribution to the city's aura. The architecture developed with elements of French Colonial style from Quebec into a Creole vernacular of its own after the majority of original French buildings were destroyed in the fires of 1788 and 1794.

Jackson Square is the center of the Vieux Carré, dominated by the Neo-Classical elegance of the St. Louis cathedral. It was erected in

1794 on the foundations of two churches that had been destroyed by fire and hurricane.

The finest examples of Creole buildings are along Royal Street and the side streets running off it. The roofs extend far over the balconies with their richly decorated wrought iron grilles that were fashioned by skilled slave hands. While apartments are hidden behind the graceful arched windows of the upper floors, the street-level is teeming with stores dealing in antiques, curiosities, and voodoo cult paraphernalia. The side streets are lined with boutiques, perfume stores, sidewalk cafés, tea rooms, and countless art galleries.

Then after World War II New Orleans became one of the most im-portant centers for art dealing where many artists and galleries offered original works. The Museum of Art has collected many of these modern treasures and behind the Grecian facade are departments for Dutch Painting of the Seventeenth century, Spanish Colonial art of Latin America, and a collection of photography of special significance.

Street Musicians in the Vieux Carré quarter of New Orleans (top left)

Paddle steamers became widespread public transport on the Mississippi after the turn of the nineteenth century. Today they are mainly tourist attractions (top right)

The Royal Café in the Vieux Carré gets its special atmosphere from architectural detail from colonial times

City paradise on the sea

Eternal sunshine and the sea ensure a great life style in **SAN DIEGO**

USA
• San Diego

Pacific Ocean

Atlantic Ocean

GETTING THERE
Internal flights into Lindbergh Field airport. International connections via Los Angeles. Greyhound bus and Amtrak routes along the Californian coast

BEST TIME
It is almost always sunny in San Diego. Even in the colder months it reaches 68 °F (20 °C)

ACCOMMODATION
San Diego is a popular tourist destination and for this reason prior booking is recommended. Every category hotel from $60 to $200 or more available

TIPPING
15 %. Taxis 15 % plus change

Sail boats are just as much a part of San Diego's skyline as the skyscrapers of modern city architecture (top)

Among the most historic monuments in the Old Town is the Church of the Immaculate Conception (bottom left)

The Sea World aquarium with its dolphin show is one of the city's visitor attractions

Joggers, roller-skaters, and mountain bikers in the peak of condition and skimpily clad dart by in hordes along the promenade. At sea, where the towering waves of the Pacific roll in surfers lithely let the breakers bring them back to shore on which thousands of sun worshippers are tanning themselves. San Diego is the second largest city of California and has the fastest heartbeat of the lively Californian coastal life.

Vacationers that throng Seaport Village enjoy the many cafés, restaurants, and souvenir stores. It is new, in the style of a turn of the century harbor village on Embarcadero. Even if the harbor never had any major commercial significance the Maritime Museum and the warships of the naval base lying at anchor on either side of the harbor bar of silver sand ensure a nautical romantic scene and atmosphere for the area down by this harbor.

After Juan Rodriguez Cabrillo was the first European to tread this land on 28 September, 1542 and named the area San Miguel, it was more than two centuries before a Spanish mission was established here. Sixty years later Sebastian Vizcaino renamed the area San Diego de Alcala when he mapped the coast of California.

Out of fear that Russian fur trappers from the north or the English to the east might seize the land the Spanish built a church and a Presidio to the south of the San Diego River in 1769. The ruins can still be seen.

War with Mexico

When Mexico took control a village was built in 1834 outside the fortifications. After the American war with Mexico this Pueblo or Old Town was extended. In 1867 the real estate trader Alonzo Erastus Horton bought an area south of the Old Town and began to build a "New Town" there. Two years later Horton constructed a quay on the waterfront that forms the nucleus of the Gaslamp Quarter. The most lucrative types of enterprise of those days established themselves here: 120 bordellos and 71 gambling dens. When the Santa Fe Railroad linked the town with the east in 1884 the future seemed secure. Despite this the property-speculation boom suddenly ended in 1888 and about half the population left the town so that the Old Town and Gaslamp Quarter declined.

Things started moving again only from 1900 onwards helped by the increase in importance of the Coronado US Navy base in both world wars and shipbuilding, aerospace, and electronics industries establishing themselves here. In the 1960s a start was made to restore the few remaining historical buildings of the Old Town.

Light from Gas lamps

Above all, the attractive Gaslamp Quarter now began to enjoy a renaissance. The old attractive Victorian brick buildings from the years between 1880 and 1920 are now perfectly restored and create a great atmosphere of the turn of the nineteenth century by gas lamp for the many visitors. In this part of town, that was still considered disreputable into the 1970s, antique and souvenir stores, small theaters, restaurants, bars, and discotheques provide a relaxed blend of gastronomy, fun, and culture.

The Balboa Park offers living elephants but also theater evenings of Shakespeare and other cultural events. Imaginative city fathers reserved this leisure-time area in downtown San Diego back in 1868 and saved it from property speculation. Today fifteen museums, four theaters – including the Old Globe replica of the former London Shakespeare theater of the fifteenth century – and most of all the famous zoo, set amid gardens of roses, palms, and cacti, beckon one to the varied experiences.

The land between the mission bay and downtown San Diego that was once a swamp is now a popular beach and sailing paradise between lagoons, small bays, and dreamy islands. On the southern shore the commercial entertainment aquarium of Sea World was opened in 1964. It is one of the world's biggest, with perfected shows by sea mammals and a gigantic underwater tunnel.

On the other side of the bay, where the lighthouse at Point Loma is situated above steep cliffs, there is a superb view across the harbor to the skyline of San Diego. From here you can also watch the more than 15,000 Gray Whales that pass off the point between December and March when they migrate along the Californian peninsula from the feeding area in the Arctic to their breeding area.

The metropolis of the West

SAN FRANCISCO is a modern legend with its Golden Gate Bridge, cable cars, and sea lions

San Francisco
USA

Pacific Ocean

Atlantic Ocean

GETTING THERE
Only San Francisco airport in the Bay Area (including Oakland and San Jose) has international flights

BEST TIME
From mid-September to mid-November. A lot of rain in winter and spring. A lot of sea mist in summer

ACCOMMODATION
Prior booking recommended. Hotels in categories from $ 60–200 and above. Cheaper hotels in Chinatown

TIPPING
15 % or more in restaurants and the better hotels

The unique lifestyle of San Francisco is formed by many different cultures and ethnic backgrounds. Perhaps this is why the city became the center for the beatniks of the 1950s and the Flower Power generation in the 1960s. Today it is a picturesque city in which to live and a meeting place for the computer brains of Silicon Valley and for homosexuals from the entire world.

San Francisco sits on a peninsula of more than 30 miles (50 km) in length on the southern side of the sea channel between San Francisco Bay and San Pablo which is spanned by the famous Golden Gate Bridge. The settlements on the shores of the Bay Area have become among the most important economic centers of the USA in the past one hundred years. Today more than six million people live here.

When the Gold Rush began

The great explorers of the sixteenth century all sailed on by the bay. The first landing by a white man within San Francisco Bay was made by Gaspar de Portolá of Spain in 1769. The first settler came seven years later in 1776.

Just under two miles to the east the Englishman William Anthony Richardson founded the first built-up area in 1835 at Yerba Buena Cove. Following unsuccessful negotiations to purchase the cove in 1846 the USA occupied it and named it San Francisco.

Fewer than five hundred white, black, Hawaiian and native American people lived here in 1846. The population exploded with the start of the Gold Rush in 1849. Within the space of a few months 40,000 arrived by ship and just as many came by foot over the mountains.

When silver was discovered ten years later in Nevada the city of tough gold prospectors had become an up-and-coming metropolis of cunning bankers, speculators, and lawyers, followed by expensive fashion stores, restaurants, and hotels. The great earthquake on 18 April, 1906 put a brake on the city's growth and destroyed the business areas. The fires that followed the earthquake and raged for four days were far more devastating, destroying 28,000 buildings and making a quarter of a million people homeless.

Wooden Gothic in Fillmore Street

The next stroke of fate came in World War II. Half a million people came to the city to work for the war industry, including ten thousand of African Americans who moved into the old timber Gothic buildings in Fillmore Street. These were previously occupied by Japanese who were interned in 1942.

When the attractive-looking old houses were renovated in the 1980s, many of the poor African Americans had to move to the already overcrowded slums in the southeast of the city.

Present-day Japan Town is a couple of blocks from Fillmore Street. It is a small financial and cultural center that many Japanese Americans only come to as visitors.

Chinatown that is further east is quite different. With its 30,000 inhabitants it counts as the largest Chinese community outside Asia. In the small streets with dual language name signs that are highly decorated with Chinese lanterns you can experience everyday Chinese life and try Chinese food.

Many of the well-established Chinese are now in North Beach that was once the Italian quarter and the birthplace of the beat generation. This lively part of town with its night clubs and many bars and cafés remains Italian leaning.

The Coit Tower on nearby Telegraph Hill provides an all-round panorama of the city and the bay – provided the weather is accommodating.

Nostalgia of the cable cars

The last three remaining lines of the famous cable cars run up the steep hills of this northeastern part of town. The tram-like cars without motors were introduced in 1873 and since then have become a symbol of San Francisco. They are operated by a continuous cable that winds beneath the street at a rate of about 10 mph (15 km/h). A visit to the Ca-ble Car Museum on the corner of Washington and Mason Streets is rewarding because the entire cable system is also operated from here.

One should also ride the cable car to the tourist center of Fisherman's Beach at the northern end of North Beach. Trips to Alcatraz leave from here to visit the prison that was the most secure in America between 1934 and 1963. Even though the locals turn their noses up at the tumult on the pier and you must not overlook the fun-fair mood and pantomime bustle of the musicians and clowns – especially since the sea lions bask themselves on Pier 39 in spite of the hurly-burly and the many attempts to resettle them.

The Golden Gate Bridge is the landmark of the city. The giant steel structure was built in the 1930s to span the channel from the Bay to the Pacific Ocean at a height of 220 ft (67 m). The city can be seen behind in the light of evening

The cable cars still ride the hills of San Francisco. Here the nostalgic curiosity is in lively Powell Street

Inlets, mountains and Vancouver

Canada's largest city on the Pacific is famous for its unique location

GETTING THERE
Daily International flights from throughout the world

BEST TIME
The best time to travel is June-October when the temperature averages 68 °F (20 °C). March to May and September to November are good times to see whales

ACCOMMODATION
Every category of hotel is available. Many offer great sea views. Prior booking is advisable

TIPPING
10-15 % of the bill for services (restaurant, taxi, hairdresser). Hotel personnel Canadian $2-3 per item of luggage

Vancouver is situated within shimmering inlets and the Fraser River on a deeply-fissured peninsula set against the backdrop of snow-covered peaks that soar to 3,937 feet (1,200 m). Its big city heart beats on a peninsula that is washed by the waters of English Bay, Burrard Inlet, and False Creek.

Chinatown is like a portal in front of the lively business area immediately on the land link and gives a foretaste of the cosmopolitan atmosphere of this city. Vancouver's British aura has been formed into an individual character through exposure to many cultures, especially Asian. From time immemorial this Pacific city of two million has had considerable attraction for countries on the other side of the oceans. Yet it is not yet 150 years since the first white lumberjack settled here among the Salish native Americans.

Gold along the Fraser River

The way for Europeans was prepared by James Cook who landed on Vancouver Island in 1778. Jose Maria Narvez found the mouth of the Fraser River in 1791 and the following year Captain George Vancouver returned having accompanied Cook fourteen years earlier. In 1793 Alexander Mackenzie reached the Pacific Ocean here after crossing the Rocky Mountains.

When gold was discovered along the Fraser River in 1858 thousands of fortune-hunters answered its call. One day in 1867 John Deighton appeared on the southern shore of the Burrard Inlet with a barrel of whiskey. He promised the lumberjacks hard liquor if they helped him to build a bar. The saloon was ready in twenty-four hours.

While Gastown grew up around the bar of Gassy Jack – as he became known – the Chinese built their Chinatown alongside and on a small island in the swamp in False Creek Inlet on the other side the lumberjack community of Granville arose.

The railroad crossing Canada reached the settlement in 1886 which became a town as a result, taking the name of the explorer of this coast, Captain Vancouver.

Now began the economic growth. As early as 1887 the first ship from China entered the harbor and with the opening of the Panama Canal in 1914 the markets on the east coast and in Europe became more accessible.

The tolerant and multicultural society that makes Vancouver so fascinating today first developed after World War II. This has been furthered by ten thousand wealthy Hong Kong Chinese who moved to Vancouver before the Chinese took over the British colonial enclave in 1997 and settled in the hilly suburbs.

The original Chinese life throbbed in Chinatown, the quarter of snack-bars, restaurants, and junk stores. On its edge is the only classical Chinese garden outside China. In the seclusion of the Dr. Sun Yat-Sen Garden one can follow the Taoist principles of Yin and Yang in peace.

Restoration of Gastown

The nearby and once shabby Gastown was cleaned up after 1970 and is now a bright and shiny business area in Neo-Victorian style. The offices of the nineteenth century have become restaurants, bars, boutiques, and galleries. The colorful life on the brick-paved streets, lined with antique street lanterns, includes street traders, musicians, and artists. The attraction of the area is the steam clock on Water Street that tourists believe is operated by natural steam from out of the earth. In reality of course it is operated these days by electricity.

Between Gastown and the upmarket shopping streets around the Pacific Center there is a former court house. Today this houses the Vancouver Art Gallery. This fine domed building extends for an entire block. The permanent exhibi-

tion of work by the famous Canadian painter Emily Carr on the second floor is certainly worth seeing. The broad open area on the northern side is a gathering place for those wanting to express political opinions while on the southern side the city's young people, passers-by, and chess players mix with suited business people lunching on the gallery's steps.

The extensive Stanley Park covers the remaining half of the peninsula. It was laid out by Frederick Law Olmsted who was also responsible for New York's Central Park.

Here the people of Vancouver enjoy extended walks, quiet picnic places, and the promenade along the shore with its magnificent views of the varied silhouette of their city.

Vancouver presents a modern face to the sea. At the center of this skyline is Canada Place (top)

Sail boats and motor boats form park of the cityscape (bottom left)

View from Stanley Park of the Lion's Gate Bridge

A true metropolis

People from 60 nations live together in **TORONTO**

GETTING THERE
Toronto is easily reached by air, road, or rail. Its Lester B. Pearson International Airport is one of the world's major airports

BEST TIME
Canada has a harsh continental climate. Summer temperatures climb to 95 °F (35 °C)

ACCOMMODATION
All categories available. The closer to the center the more expensive they are

TIPPING
10-15 % of the bill for services

The first rays of the sun in spring have barely touched the sidewalks between the skyscrapers before tables and chairs appear outside every bar. When thermometers in summer register above 86 °F (30 °C) in the canyons between the skyscrapers, which they often do, people escape to the shore of the lake to the south of downtown Toronto, where a light breeze from Lake Ontario makes the heat more bearable.

The long sandy beaches and promenade along the shore create an almost Californian atmosphere. Roller-blade skaters and joggers speed past the grills, sports boat marinas, swimming pools, and amusement joints. Armed with picnic baskets, families and groups queue for the small ferries to take them to little islands off shore from which there are superb views of Toronto's skyline.

The colorful mixture of every skin tone, ethnic origin, and language is striking. Toronto is the most ethnically diverse city in the world. Forty percent of its inhabitants were born overseas. People from sixty different original nations live together in harmony in this metropolis and impart it with a very special character.

When the first European trappers reach Lake Ontario along the trails of the native Americans they found the settlement of Teiaiagon of the Mississauga native people. In 1720 the French built their trading station of Toronto on the natural harbor, defended by a small fort.

In 1763 Canada came under British rule and following the American Civil War Toronto experienced its first wave of immigration with many colonists from the south preferring to remain under British rule rather than remain under an American administration.

Hard liquor for land

The British bought more than 40,000 acres (100,000 ha) of land from the Mississauga for hard liquor, weapons, and £1,700 in order to extend the settlement at the harbor. The Governor of Ontario, Lieutenant-Colonel John Graves Simcoe named the settlement York in 1793 and made it the capital of Ontario.

Two years later the government settlement on the edge of the wilderness consisted of twelve huts.

When the Napoleonic War ended in Europe and England sank into a deep economic depression, many sought a new future in the Canadian York. While only 700 lived in the settlement in 1812, by 1834 this had risen to 9,000. York had truly become a town but now returned to the name of Toronto.

There was an economic upturn in the mid nineteenth century with the coming of the railroad. The Canadian nation's identity became established after the turn of the century and between 1908 and 1915 art and culture blossomed in Toronto. The first skyscraper shot into the sky at this time on the shores of Lake Ontario and this de-

velopment increased apace in the 1960s and 1970s. Many of the fine old buildings from the later nineteenth century that had survived the fire of 1904 had to give way to the high-rise buildings.

Many towns within the city

But not everything has disappeared. At first glance the financial district is a collection of exciting glass and concrete architecture but between these there are still gems from the past to be discovered.

In the area known as Cabbagetown close to the financial district the graceful charm of Victorian architecture is still full of life. This suburb that was once a workers' town and later the "largest Anglo-Saxon slum of North America" is today a lovingly restored and tran-

quil neighborhood with well-tended small parks.

Toronto is a fascinating mosaic of completely different parts of the city. Some are dominated by a single ethnic group while others merely reflect a certain lifestyle. The arrival of new inhabitants often changes the character of a neighborhood. Hence Little Italy arose after World War II from the former Jewish quarter whose occupants had moved to more prosperous parts. Today despite its Italian atmosphere Little Italy is in Portuguese hands. The Italians have created their Corso Italia, a quarter renowned for top fashion houses, select restaurants and cappuccino bars.

China lives meanwhile in six parts of the city. Chinatown in downtown Toronto came into being in 1935, then dominated by north-

ern Chinese. Today it is mainly Hong Kong Chinese who live here. Fairly close by in the historic Old York Town are the neighborhoods of Korea Town, Greek Town, Indian Bazaar, Little Poland, Portugal Village, and York Village, the only hippie community. Each neighborhood is a lively reflection of the people's homeland.

Casa Loma is an architectural curiosity. It is the ninety-eight room mansion of the industrialist Sir Henry Pellat. Not only did he furnish the rooms magnificently, he also had secret passageways and doors built. The house is now open for visitors as a museum.

Toronto's position on the shores of Lake Ontario make impressive views of its skyline possible. To the left of the picture are the covered baseball stadium and CN Tower (top)

Isolated buildings that survived the fire of 1904 can be found among the modern skyscrapers

Three cultures in Mexico City

This Latin American metropolis rose from the ruins of an Aztec city

If a city has a soul then in the case of Mexico City – with its more than twenty million inhabitants – it can be found in the Zócalo beneath the enormous expanse of the Plaza de la Constitución that is paved with blocks of black stone. The expanse of this Constitution Square is reminiscent of Venice's Piazza San Marco and in a similar manner important buildings such as the largest Baroque cathedral of Latin America and the enormous government building, with its famous murals of Diego Rivera, line its rim. Although invisible but nonetheless firmly fixed in the minds of the Mexicans, the Zócalo delineates the square with an Aztec temple and residences of their nobility since the Aztec city of Tenochtitlán once had its center here.

Mexico City sits at a height of 7,800 feet (2,240 m) above sea level in a high altitude basin that some five hundred years ago was covered in lakes. According to Aztec legend the México tribe found a mythical eagle sitting on a cactus on one of the larger islands with a serpent in its beak. This fulfilled a prophecy of a sign from the god Huitzilopochtli that the México should settle at this place. The Aztecs did settle here on a large island in 1345 to found the city they called Tenochtitlán.

Montezuma's mistake

When the Spanish conquistador Hernán Cortés reached the high altitude valley in Mexico in November 1519 the Mexicá's city was only accessible by means of a raised causeway and had a population of about 300,000. The Spanish were astonished by the beauty and wealth of the place, the central assembly area of which reminded them of Seville. It had a number of pyramid temples and towers, thousands of stone-built buildings, and fine gardens everywhere. The conquistadors quickly discovered that gold and silver were kept in Tenochtitlán.

The Aztec emperor, Montezuma II invited the bearded strangers with friendship into his palace, believing them to be gods of whose appearance priests had foretold. The Aztecs recognized the rapacity of their guests too late. The Spaniards took Montezuma as a hostage in order to extort treasure, committed terrible massacres with their firearms and after a struggle lasting many months pillaged the Aztecs of not only their gold but also of their land that was declared a province of Spain. Montezuma probably died in 1520 at the hands of his own people.

After the plundering the badly damaged Aztec city was razed to the ground. The stones from the "heathen" temples were used by the Spanish to build Christian churches and grand homes. Cortés had his own palace built using stones from the "New Palace" of Montezuma II. The Palacio Nacional was built on open space in front of the demolished Aztec buildings which later became an unfinished monument known as El Zócalo (the plinth).

Remains of the Templo Mayor

In order to gain a realistic impression of the former cult centers of the Aztecs it is worth paying a visit to the famous temple pyramids of Teotihuacan, half an hour's drive to the north of Mexico City. Some of the buildings that are monumental in scale and abandoned before 700 AD served as an example for those building who built the Aztec city nearby. Meanwhile in the northeastern corner of the Zócalo a section of the foundation wall of the Templo Mayor Aztec cult temple has been uncovered.

Mexico City proudly presents itself today as custodian of three cultures: that of the Aztecs, the Spanish, and the Mexican culture derived from the other two. The museums are richly supplied with priceless artifacts of the Aztec empire. Spanish Colonial style at its finest can be admired at the Plaza Santo Domingo where one of the finest Baroque churches of Mexico also attracts attention. The grand boulevard known as Paseo de la Reforma is reminiscent of Europe during the Belle Époque and the Palacio des Bellas Artes is an enchanting embodiment of Art Nouveau. The 580 foot (177 m) high Torre Latinoamericana is a modern landmark from which at night the sea of houses below can be seen as an ocean of light.

This is the best time to visit the Plaza Garibaldi with its Mariachi bands playing late into the night. At least they will play if you throw them a few Pesos.

GETTING THERE
Good flight connections with all parts of the world

ACCOMMODATION
Hotels in every category

BEST TIME
October to January

TIPPING
15 % of bill in restaurants and bars. Give chambermaids a few Pesos on arrival to improve service considerably. Porters expect a US dollar or two.

EXCURSIONS
Take a taxi or bus to the ruined city of Teotihuacan thirty miles to the north of Mexico City for its famous pyramid temples

Latin America's largest cathedral dominates the gathering place of El Zócalo in Mexico City. The Spanish used stone from the Aztec temples to build it in 1573 (top)

Folklore groups nowadays honor the Aztecs by performing their dances in costume (bottom left)

The great example for Aztec builders were found by them at Teotihaucan with its pyramid temples

121

Legends from Havana

The Cuban capital retains its heritage. Many Baroque buildings have been restored

GETTING THERE
Mainly by charter flights

BEST TIME
Pleasant climate
throughout the year.
January & February
71.6 °F (22 °C), August
82.4 °F (28 °C)

ACCOMMODATION
Little accommodation
for those traveling
outside package
arrangements

TIPPING
Customary for all
services up to 10 %

The Italianate Baroque cathedral in the center of the old city.

Havana cigars are regarded as the best in the world. In the Partagas cigar works workers roll cigars by hand (bottom right)

The architecture of the National Theater recalls a colonial past. Ancient American cars are still popular means of transport

Hemingway enjoyed his whiskey in this bar. Interior of the Bodeguita del Medio

A merican street cruisers from the 1950s and 60s dominate the narrow streets of old Havana. This recalls the heady days when corrupt politicians ruled Cuba. Mafia bosses like Lucky Luciano and Meyer Lanski stashed their dirty money here and writers like Ernest Hemingway drank until morning.

The colorful and exciting night life still pulsates in the many cinemas, theaters, cabarets, night clubs, and music halls. It may be more modest than fifty years ago but it does possess authentic Cuban soul and is far less commercialized than in any other city.

Havana is on the western side of a deep and blue bay with only a small channel to the Atlantic. This was an ideal position for Spanish conquistadors because the entrance could easily be defended. Admittedly the conquistador Diego Velázquez de Cuéllar built the first version of Havana on the southern side in 1515 but this was deserted in 1519 and moved to its present site since the initial site was too marshy and plagued with mosquitoes.

Spanish gateway to the west

Havana quickly became the preferred choice as port of call for Spanish ships before setting sail on course for home laden with treasure from Mexico and Peru. It was also the gateway to America for the Spanish conquerors and for the political and economic domination of their vast colonial empire.

This of course made the town a desirable objective for English, French, and Dutch pirates. Therefore fortifications were soon built such as the Castillo del Morro that was completed in 1610 and formed the center of a network of fortifications. Together with the Castillo de la Punta its still commands the entrance to the harbor today.

When the city walls were also

completed in 1700 it was deemed impregnable until the heavy cannons of English ships appeared and took the city after a siege lasting three months at the end of August 1762. The besiegers did not stay more than a few months though because in distant Europe the warring states had just ended the Seven Years War and Spain got Havana back in exchange for Florida.

Neglected old town

The war of independence broke out in 1895 and with the USA acting as go-between Cuba finally gained its independence in 1898, only to find itself with a new kind of dependence from its overpowering neighbor. Havana increasingly became a US-style American city.

The corrupt rule of three dictators finally provoked the Revolution of 1 January, 1959 when Fidel Castro marched into Havana. The USA cut all connections to the island from the outside world and sealed the (often illegal) stream of money.

Because the new government was strapped for cash and invested in the badly neglected interior the old city of Havana was virtually neglected. But the rough beauty was spared from both destruction and building transgressions and remains one of the most unified townscapes of Baroque and Neo-Classical architecture. Increasingly the fanciful old colonial buildings are being restored since the Cuban government implemented a multi-million dollar restoration program in the 1980s.

One of the first buildings to be restored was Havana's cathedral that is dedicated to the patron saint of San Cristóbal. It was constructed close to the water in the eighteenth century by Jesuits and is regarded by art historians as one of the finest examples of Italianate Baroque.

The center of Cuban life at the end of the nineteenth century was the Plaza de Armas. The showpiece is the Palacio de los Capitanes Generales that was the seat of the Spanish Captain General from 1793 and of the President from 1909. Today the Museo de la Ciudad clearly presents the city's history from the discovery of Cuba by Columbus in 1492 to the Revolution of 1959.

Mountain air in Quito

The Ecuador capital's well-cared for city center is a world-class monument

GETTING THERE
Good flight connections, usually via other cities in South America

BEST TIME
Spring-like 59-71.6 °F (15-22 °C), changeable but mainly dry. High season is December-January and June-August

ACCOMMODATION
All standards available. Simple hotels in the old town, medium to top quality hotels in the new town. Book a week in advance during high season and the many feast days

TIPPING
10 % service charge. Do not leave the tip on the table in restaurants. Taxi drivers do not expect a tip

The oldest capital city of South America is set in a wide valley not far from the 15,728 feet (4,794 m) Pichincha volcano. At an altitude of almost 9,514 feet (2,900 m) the air is extremely thin and takes some acclimatization for visitors. But the ever present marvelous spring-like weather, peaceful squares with their fountains, the steep and narrow streets of the old town, and the spacious ones of the new town compensate completely for the initial shortness of breath.

In the northern part of Quito the noisy sound of dense traffic in the wider Avenida 10 de Agosto and its partner of 6 de Diciembre intrudes. At the main meeting place of the city on the Avenida da Amazonas business people with mobile telephones, students, and Quiteños hurry past the row of different enterprises or relax in the many sidewalk cafés. In the streets of the old town on the other hand one encounters few cars. At worst ramshackle taxis and cheery colorful buses pick their way over the uneven streets and between the people.

Quito was the capital of the Inca kingdom of Quitu. Between the tenth century and 1487 when the Incas subjugated the city the Shyris were sovereigns over the native Cara people. It is said that they came from across the seas.

But Sebastián de Benalcázar, a Lieutenant with Francisco Pissaro's conquistadors only found ruins when he conquered the Inca city on 6 December, 1534 because Rumiñahui, general to Atahualpa, the last of the Inca emperors, preferred to destroy the city than hand it over to the conquistadores.

Quito was the first city in South America to unilaterally declare its independence on 10 August, 1809. But full independence was only achieved thirteen years later when republican troops finally defeated troops loyal to the crown.

Magnificent old town

Quito's old town has hardly changed from colonial times. Since it was listed by Unesco in 1978 as a world heritage site both new building and extensions in the old town have been strictly regulated. The few new buildings of the 1960s and 70s barely mar the simple white lime-wash facades of the old buildings with their stucco adornment above the windows, the decorated bays, and the hidden courtyards.

At the heart of old Quito lies the rectangular Plaza de Independencia

with the Palacio de Gobierno, the cathedral, and the shrine of revolutionary hero Antonio José de Sucre. Just a few streets away on the way to the Plaza de San Francisco you come across the best-known church of the city: La Compañia de Jesús that was dedicated in 1572. The facade alone catches the eye with the way the light plays on the columns, arches, and statues. In the semi-darkness of the interior the arched wooden ceiling of the nave is decorated all over with gold leaf and at its end the golden decorated high altar glistens above the carved wooden main altar.

At the Plaza de San Francisco a set of cloisters extend over four blocks. Within there is above all the sparkle of emeralds, the finest carvings decorate the choir stalls, and the Gothic pointed arches harmonize impressively with the Baroque altar.

In colorful ponchos

The colorful center of the old town is the Plaza de Santo Domingo with its church of the same name. Just before sunset throngs of people gather by the stops for ancient buses. Native women wearing colorful ponchos above their wide skirts and semicircular felt hats make coffee on bucket stoves and sell bread and boiled eggs.

Behind the old town the hill of El Panecillo rises up that is crowned by the statue of the "Winged Virgin." Take a taxi to the top for street robbers make the steps that lead upwards risky. The view from the top across the roofs of the Ecuador capital and to the snow-covered peaks of the distant mountains is unforgettable.

It is not just the choice of museums in Quito that is impressive, but also their quality. The enormous rounded Casa de la Cultura Ecutoriana "house of Ecuador culture" is particularly worth a visit as it houses a number of different museums. The collection in the archaeological museum of the Central Bank provides an extensive overview of the culture and early and pre-history of the early inhabitants of Ecuador. In the city's museum of art and history one can trace the development of religious art as it blossomed during colonial times. Quito established the continent's first school of art in 1552.

At the center of the historic old town of Quito is the Plaza St. Domingo. Behind on the summit of El Panecillo is the statue of the "Winged Virgin" (top)

The modern skyline of Quito set against the backdrop of the Cordillera to the north (bottom left)

The massive towers of the cathedral at the Plaza de Independencia

Market place in the Andes

Inca descendants dominate life in the Bolivian metropolis of **LA PAZ**

BOLIVIA
● La Paz

Pacific Ocean

Atlantic Ocean

GETTING THERE
International flights to the world's highest airport of El Alto from or via New York, Miami, and Rio de Janeiro

BEST TIME
The climate can seem harsh in summer. It rains almost every afternoon with a temperature around 64.4 °F (18 °C)

ACCOMMODATION
Wide choice of inexpensive hotels and bed & breakfast places. Prior booking is unreliable so arrive early in the morning. Also choice of luxury and top hotels

TIPPING
A service charge of usually 10 % is included in hotel bills

The Plaza San Francisco is a popular hang out for street traders (top)

Traders offer magic ingredients to ward off evil spirits at the Witches' Market or market for alternative therapies

Around 13,000 feet (4,000 m) above sea level the Altiplano high plateau extends for more than six hundred miles in southern Peru to the southern corner of Bolivia. Not far to the southeast of Lake Titicaca the impressive canyon of the La Paz river cuts 1,300 foot (400 m) deep into the Altiplano.

In this wide basin protected from the freezing winds of the high plateau one finds the red roof tiles of the extensive swathe of buildings of La Paz that rise up the slope. In between are a few skyscrapers dotted around and in the distance the snow-covered peak of the more than 20,900 foot (6,400 m) high Nevado Illimani.

This valley, in which an Inca village already stood, was chosen in 1548 by the conquistador Alonso de Mendoza as the site for the town of Nuestra Señora de La Paz after gold had been found in Choqueyapu. The gold rush did not last long but the main route for silver transport from Potosi to the Pacific coast also passed through this valley and ensured the town a stable economy for some considerable time.

World's highest city

The town was renamed La Paz de Ayacucho in 1825 in memory of the last battle for independence. In 1898 Bolivia moved its seat of government here but Suvre in southern Bolivia continued to be the capital. When La Paz became a railroad junction at the end of the nineteenth century the number of inhabitants increased enormously.

Today about one million people live in the thin air of this highest city in the world. But visitors need not concern themselves about getting lost in the jumble of streets and buildings because there is only one main street that follows the course of the Choqueyapu valley. If you get lost then simply go downhill.

The center of La Paz is the Plaza Murillo to the northeast of the river, bounded by the cathedral – built in 1835 – the impressive parliamentary buildings, and the government palace.

In the old town few buildings have survived from the colonial era, but a few blocks north of Plaza Murillo one of the streets has been restored with great care. There are also four small museums that are worth a visit here. In the Museo de

Metales Preciosos Precolombinos there is an astonishing collection of gold and silver finds dating from before Columbus. The Casa Murillo museum displays treasures from the colonial era and the Museo del Litoral Boliviano documents the "Saltpeter War" of 1879–1883 when Bolivia lost its Pacific coast. Finally the Costumbrista Juan de Vargas museum reflects the entire history of La Paz in the colonial era.

Bizarre prison customs

A new attraction is the Coca Museum on the Calle Linares. Its informative and objective exhibition describes the position of this drug in traditional society, its use, its use in refreshing drinks and medicines, and the stigmatization and its extension as the illegal cocaine.

One of the most bizarre tourist attractions is a visit to the San Pedro prison. The around 1,500 inmates attempt anything possible to earn money. The most successful of them – or the least considerate – live in well-appointed cells with the comfort of a good hotel. At the main gate one can speak to prisoners who give guided tours for a couple of dollar bills, under strict watch of guards. One can also buy toys and other handicrafts of the prisoners during the tour.

The descendants of the native people dominate life in the city more strongly than in any other city in South America. This is clear from the impressive, colorful, market with its abundant assortment of articles. They display high on the western slope, leading from the Plaza San

Francisco with its church of the same name. The local native people have gathered in front of the church on Sunday mornings for weddings since its building started in 1549. It was not completed until the middle of the eighteenth century.

Colorful market splendor

The Calle Sagárnaga is lined with handicraft stalls and kiosks that sell native woven items, musical instruments, silver jewelry, and also a range of tourist mementos.

An entirely sumptuous colorful and diverse Bolivian market sets out its wares on the other hand at the enormous Mercado Negro. The labyrinth crammed with stalls and small stores extends over several blocks.

In a side street one can probably find the rather strange Witches' Mar-

ket, the Mercado de Brujos or Mercado de Hechiceria as it is officially known. Traders here hawk their magic ingredients, herbs, seeds, little effigies, and such unusual items as llama fetuses. These items will work against all manner of diseases and protect you against evil spirits that populate the world of the Aymara people native to this region.

Chile's most important port

VALPARAISO has long been the "pearl of the Pacific". The city has a checkered history

Pablo Neruda knew precisely why of all places he bought a house on one of the city's fifty hills. The somewhat choosy humorous poet had already bought himself a house in the capital Santiago and a beach villa on the Isla Negra 50 miles (80 km) to the south of the port city when he returned to Chile from exile, rich and famous in 1952. But the fabulous view from the La Florida hill of the city and its extensive harbor must have fascinated this ship obsessed man as much as his visitors and admirers who today overcome the obstacles to find their way here.

The often colorfully-painted houses seem crammed together on the steep slopes encircling the city and that rise sharply from the narrow Pacific shore. The coastal strip is so narrow that land had to be created by tipping soil into the bay to create the city center.

The wide bay where the city was founded in 1536 was regarded in the first instance as a good anchorage by the Spanish conquistador Juan de Saavedra. He named the settlement for the town of his birth in Spain. The hills gave protection against the prevailing and often stormy southerly and southwesterly winds.

When the merchants arrived

The small port suffered under the trading regime of the Spanish colonial rulers for a long time. This changed almost immediately following independence in 1818. Merchants came to Valparaiso, shipping lines linked the city with Europe, and the port became an important staging post for ships rounding Cape Horn. It also became the base for the newly formed Chilean Navy.

The golden age ended with the opening of the Panama Canal in 1914 with ships no longer rounding the Horn. Meanwhile Valparaiso has subsequently become Chile's most modern and most important port.

The romantic corners remain. In the smaller harbor basins there are many – predominantly yellow painted – wooden boats of the coastal fishermen who sell their catches direct from their craft.

As dreamlike and picturesque as the city's position is, it has constantly been tried by acts of fate. Only a few of the former colonial buildings have survived pirate raids, the many severe storms, fire, and earthquakes. After the devastating quake of 1906, a great deal of the city had to be rebuilt and the latest quake of 1971 leaves many buildings heavily restored. Despite this there are still many Victorian and Neo-Classical buildings in the center of the city.

At the beginning of the twentieth century Valparaiso was known as the "pearl of the Pacific." With almost twenty luxury hotels, its animated life, busy trade, and international air, the city put the colorless capital of Santiago in the shade.

Steep old town quarter

The modern Valparaiso with its port facilities, warehouses, banks, and shopping center extends the length of the harbor. Its central points are the park-like Plaza Sotomayor surrounded by administrative office buildings and the Puerto railroad station. Close by are the cathedral, parks, avenues, theater, and many closely-packed cafés. In the adjoining streets the occasional building from colonial times can be discovered and also the La Matriz church that is worth a visit.

Traders cover the streets on market days with their stalls and kiosks and on the other side of the Puerto rail station at the long and wide Muelle Prat pier in the harbor numerous indigenous craftsmen and women offer their work at weekends.

Down here by the ocean the shape of Valparaiso can easily be seen. Wide streets largely run in wide parallel arcs from the shore. But on the slopes of the hills and in the city center there is an almost Medieval jumble of steep footpaths, steps, alleys, hairpin bend streets, and dead-end streets. One needs to have been born here not to get lost for even the best town map fails.

Among the landmarks for orientation there are fifteen Ascensores or funicular railways/cable cars still functioning that for a few Pesos take the trouble out of climbing the steps. Admittedly one sees the red or yellow cars from wherever you look but the end stations are often difficult to pick out. There were originally twenty-eight elevators built between 1883 and 1932 and some of them are a masterly example of engineering.

With their help you can explore the hilly parts of the city on foot for hours, since vehicles hardly venture here. The narrow streets are too winding and steep and at any moment they can become steps or just come to a dead end.

GETTING THERE
Rail and bus from Santiago, internal flights

BEST TIME
Best time is October-January. Rainy season is May-August

ACCOMMODATION
Hotels of every type in city center and close to the harbor

TIPPING
Restaurants 10 %. Taxi fares just rounded up

The boats of the coastal fishermen also bob up and down in the harbor (top left)

The densely-packed area of La Matriz extends uphill (bottom left)

Funicular railways are still a popular means of getting up the hills

131

The stunning beauty of Rio

South America's secretive capital gets its zest for a full life from its citizens

The carnival is merely the grandest volcanic eruption of intoxicating joie de vivre. Dancing, alcohol, beach, sport, and sun are the elixirs of life of the close to six million inhabitants of Rio de Janeiro. The extensive beaches, capped by Copacabana beach, are the center of this hunger for life.

Along the Atlantic shores of Copacabana, Ipanema, and Leblon there are tall apartment blocks of the well-heeled middle classes. Higher on the slopes of the steep hills like an admonition are the homes of the poor in the Favelas. A cable car runs every half hour from Praia Vermelha between Flamengo and Copacabana up to one of the two landmarks of Rio, the over 1,300 foot (400 m) high Sugar Loaf.

Christ watches over the city

The other landmark is the around 130 foot (40 m) tall statue of Christ that stands on top of the approx. 2,300 foot (700 m) high Corcovado rocks to the west of the Sugar Loaf with his arms stretched out over the city. A winding road through a section of ancient rain forest and a rack railway reach the top. The mountain ridge from which the Corcovado rises separates the southern part of the planned rich suburb of Barra da Tijuca from the northerly National Park da Tijuca.

Rio de Janeiro owes its stunning beauty to its position on the western shore of the wide Guanabara Bay, at the foot of the slopes of the Morros, and the foothill of the Brazilian mountains that is covered in lush vegetation.

This surely also impressed the Portuguese discoverer, André Gonçalves when he entered Gunanabara Bay on New Year's Day 1502. He mistakenly imagined there to be a river and named it Rio de Janeiro or "January River." Because the bay is an ideal natural harbor Gonçalo Coelho built a Portuguese settlement at Urca, the hill below the Sugar Loaf. The first foundations of Cidade de São Sebastião do Rio de Janeiro were laid in 1565 in the place that is now the center of the city.

When gold was found in the early eighteenth century at the Gerais mines to the south of present-day Brasilia it led to a wave of immigration from Europe. The town quickly grew beyond its walls and replaced Bahia as the colonial capital in 1763. The gold mines were soon exhausted but after a short economic downturn the country turned to exporting coffee. When the Portuguese Royal family fled here to escape Napoleon in 1808 the colony grew even faster. New buildings were constructed, old ones were restored, new streets were driven through the town, and the public water supply was extended.

Catedral Metropolitana

After King John VI returned to Portugal in 1821 and Brazil became independent in 1822, a new building boom began. By the end of that century the city had implemented the latest modern technology with a race track, railroad connection, street lighting, sewage system, radio telegraphy, and a telephone system. After the turn of the century many older colonial buildings made way for wider new roads and increasingly high rise buildings. Even as late as the 1960s colonial buildings were demolished to make way for the impressive avant-garde Catedral Metropolitana that was inaugurated in 1976. Yet some old alleys are hidden away on either side of the central pedestrian street of Avenida Rio Branca. Throngs of people pass hundreds of small stores here. There is not a space free in the numerous restaurants during lunch-time because it is less expensive to eat here, and often better than in the tourist restaurants of the southern zone.

Time stands still on the Ilha Fiscal (Customs Island). The greenish building was constructed in 1880 in Neo-Gothic style. The expensively and carefully restored palace has housed the Museum Cultural da Marinha since 1999 in which the clothing and items of practical use from the royal family can be seen.

The botanical gardens (Jardim Botànico) in the Tijuca National Park are an oasis in the midst of this hectic metropolis. It is one of the finest tropical botanical gardens and arboretums of the world. John VI had plants of economic importance from other tropical parts of the world planted here. Today there are around seven thousand species growing there.

View across the city to Guanabara Bay and the Sugar Loaf (top)

The statue of Christ the Redeemer with its outstretched arms is 131 ft (40 m) tall and a landmark of Rio (bottom left)

Ipanema Beach is a Mecca for everyone, not just the rich and the beautiful

On the shores of the Plate

Uruguay's capital of **MONTEVIDEO** has remained tranquil yet moves to a modern beat

URUGUAY

Pacific
Ocean

Montevideo

Atlantic
Ocean

In contrast with other South America major cities it is remarkably tranquil in Montevideo with none of the bubbling extrovert Latin gaiety, and no tourist areas. Modern bright computer stores, exclusive fashion boutiques, and glistening malls can be found harmoniously alongside dusty booksellers, dimly lit cabinetmakers, and general stores crammed with goods. The contrast of old and new alongside one another is characteristic of the entire city, the buildings of which are a blend of Spanish Colonial, Italianate, and Art Deco styles. Somewhat moribund perhaps but full of charm, especially as the older buildings are increasingly being restored.

In his quest for a channel to the Pacific, Fernão de Magalhães was the first European to see this place in 1519 when he sailed up the mouth of the Rio de la Plata (River Plate) which is around 60 miles (100 km) wide at this point. The area seemed to have little to offer the explorer with neither mineral resources or the native manpower who could be forced to work them.

Base for smugglers

The first Spanish garrison at this favorable anchorage on the eastern side of the River Plate was not established until the eighteenth century. The Portuguese had already created the town of Colônia do Sacramento further upstream opposite Buenos Aires before 1680. This was a trading post that lived off smuggling to its Spanish neighbors. The Spanish colonial powers decided to prevent this by blockading the access to the Atlantic and authorized the Governor of Buenos Aires to establish a garrison to the south of San Felipe de Montevideo in 1726.

Between 1807 and 1830 the settlement was occupied in turn by English, Spanish, Argentine, Portuguese, and Brazilians, to the disadvantage of trade that had just begun and the inhabitants hurriedly deserted the settlement.

Between 1843 and 1852 the settlement was occupied by the Argentine/Uruguay army of dictator Juan Manuel de Rosas while the French and English in a countermove blockaded Buenos Aires. This time however trade nevertheless flourished and Montevideo became the most important port on the River Plate.

In the vicinity of the jetties for the ferries to and from Buenos Aires on the northern side of the Mercado del Puerto peninsula there is a gastronomic Mecca. Beneath the roofs of the former market hall of wrought iron there are numerous snack stalls, bars, and also some fine restaurants. Offal and massive chunks of meat sizzle on giant grills and the smell of fish and mussel soup fills the air.

By way of the narrow streets of the old colonial town or Ciudad Vieja one reaches the parks and places that form a line towards the east through the center of Montevideo. On the other side of the old town the expanse of the southern shore of the peninsula with green parks and dreamy beaches stretches along the coast in front of high-rise apartments and the beach-front street of Rambia Gran Bretaña.

In the region of the Plaza Zabala and the Plaza de la Constitución there are interesting museums and superbly-restored colonial buildings. On the western side of the tree-shaded Plaza de la Constitución is the cathedral of Iglesia Matriz. The great people of Uruguay history are buried in this church built in 1799.

Wide variety of architecture

Opposite the cathedral a pedestrian street leads past small boutiques and sidewalk cafés to the old city gate at Plaza Independencia, the new city center of Montevideo. Surrounded by large green squares the freedom fighter and national hero José Artigas surveys the big city bustle from high-up on his horse on his mausoleum. The collection of buildings around here are in diverse architectural styles, from the hyper-modern Palace of Justice to the Classical buildings of the former government buildings and the chamber of commerce, to the Neo-Classical of the Teatro Solís.

Perhaps the most controversial but also the most fascinating building of Montevideo thrusts twenty-six storeys in its wedding cake style above the south side of the square. This building, with its strange windows and countless turrets and bay windows was built in 1928 and was the tallest building in South America for many years and has become a landmark of Montevideo.

GETTING THERE
Many international flights to Montevideo. Regional flights to and rapid ferry links with Buenos Aires

BEST TIME
June-August 46-62 °F (8-16 °C), January-March 64-82 °F (18-28 °C)

ACCOMMODATION
Many top-class hotels in Montevideo and the nearby vacation resorts. Cheaper hotels in the old town. Pre-booking during the southern summer and carnival is recommended

TIPPING
10 % for taxis and restaurants

Plaza Independencia is Montevideo's new city center. Behind the mounted statue of national hero José Artigas towers the Palacio Salvo, the city's most striking landmark (left)

The old port with the tower of Palacio Salvio (bottom right)

View across the bay of the Rio de la Plata (River Plate) and Montevideo

The tango capital of the world

BUENOS AIRES has the world's widest avenues and set's the pulse of Argentina

Atlantic Ocean

Pacific Ocean

• Buenos Aires

ARGENTINA

GETTING THERE
International flight connections with most major world cities. An attractive alternative is a passage on a container ship

BEST TIME
Best time is the northern winter with temperatures of 70-79 °F (21-26 °C) in winter and spring, and 50-64 °F (10-18 °C) in summer and fall

ACCOMMODATION
All categories. Competent booking help at the airport

TIPPING
5-10 %. Porters and hotel boys 0.50-1 Argentine dollar

The Porteños, or old-established inhabitants of Buenos Aires, claim their Avenida 9 de Julio as the widest boulevard in the world. It is probably also the most densely-packed with traffic. The many Colectivos, that are the Argentinean solution to public transport and a symbol of Buenos Aires, stand out amid an impenetrable mass of vehicles. The drivers of these small buses chat with a lively commentary about everything and everyone to their packed in passengers. Their rather aggressive yet extremely safe manner of driving is legendary. They are symbolic of the rapid pace of life in this city.

An obelisk of around 230 foot(70 m) high that is visible from far and wide was erected in the middle of Avenida 9 Julio in 1936 to commemorate the first but unsuccessful founding of the city.

The present-day major city of around eleven million inhabitants had a very troubled early history over four hundred years. The first efforts to found a settlement here in 1536 failed because of action by the native people but also from the lack of foodstuffs.

Viceroyalty of Rio de la Plata

The second attempt in 1580 was more successful. The participants in the founding expedition received large estates and caught the pasture animals that had been left by the first settlers and had in the meantime significantly increased in number.

Yet Nuestra Señora de Santa María del Buen Aire as the first settlers named the place, first eked out a shadowy existence. The Spanish did not permit any trade from here and hence the settlers quickly went

their own way and in addition to intensive cattle ranching also engaged in lucrative smuggling. This was so rewarding that at the end of the seventeenth and in the early eighteenth centuries countless settlements sprang up along the fertile area of the Paraná with its numerous small rivers that were accessible for the small boats of smugglers.

Since the results of trading were enormous, Buenos Aires became the capital of the newly-form Spanish viceroyalty of Rio de la Plata in 1776. The now official trade established the importance of the town as the administrative center.

With the increasing wealth came immigration mainly from Spain and Italy but also countries in central Europe and particularly from Germany. They established their warehouses and slaughterhouses in the southern

parts of the town close to the harbor that was vacated by the local middle classes following an epidemic of yellow fever in 1870.

On the Plaza de Mayo

The historical center of Buenos Aires is the Plaza de Mayo that is dominated by the Casa Rosado government building of the President. The Presidents of the country make their addresses to the people from a balcony of the red building. Many hundreds of thousand Argentineans protest, celebrate, or demonstrate once more on the square in front of this building.

On the western side of the square the more than a mile long Avenida de Mayo directly links with the Congress building just like the Capitol in Washington.

All distances within Argentina start at the kilometer zero stone in the Congress square. Opposite this the monument to the "Second Congress" symbolizes the Andes with its granite steps and the river and the sea with its fountains.

The modern rhythm of Buenos Aires pulsates to the north of the Plaza de Mayo on the right and left of the pedestrian streets of Calle Lavalle and Calle Florida. Here numerous well-dressed business persons rush past the arcades with their mobile phones to their ear to the financial and banking areas, and throng the meat grills in restaurants and stand in line for the theaters and cinemas in the evening.

Artists' quarter of San Telmo

A popular place to visit is the workers' neighborhoods of San Telmo and La Boca south of the Avenida de Mayo. Artists and craft specialists live and work in the restored colonial buildings of San Telmo and in colorful La Boca the gaudily painted buildings of timber and tin are an original setting for many parties and the countless tango events.

The wealthy have withdrawn to Recoleta, Retiro, and Palermo in the north. Here one can find peaceful refuge in a stroll through the botanical and zoological gardens between luxury villas from colonial times and those ultra-modern ones of glass and concrete and through the cemetery of Cementerio de la Recoleta where generations of Argentinean elite rest.

The Congress building is a close copy of the Capitol in Washington (top left)

The Republic Square with its obelisk is center of the modern city (top right)

Gaudy colors are part of the charm of the houses in the area of La Boca

ASIA

The holy city of Jerusalem

Christians, Jews, and Muslims share the holy sites of three religions

There is no more enchanting view of Jerusalem than from the Mount of Olives at sunrise. Firstly the sun glistens on the golden Dome of the Rock. Then the sun shines on the minarets and churches, the cube-form buildings of the Muslim, Christian, Jewish, and Armenian quarters and then finally on the yellow blocks of stone of the city walls. And while the Kidron valley remains in darkness the Holy City seems to float light as a feather between heaven and earth to form a tranquil image.

The uniformity of building materials of the old city of Jerusalem contributes to this picturesque scene. The buildings are from the same limestone as the almost 50 foot (15 m) high city wall or are at least clad with this material. This retains the ancient magic of this place of pilgrimage for three major religions with the architecture of Jerusalem forming a perfect collective work of art, which God according to the Talmud provided nine tenths of all the earth's beauty but also gave nine shares of all suffering and grief.

For all Jewish believers the history of Israel began more than three thousand years ago on the Temple Mount. This is when King David of Israel and Judea stormed Jerusalem that was defended by the Jebusites and on the Temple Mount declared Jerusalem the holy capital city of Judaism. His successor King Solomon completed the city's foundation by building a palace and the legendary temple bearing his name. An extensive temple complex was built on the high plateau in 37 BC in the reign of King Herod of the Jews, under the Roman occupation.

Barely a stone was left standing from all these major buildings over the course of the centuries. Arab conquerors pulled down the walls of these – for them alien – religious structures. Only the western wall of the Temple Mount survived the original Jewish era. It is built of massive stone blocks piled to a height of almost 60 feet (18 m) and is now the most important sacred place for Jews: the Wailing Wall. Opposite on the Mount of Olives the prophets of Israel foretold of the coming of a Messiah who would open the door to a heavenly Jerusalem.

Beginnings of Christianity

Instead of a Messiah recognized by the Jews the Savior or Redeemer of the Christians once wept here as described in the Bible overlooking this city that has suffered much from conquest. Jesus was thirty-three years old when he was crucified for his teaching in the holy city. Seventy years after his death the first formation of a Christian community began in Jerusalem that has triumphed into a world religion present in virtually every country in the world. In the fourth century believers built the Church of the Resurrection on the site of his rock sepulcher that was replaced in 1149 by the Crusaders with a Romanesque basilica, the present day Church of the Holy Sepulcher. Many thousands of pilgrims since then have dragged heavy wooden crosses on their shoulders along the Via Doloroso to this most Christian sacred shrine to share the

suffering of their Redeemer on his last journey.

Jerusalem is also holy for the Muslims because the Prophet Mohammed is said to have ascended to Allah on a winged steed Al-Buraq from a rock outcrop here. When Caliph Omar I conquered the city in the seventh century he converted the Temple Mount into the most holy Islamic shrine after Mecca and Medina. Where Mohammed began his journey to heaven the octagonal Dome of the Rock arose, a masterpiece of early Islamic architecture. Since this is a memorial dedicated to the Prophet the huge seven-sided Al Aqsa Mosque was erected for Islamic worship, the principal place for Muslim prayer and religious centerpiece of Muslim Jerusalem.

Jerusalem long ago spread beyond the old city with its churches, chapels, monasteries, and places of prayer. Of the more than 600,000 inhabitants, two-thirds are Jewish, approx. 180,000 are Moslem and 20,000 are Christians of various denominations, but predominantly Melkite (Greek Catholic). The fact that Jerusalem is the Holy City for three faiths has led to religious conflict, past and present. A quick resolution of the conflict can only be hoped for, so that all nations can find the much needed peace.

Panoramic view from the Mount of Olives across the holy city of Jerusalem (top)

Jewish believer praying at the Wailing Wall (bottom left)

The Temple Mount with the golden cupola of the Dome of the Rock

The white city on 18 hills

AMMAN is capital through rise of the kingdom of Jordan

**Ruins of the Forum
Romanum (top)**

**Dome and minaret of
the Abdullah Mosque
(bottom left)**

**View of Amman from
Citadel Hill (bottom
center)**

**Astonished tourists in
the huge Roman
theater**

For a first view of Amman climb the 2,720 foot (837 m) high Citadel Hill of Jebel Ashrafiah. The built-up area spreads itself across eighteen hills with most buildings painted white in accordance with royal wishes. To the east of the Jordanian capital a section of the Syria–Egypt highway can be seen and beyond this the dusty haze of unending desert. To the west though the land is green where the land drops to the fertile Jordan valley.

The Citadel itself is part of the city's history. Archaeological finds have shown that people settled here more than four thousand years ago. Around 1200 BC it became the center of the Ammonite kings. The Jewish King David also left traces behind here as did the Assyrians, Babylonians, and Persians. The citadel from Roman times remains. There are masonry remnants of Byzantine churches of early Christianity. An impressive seventh century gate house – the Qasr – remains from the Muslim Umayyad dynasty.

Present-day Amman is a product of the twentieth century. The population first climbed within the past one hundred years from two thousand to 1,700,000 people. Firstly, Circassian and Chechen Muslims came from areas now within the Russian Federation and proved themselves in the repulsion of Bedouin tribes who extorted money. The connection of the city with the desert highway between Damascus and Medina in 1908 proved of economic importance. Since then Amman has been an important staging post each year

for thousands of pilgrims heading for Medina. There was a further upswing with the end of Turkish rule following World War I and then in 1952 the Hashemite Kingdom of Jordan made Amman its capital.

The successful monarch

The first monarch of the Hashemite throne was King Abdullah in 1950 but three years later the eighteen-year-old Hussein followed after his father was assassinated in Jerusalem. This was a stroke of luck for the new nation since King Hussein – the "little king", as the diminutive monarch was known – proved to be politically astute in the explosive situation of the Middle East. Unharmed by the war in the neighborhood, Amman developed into a modern large city with its own university, international airport, trade settlements, and tourist industry. Until his death Hussein himself was the best possible advertisement for travel to his country through the sympathetic manner of his appearances in the media.

The center of Amman lies in a valley between the Citadel Hill and three other hills. Public buildings are found close together here such as the main post office, luxury stores, and an Arabic souk or market and religious sites like the Al-Hussein Mosque that was built in 1924 on the foundations of an Umayyad Mosque. The main sites in the city center are the Forum Romanum, a Roman amphitheater with superb acoustics for six thousand people in which performances are still given. A mussel-

shaped Odeum where musical performances are given completes the Roman ensemble.

Very well worth seeing but not visible from the street are the fantastic grand houses of the upper classes from the 1920s and 1930s at Jebel Amman. Only the modernist building of Jordan River Designs is open for visitors. This organization promotes indigenous arts and crafts. King Hussein's family also lived in Jebel Amman before moving to the royal residence further east at Jebel Al-Qusur. Meanwhile further parks are found there by the Basman and Raghadan palaces.

Numerous hotels have been built in the government and diplomatic quarter of the city in recent years to cater for the increasing numbers of tourists who use Amman as a hub for their excursions to famous ruins. The air-conditioned tourist coaches also set out from here to Jordan's interior. The main objectives for tourists are the ruins at Petra, the mosaics at Madaba, the Crusader's fort at Kerak, and the ancient Jerash, and also seaside resorts on the Dead Sea.

Heavenly Damascus

Syria's capital is one of the oldest places on earth

GETTING THERE
International flights to Damascus

ACCOMMODATION
Two to five-star hotels

BEST TIME
Best time is April-May and September-October

TIPPING
10 % of bills. In restaurants tip not only the head waiter but also the poorly paid assistant waiters

The finest and strangest compliment ever paid to the Syrian capital of Damascus is attributed to the Prophet Mohammed. When the founder of Islam approached the oasis city – of cypresses, palms, colorful bazaar, towers, and domes – from a mountain after a long journey he was so deeply impressed by its beauty that he would not enter the city. There could only be the one paradise for him, he declared to his companions, and that was with Allah in heaven and hence he made a wide detour.

Archaeologists regard Damascus as the longest continuously settled town on earth. Long before 12,000 years ago, according to finds, the first people settled here, drawn by natural oasis on the Barada river. It was an ideal resting place for caravans on their way from the desert to the Mediterranean or before climbing the Antelebanon mountains. Around 2500 BC Damascus acquired town rights and in 1480 BC the Egyptian Pharoah Thutmosis III entered Damascus in the list of cities of his Egyptian realm.

Struggle over the sacred buildings

The first major sacred building was a shrine constructed by the Aramaeans to their god Hadad in what later became the city center that the Romans then replaced with a massive temple to Jupiter, which in turn was replaced by a Christian basilica. Close to this at the beginning of the first millennium a Jewish synagogue was built. The Assyrians, Babylonians, Persians, and Greeks have all left traces of their culture behind in Damascus.

In the eighth century Damascus increasingly became an Islamic city. The Byzantine Basilica of Christ was converted to the Umayyad Mosque, a masterpiece of Islamic architecture that exists to this day. Next to an elongated triple nave prayer hall there is a large inner courtyard that is lined on three sides by colonnades. Precious mosaics, wood carvings, sculpture, and wrought iron-work emphasize the importance of this structure as the most important mosque of this city.

One of the relics in the mosque from early Christian times is said to be the head of John the Baptist who is revered by Muslims as the Prophet Yahua. According to tradition the forefather Abraham was born in Damascus and it was here that Cain slew his brother Abel. In the eastern old town a chapel of St. Ananias recollects the believer whom Christ ordered to restore Saul's sight following which Saul the hater of Christians became St. Paul the Apostle.

Highly-developed medicine

Damascus played a mold-breaking role in the treatment of illness in the Middle Ages. With the construction of the Maristan Nuri hospital in 1154 the city had one of the most modern hospitals of the age. The clinicians divided their activities into specialties such as surgery, orthopedics, fevers, and mental illness. For education the establishment had access to an extensive library of works about medicine. Unlike the backward hospitals of Christendom mentally handicapped were not separated off into a secular place of refuge.

The forward-looking Damascus had a major set-back in the thirteenth century when it was pillaged by Mongols. Even more serious devastation was done in 1400 by Tamurlane when he and his forces entered the city. From the sixteenth century until the end of World War I Damascus was a provincial capital within the Ottoman empire under Turkish rule. In 1920 the League of Nations gave France the mandate over Syria. The country became independent in 1946.

Damascus in the twenty-first century is a city of two million and once again a "pearl of the Orient" – as the Roman Emperor Julian described it in the fourth century – if you ignore the many building mistakes of recent years and the daily traffic chaos. The ancient center beneath the dominance of the towering citadel is a timeless gem of city architecture. On the edge of the street that is called Straight with its many stores and neighborhood souks there are ornate villas and patrician houses and Medieval city gates to admire, dome covered mausoleums of deceased rulers, and the ancient Nuredin bath house recalls the pleasure of early hygiene.

The major buildings are mosques and Islamic madrasahs, the tall towers of the many skyward thrusting minarets. According to an Islamic prophecy Jesus will come again from heaven to the highest and finest minaret of the Umayyad Mosque in Damascus to begin the Last Judgment.

Believers in the courtyard of the Umayyad Mosque (top)

Wood turner in front of his store (bottom left)

Panoramic view of Damascus

Discoveries in Baghdad

Fine mosques recall a Thousand and One Nights

Where the Grand Caliph Harun al-Rashid once mingled with his people in disguise one encounters an entirely different ruler at the start of the twenty-first century in the dictator Saddam Hussein. The dictator with his black mustache waits at the edge of the street in his white shirt. He lets himself be seen kneeling in brown uniform on a prayer mat, looking statesmanlike into the future in a dark suit, or as a Bedouin, or bearing a saber and with a red sash at the generals' full mess dress evening. Saddam monuments, Saddam statues, and Saddam murals in the Iraqi capital of five million people massage history with a fairy-tale view.

This city on the west bank of the Tigris was founded in 762 by the Abbasid Caliph al-Mansur (The Victorious). Following the example of Firuzabad in Persia he established a circular ground plan for his residence. A double circular wall also finally enclosed the new city with a deep defensive ditch. At the center were built the Friday Mosque and Caliph's palace. The circular plan was cut across by two diagonal avenues which divided the town into quarters and accordingly the city gates were set at the four main points of the compass.

Tree of gold and silver

Caliph al-Mansur named his town Medinet as-Salaam (City of Peace). But under one of his successors, Harun al-Rashid, the shape of the city was reflected in its name in the eighth century. Baghdad is "The Circle." The city quickly gained prosperity with its gold and silversmiths and weavers of precious fabrics. Arabic sources report immeasurable luxury for the upper classes.

In the Caliph's palace alone there were 38,000 valuable drapes and 22,000 carpets. The "Hall of Trees" in which audiences with the Caliph took place was embellished with a magnificent gold and silver tree as the centerpiece.

By the start of the thirteenth century two million people lived in Baghdad. They were mainly Muslims and Christians but there were also many Jewish craftsmen and traders. In 1258 and 1401 the Mongol hordes butchered a large part of the population and reduced the city to rubble and ash both times. In later times and under a variety of rulers the city's population was decimated by the plague, famine, and floods and at the end of the nineteenth century was only 150,000.

Baghdad's newly-built modern image follows the relinquishing by Great Britain in 1932 of its role as Protector and then the Coup in 1968 with the nationalization of foreign oil assets. There are broad palm-tree lined avenues, areas of high-rise buildings and some impeccably restored historic buildings. Only a few old streets in the old town on the left bank of the Tigris are oriental in the conventional sense. The bridges that were heavily damaged during the Gulf War are fully repaired.

One major example of early Islamic architecture by the Tigris is the mosque and Islamic madrasah of al-Mustansiriya that was built by the Caliph of this name in 1234 and divided into the four schools of jurisprudence. Numerous external restorations have ensured the building retains its original pointed arch and two-storey arcades. The same is true of the Abbasid palace of the thirteenth century, the Maryan

Mosque with its richly-decorated high brick gateway of the fourteenth century and the Casimain Mosque with its superb mirror mosaic and decorated tiles from the sixteenth century.

Dome for the dead

Some of the most important monuments are the memorials to the dead. Above the grave of Sheik Omar, a holy man who died in the thirteenth century, a spire of honeycomb pattern was erected that is worth visiting. Fine domed mosques also embellish the resting places of famous Imams. The Martyrs Memorial by Ismael Falah al-Turk is an architectural masterpiece in turquoise from 1983 as a memorial to the fallen of the Iran-Iraq war of 1980–1988. It has the form of a divided dome that when viewed from a distance the two halves come together.

The original core of Baghdad, the initial circular settlement, can be found on the western bank of the Tigris close to the main rail station. Everything ancient has long since been built over. All that remains from Harun al-Rashid's time are the remains of a city gate (Bab al-Wastani) and a tomb dating from 1202 for the mother of the Caliph al-Nasir but which many Iraqis believe houses Harun al-Rashid's favorite wife, Zubayda.

GETTING THERE
Because of post Gulf War sanctions there are only flights via Amman, Cairo, and Damascus. Most nationalities require a visa only available on invitation or through a travel agent

ACCOMMODATION
Hotels in all categories up to the 5-star Al-Rashid

BEST TIME
March-May and September-December

TIPPING
Restaurants 5-10 % of bill. Tourist guides expect $1-2

The Fourteenth Ramadan Mosque (left) with successful combination of traditional and modern architecture in one of Baghdad's new suburbs

The al-Mustansiriya Mosque and Islamic college of the thirteenth century in which Islamic law is studied

San'a' is a Yemeni work of art

The "pearl of Arabia" retains its Medieval appearance

GETTING THERE
Flights to San'a's international airport (Al Rahabaa)

ACCOMMODATION
Sufficient hotels in the various price classes. The lower categories rarely suit western tastes

BEST TIME
October and November

TIPPING
Not customary in restaurants and hotels

EXCURSIONS
Half-day excursions to Kawkaban and Thula. Day excursions to Hajjah, Mahwit, Hajarath, and Dhin Bin

The entire old town of San'a' is a work of art. No two of the four thousand houses are the same. They differ in height, the parapets of their roof gardens, and the decorative stucco work of their facades. The greatest diversity is in their windows: circular, rectangular, arched, or roseate. Some have filigree railings and with the oldest there are neither panes of glass or slices of opal. The building materials are natural stone and clay bricks in the brown tones of the Yemen highlands. And because the masons have retained the same techniques for centuries ancient San'a' has retained its Medieval appearance.

There are only presumptions about the origins of the Yemeni capital over 2,500 years ago. One legend deals with Sem, the oldest son of the biblical Noah. He is said to have been distracted by a bird which picked up a twig in its beak while he was building a house on Mount Alian. Sem regarded this as a sign from God and followed the bird which eventually dropped the twig at the foot of the 9,400 foot (2,892 m) high Jebel Nukum. Sem is said to have built a house at this spot and to have founded a settlement that originally bore his name, later was called Azal, and finally San'a'.

Minarets above the roofs

Archaeologists believe that the building of a fortress in the time of the kingdom of Sana led to people settling here at a height of 6,500 feet (2,000 m). It is possible there was a temple in the area of the old town before 2,000 years ago. Jews later built a synagogue on its site which then gave way to a church of Coptic Christians. In the seventh century San'a' was conquered by Muslims who built the Al-Cabir Mosque that was rebuilt and extended much before it was succeeded by the Grand Mosque. Since then this "pearl of the orient" that is steeped in legend has become an Islamic city with collectively forty-five whitewashed or Arabesque decorated minarets towering above the sprawl of buildings.

Resting place for the caravans

Sitting at the junction of caravan routes San'a' was a prosperous trading center in the first millennium. The prosperity was aided by gardeners, silversmiths, alabaster carvers, and weavers of precious fabrics. About half the city's wall still exists and the oldest part dates from the third century. The city gets its name from the 7 and half mile long, 45 foot high and 16 foot thick (12 km, 14 m and 5 m) defensive wall for San'a' means "well-defended." There are five city gates and their heavy gates are bolted and guarded at night by soldiers.

One of the first European visitors to San'a' was the Italian, Ludovico di Varthema in 1503, who described the city as a large town with four thousand buildings, many gardens, and a massive city wall. The German Ulrich Jasper Setzen, in the service of the Russian Czar, confirmed in 1801 the praise of many travelers when he described San'a' as the most beautiful city of the orient. This was supported in more modern times by the German globetrotter and travel writer Hans Helfritz in 1930 when he said Sana'a' was one of the few cities in the world that did not disappoint on a second look.

Yemeni capital since 1990

After heavy damage during the recent civil war San'a' became the capital of the united Yemen in 1990 and since then there has been a slow upturn. With now more than 900,000 inhabitants, the "well defended" city today is modern outside its historic center, with a flourishing cotton industry, university, radio station, and international airport.

Tourism has increased significantly in recent years. Today's visitors likes those of old are enchanted by the wide-ranging forms of creative expression in the old town. The historic heart is a collective work of the art of town planning and every building is a testimony to the heights of Arabic culture. In addition to the Medieval houses the sites worth seeing include the city's Al Kasar castle, the caravanserai, and warehouses with sesame mills still operated by camels, the Bab al Yemen city gate, the thirteenth century custom's house, and various souks and mosques. Turkish occupiers left behind the Imam's palace that now serves as the Yemen National Museum. The oldest exhibits are tools of flint and obsidian from the early Stone Age when

San'a' was hunting territory.

Unesco has done its best to ensure the heritage of this "pearl of Arabia" is protected. Praise is also due for countries such as Germany, Great Britain, The Netherlands, and Norway who are involved in an international project to preserve and restore the Medieval built heritage of San'a'.

The old town of San'a' at the foot of the biblical Nukem mountains. Different styles of adornment and windows make each building distinctive (top)

The Medieval market place in the historic center (bottom left)

A modern traffic island in front of an ancient city gate

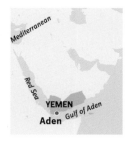

Life from a volcano

ADEN at the southern tip of the Arabian peninsula welcomes tourists once more

GETTING THERE
Aden has an international airport

ACCOMMODATION
Many simple hotels but also better class establishments such as the Aden Mövenpick and the Al-Amer

BEST TIME
The winter months

TIPPING
Was not customary but becoming happily accepted in the tourist areas

The most attractive thing about Aden is its position. It is as if nature – or as they would say here, Allah – engineered a huge volcanic eruption in order in one blast to create a safe natural harbor, a rocky fortification, together with sandy beach bays and a backdrop of picturesque mountains. Aden sits on the lava of a volcanic island that is attached to the Yemeni mainland by a strip of land that provides protection from storms for ships.

The inhabitants of this harbor town that is mentioned in antiquity knew Islam during the lifetime of the Prophet Mohammed (570–632). As the most important anchorage between the Red Sea and the Indian Ocean Aden already had a population of 80,000 and many mosques in 1267 according to a report of the world traveler Marco Polo. From early on this trading place with its ideal position aroused the greed of foreign powers. Occupations, plundering, and the diversion of ancient trade routes eventually led to a decline. The city crumbled and the population dropped to about one hundred.

Profit from the Suez Canal

The former trade flourished once more when British troops occupied Aden in 1839. Following the opening of the Suez Canal more ships entered the harbor than ever before. In the late nineteenth century Aden was the world's third largest port behind New York and Liverpool. The run of success ended in 1967 when the British withdrew and Moscow and Peking showed interest in the former Crown colony. Aden became the capital of the Socialist Peoples Republic of Southern Yemen in dispute with North Yemen which was finally settled when the two parts of Yemen united in a single independent republic in 1990.

Although no longer a capital, Aden remains economically important and now has a population of 600,000 and a leading role within Yemen. Tourism was one victim of the civil war but is booming again. More than 100,000 visitors are attracted each year to this country on the southern tip of the Arabian peninsula. The majority of these come from Germany and they also explore the interior.

The main attraction of Aden is the Crater district of the city that lies at the center of the old volcanic crater that is surrounded by precipitous rock walls of solidified lava like the walls of a fortification. In this oldest part of the city there is a typical oriental souk with workshops, tea rooms, and places selling snacks. The colorful display of wares are added to by the great ethnic mix of people thronging the souk, with Arabs traditionally attired, Africans in colorful clothes, Indians dressed all in white, and disheveled backpackers from all over the world.

Marvel of early technology

The monuments of the old town include a solitary white minaret remaining from an eighth century mosque and in the oldest quarter the around five hundred year old al-Aidrus Mosque. Inside this mosque there is the sarcophagus of the patron saint of this city, Sayyid Abdullah al-Aidrus in whose honor a great pilgrimage takes place each year. An imposing palace of a former Sultan of Aden is now the National Museum, although the most valuable parts of its collection have been plundered. A marvel of pre-Islamic engineering are the Tawila cisterns with their eighteen catchment basins that can store 90,000 cubic meters of rainwater. Close by is the "Tower of Silence" that is open at the top on which the followers of Zarathustra from the former Persia, known as Parsa, leave their bodies for carrion birds.

The western shore of the Ma'allha neighborhood retains a highly mannered feel in the English style with its large mansions. On the nearby Gold-Mohur beach that is one of the finest, widest, and longest, the many sharks are prevented from attacking swimmers by a net strung right across the bay.

This bathing paradise in the Gulf of Aden is towered over by the 1,820 foot (560 m) high Jebel Shamsan a somber part of the volcano that once rose out of the sea at Aden. This happened in 67 AD and probably first occurred more than 1,500,000 years ago. Only Allah knows if such an eruption will be repeated. When this happens, according to the French writer Paul Nizan in 1931: "The new eruption of the volcano of Aden would cause hell on earth and proclaim the end of the world."

Aden's old district of Crater is within a volcano crater surrounded by steep lava walls. Steps lead through a white gate to the "Tower of Silence" in which the Parsa lay their corpses to rest (top)

There is a lively bustle in the souk in the center of town (bottom left)

The ancient cisterns are guarded by a mosque

Dubai is not a mirage

Holiday oasis and shopping paradise on the edge of the desert

The freeways are dead straight in the Emirate of Dubai and as hot as an oven. To the east the land is bounded by mountains of bare rock and to the south by endless sand dunes. From here the route out of the desert leads to the Persian Gulf. To the northwest shrouded in a shimmering haze one sees strange shadowy outlines of parts of a pyramid-like or mussel-like object or perhaps even the Tower of Babel. A mirage perhaps?

This hallucination on the horizon proves on closer inspection to be constructed of steel, glass, and concrete. Tens of thousands of immigrant workers have constructed hundreds of ultra-modern buildings on the coast line of more than 40 miles (70 km) of the Emirate. There are barrel-like twin towers, pyramid shopping temples, giant office blocks, and towering hotels with curvilinear exteriors that remind one of a sail.

Posters proclaim "Our city is getting bigger and better." Dubai is one of the states forming the United Arab Emirates, about one and a half times the size of Luxembourg and the ruling Al Maktoum family wish to turn it into the world's most modern city. With its World Trade Center, Dubai is the most important trading center of the region, has the most competitive airport, and the largest artificial container harbor.

It rains Petro Dollars

The dream blossoming began to develop when oil was found in the sea. With the successful offshore drilling Dubai overnight joined the club of oil extracting nations. The daily yield is in the region of 1,500,000–2,000,000 barrels and for the state's treasury it continuously rains Petro Dollars.

Part of the wealth was shared with members of his tribe in 1990 by the ruler Sheik Rashid bin Zayed Al Maktoum, the 180,000 original inhabitants of Dubai. None of these descendants of Bedouin is forced to breed camels, fish, dive for pearls, or get involved in smuggling to make a living. They all live in luxury villas and have at least a Mercedes 600 parked by their gate.

The Sheikh was concerned with engineers' reports that calculated Dubai's oil fields would be exhausted in the near future, perhaps as soon as 2025. In order to continue to profit from the blessings from Allah billions of dollars have been invested in major projects to yield major profits when the final drop of Dubai oil is drained off.

In Dubai City two ages clash head on with each other. The area around the harbor was once an Arab settlement on either side of a small sea inlet that stretches for 7 and half miles (12 km) inland. Wide-beamed Arab dhows – trading vessels little changed since the Middle Ages – still moor at the quay. There are also oriental souks and old quarters such as Bastakia with its wind tower houses with decorated roofs that let fresh air into the living areas. This is all within a couple of hundred yards of the shaded business center and high-rise bank buildings with full air conditioning and marble clad temples of consumerism with their conspicuous design, sometimes ancient Egyptian, sometimes Belle Époque, and sometimes futuristic.

Tourism is also booming. For the wealthy there is an extremely modern cruise terminal and in winter the international airport conveys a virtually never-ending stream of pale westerners to the Marina. More than two hundred luxury hotels offer rooms and suites of more than 500 square feet up to 5,800 square feet. The star of these grand hotels is the 1,043 foot (321 m) high Burj Al-Arab, a seven star hotel tower in the form of slightly billowing sails. Eco tourists can stay in a sort of improved Bedouin encampment of the Al-Maha Resort amid the dunes. The Jumeira Hotel with its ocean wave design also offers superb views.

Man-made vacation island

The ultimate in vacation architecture is still being built. Five thousand workers from the Indian sub continent have poured eighty million cubic meters of rocks and sand into the Gulf in order to create an island with its own yachting harbor, fine restaurants, and exclusive places to stay. Some one thousand villas and three thousand vacation apartments on this oasis created from the sea are being sold, at prices starting at 500,000 Euros.

GETTING THERE
Wide choice of international flights

ACCOMMODATION
Discerning middle class hotels and luxury hotels for the very well connected. Packages available through travel operators

BEST TIME
November to March

TIPPING
Foreign service personnel 10 % of the bill. Most Arab staff, especially from Dubai, frequently expect none

EXCURSIONS
The Hatte Oasis, Sharjah Emirate, and Abu Dhabi

The 1,043 ft (321 m) high Burj Al-Arab Hotel on the Gulf beach offers 7-star vacation accommodation (far left)

Dubai's race track on the edge of the desert (top right)

High rise architecture on Dubai Creek, a sea inlet once used as harbor

Teheran's shining heritage

The palaces are open to view in Iran's capital city

GETTING THERE
Virtually all main
international airlines
serve Teheran

BEST TIME
The temperatures in
Teheran are similar to
those of western
Europe. The coldest
month is February with
an average of approx.
31 °F (0.5 °C) and
warmest in July and
August, on average
72 °F (22 °C)

ACCOMMODATION
Guest houses and hotels
in every category. From
3-star and above tourists
must pay in US$

TIPPING
Tips are not customary
in Iran with the
exception of restaurants
frequented by the
prosperous and luxury
hotels

The Persian cartographer Ibn Houqual was puzzled. On a tableland rising from the Elbur mountains to the north of the great desert he found many fruit gardens close to one another without any other apparent sign of human habitation. He recorded the solution to this riddle in a note. "The inhabitants live most of the time in underground caves and their main occupation is the robbing of passing caravans." The geographer named this place Teheran in the year 924. It is the first mention of the place that was to become the Iranian capital city.

More recent chronicles describe Teheran favorably as the popular summer residence of members of the royal family from the royal town of Rey. The green settlement on a rising plateau at a height of 3,900–5,525 feet (1,200-1,700 m) developed into a flourishing trading center with the help of refugees who sought protection from the Mongols. When the Kadjaren ruler Aqa Mohammed Khan had subjugated all of Persia by 1789 he made this high place his capital and had himself crowned as Shah. From then on Teheran was the royal seat of government until the last Pahlevi Shah fled into exile in 1979 at the time of the Iranian revolution.

A few years before his enforced abdication Shah Rez Pahlevi had ordered the erection of a 146 foot (45 m) high tower to mark 2,500 years of monarchy. The tower which serves as a triumphal arch has the shape of an upside-down upsilon or "Y". Renamed the "Freedom Tower" the futuristic buildings provides a panoramic view across the sprawl of Teheran to the snow-capped mountain slopes to the north.

Crown jewels on view

With a population estimated between nine and fourteen million the present-day Iranian capital of the Islamic Republic is one of the most densely populated communities on earth.

Teheran's great attraction for tourists is in part due to the artistic feeling but also the grandeur and limitless extravagance of the previous dynasty. During the time of the revolutionary leader Ayatollah Khomeini the majority of royal palaces were turned into museums. Astonished visitors can now view the royal salons in which the Shah and his family held court, granted royal privileges, titles, and orders. On occasions the host was seated on the sun throne, sometimes as in the case of

Shah Reza Pahlevi he preferred the peacock throne.

While the sun throne remains in the Golestan Palace, the peacock throne that is embedded with 26,733 jewels can be seen with other treasures of immeasurable value in the National Museum of Jewels. Astonishingly there are 3,380 diamonds, five emeralds, two sapphires, and 368 pearls in the golden Pahlevi crown, a platinum diadem of Farah Diba with 324 diamonds such as the famous Darya-ye Nur (Sea of Light) diamond that is 25 mm long by 20 mm across, weighing 182 carats. Close by is the Shah's golden globe, weighing 8,118 pounds of fine gold, on which the land and oceans are represented by 51,366 gemstones.

Bazaar of 10,000 stores

The sparkle of the mirrored hall of the Green Palace surpasses all at least in terms of its size. It took craftsmen six years to cover the ceiling of this "meeting room" with mirror glass mosaic.

Life in the Teheran bazaar is livelier than in the dead palace, with the most extensive oriental shopping area of any age. More than 10,000 stores entice with their goods, fragrant spices, glittering jewelry, blaring radios, bleeping computers, and mutton so freshly slaughtered it will make you gawp.

It is calmer now in front of the US Embassy where the staff were held hostage by fanatical youths for 444 days after the flight of the final Shah. Although the building is edged with Islamic gardens the strident message of "USA is the devil" is still demonstrated outside with increasing numbers of guards while inside computer training courses are held.

There is generally a relaxed mood, even at the mausoleum of Ayatollah Khomeini. The tall concrete and steel structure in the south of Teheran with its golden dome and four minarets is the popular destination for tens of thousands on holy days. Men pray on their prayer mats in front of the sarcophagus and dedicate themselves anew to be followers. Surrounded by picnicking families, playing children, sleeping older people, and card players, the tomb of the once so strongly disapproving top Shiite now embraces life.

View of the Throne room of the Golestan Palace in Teheran. The Shahs once sat on the marble throne (top)

View across northern Teheran to the snow-capped Elbur mountains (bottom left)

Tourists in front of the National Archaeological Museum, a former royal palace

153

Isfahan "is half the world"

An oasis in the mountains became Persia's cultural capital

GETTING THERE
Daily internal flights from Teheran and rail and bus links

ACCOMMODATION
Every need of the tourist from simple tourist guest houses to 5-star hotels. An original touch is to stay in a former caravanserai converted into the Abbasi luxury hotel

BEST TIME
Mild winter and occasionally very hot in summer. Spring is the best time

TIPPING
Tipping is not customary in Iran except in up-market places

Before the end of the first millennium traveling traders told of a superb resting place on the slopes of the Zagros mountains in central Persia. At around 4,800 feet there are shady gardens of an oasis alongside the Zayandeh river. Later a small trading place was created by these patches of green and finally a rich royal residence in which hundreds of the best Persian architects were given a free hand by their clients to turn bold dreams into reality. Hence Isfahan came into being, a town with the greatest collection of the finest oriental architecture between the Caspian Sea and the Persian Gulf.

The first major building was a temple erected by disciples of Zarathustra around 500 BC on a highly-placed site for their fire cult. Only some remnants of the walls remain of this sacred place but Isfahan in the meantime has become a city of 4,400,000 people and the second largest city in Iran while retaining its beauty. Narrow irrigation canals still glitter between the rows of buildings as of old and the avenues are lined with pines, plane trees, and espaliered poplars. And the outline of the city is still of domes and the forest of minarets that dominate the old center, which has been declared a world heritage site by Unesco.

Persians, Arabs, Seljuks

The settlement by Jews and the changing rule of the town by Persians, Arabs, and Turkish Seljuks led to creativity between the fifth and eleventh centuries in the building of royal palaces, mosques, Islamic madrasahs, and mausoleums. Ancient oriental styles of decoration combine well with the Islamic influences for instance in the Friday Mosque of Masje-e-Jom'e that creates an impression of perfection with its clean lines and harmonic proportions. Around the year 1000 there were one hundred mosques in Isfahan together with Koran schools, two thousand caravanserai, and three hundred bath houses.

In the twelfth century the town suffered from terror and barbarism. Members of a Shiite sect of assassins killed leading Seljuks and in 1121 set fire to the Friday Mosque. The precious interior and the entire library were destroyed by flames. Mongolian hordes pillaged the town regularly and threatened to burn it.

There was an upturn once more in building and craft work under the ambitious Shah Abbas I. At great expense the young monarch wished to make the residence of his Safavid dynasty of Isfahan into a mirror of all the world's beauty. To this end he had a royal square created in the town center surrounded by colonnades that at 1,664 by 520 feet (512 by 160 m) surpasses St. Mark's Square in Venice many times.

The great art of craftsmen

The square was subsequently used for playing polo and animal baiting and then turned into green areas with many fountains. The shah also had a royal mosque built covered with 1,500,000 decorative tiles, an artistic palace residence, and a smaller mosque. The Isfahan carpet became a desirable object of trade with its dense pile and beige tones.

In contrast with other places the ancient architecture in the center of Isfahan is filled with life in this twenty-first century. In the arcades around the former royal square craftsmen have established their workshops, there are caskets with mosaics incorporated for sale, painted miniatures are offered, and one can see how precious fabrics are printed with traditional motifs by a block process.

The fountains outside are besieged by children and hordes of people on foot press through the north gate into the Qaisariye Bazaar that has a pleasingly cool temperature even in the height of summer thanks to ventilation holes drilled in the right places in the roof by a carpenter centuries ago.

A poem of praise from the Middle Ages refers to "Isfahan nesf-e jehan" (Isfahan is half the world). It is no longer possible to inquire of the Persian poet what precisely was meant by this. The expression has become a standard quotation for Iranians, with the explanation that of all the world's wonders, half of them are to be found in Isfahan. God or Allah be praised.

The Masdschid-i-Sheik Lotfollah (top left) and Women's mosques (left of right-hand page) with their arched domes that tower above the old town.

Craft specialties include painted decoration of cotton textiles (below)

View over the roofs of the old town of Isfahan that is a world cultural heritage site. The Shah Mosque with its minaret is one of the unique sights of interest (top)

A masterpiece of oriental architecture spans the oasis river of Zayandeh

The paradise of Samarkand

Tamurlane did not shrink from shedding blood for the beauty of his city

The wonder of Samarkand lies surrounded by fields of red poppies and white dabs of cotton fields in the southern mountains of Uzbekistan. From the old caravan routes travelers first see giant pyramidal shapes on the horizon that are brown like the rocky terrain or turquoise in the light of the sun. These are the domes of splendid Medieval buildings that still dominate the view of the town in the twenty-first century.

The Uzbeks were originally Turkoman settlers who more than 2,500 years ago named this oasis on the Zarafshan river from samar for fertile, and kand for settlement. Valuable cargoes reached the warehouses of Samarkand from Beijing and Baghdad along the northern silk route. Soon paved streets led to the central market where silk, musk, carpets, furs, and also young Turkish slaves were haggled over.

Books from Samarkand

Samarkand's most important role was the spreading of intellectual output. The orient and the occident exchanged scholarly knowledge with the help of traveling merchants, expedition reports, news about the arts and philosophical ideas. Samarkand succeeded in 751 to make paper by a Chinese process and then supplied dictionaries, encyclopedias, and medicine books in manuscript that included medicine tracts by the Uzbek genius Ibn Sina, also known as Avicenna. Under the terror regime of Tamerlane (Timor Leng or Timur the Lame), Samarkand became the center of the Mongolian empire in the late fourteenth century and the finest city in Asia of great architectural beauty, purchased literally with rivers of blood. To transform his residence into a "Paradise of the East" the clever descendant of Genghis Khan and his hordes not only made Samarkand the wealthiest place in Asia or eastern Europe but also carried off the best architects, craftsmen, and artists.

At home the plunderer of treasure had realized an ambitious building program within a few years that elsewhere would take many generations. Almost simultaneously masterfully built mosques, madrasahs (religious schools), magnificent palaces, and hospitable caravanserai rose from the ground. Tamurlane mercilessly drove people from the town center, demolished their houses, and in their stead built a covered main bazaar that soon became the principal interchange place for wares between east and west.

To build the Bibi Chanym Mosque, dedicated to his favorite wife, it took ninety-five elephants four years to drag huge blocks of stone that were then cut to shape by five hundred stone masons. Huge rectangular Persian-style towers known as iwans were tiled from top to bottom by specialists with mosaics and faience. The railings were wrought by smiths to Arabesque patterns from "seven metals." To support the four hundred prayer halls next to the dome required a forest of marble columns.

War for disturbing the dead

To glorify himself after death Tamurlane had the giant Gur-e-Amir (Prince's Tomb originally built for his favorite grandson) mausoleum built. The main section of the remaining palatial structure has a 110 foot (34 m) high melon-shaped golden dome crowning a drum-like building. The rectangular main portal to the inner courtyard is about 39 feet(12 m) high. This was created for Tamerlane by the famous Isfahan architect, Ibn Mah-

mud. Above the gate arch in decorated tiles are the words: "One is fortunate if one leaves the world before the world can do without you."

Tamurlane died suddenly in 1405 outside Samarkand in an encampment from which the sixty-nine year old intended to conquer China. His followers bore his body back to Samarkand where it was placed in the Gur-e-Amir mausoleum and words were added to the inscription to warn that any disturbance of his rest would be responded to by a fierce war. Soviet archaeologists were the first to attempt exploring the tomb in 1941 when they found the remains of a man who was lame in both legs of sturdy frame and with a Mongol skull and red beard. Within weeks Germany was at war with the Soviet Union.

The Registan main square in the center of Samarkand (top left)

The imposing She-i-Sinda cemetery (top right)

The finely decorated dome of the Gur-e-Amir mausoleum (center above)

The Registan Mosque is a popular tourist sight

157

Architecture and love in Lahore

Mughal emperors leave architecture of fairy-tale beauty

GETTING THERE
Lahore has international flight connections

ACCOMMODATION
Holiday Inn and simpler accommodation

BEST TIME
November to February

TIPPING
Up to 10 % of the amount of bills

The history of the origins of the most beautiful city in Pakistan remains in the dark. According to Hindu legend Lahore was founded before time itself by Loh, a son of Rama, the incarnation of Vishnu. Muslims derive the name of the former residence of the powerful Mughal ruler from the words Loh awar, meaning "iron fortress." It has been handed down that the city of many mosques and fine mansions once boasted from one of its grand towers: "Nothing like it has ever been nor ever will be seen this side of heaven."

Stairs for elephants

The heyday of Lahore began soon after the end of the first millennium when the population became Islamic following conquest by Muslims. Under the rule of various sultans the city developed into an intellectual center that attracted poets, artists, and scholars from Persia and Central Asia. In the sixteenth century the Mughal emperor turned Lahore into the architectural treasure of his realm. Nowhere else in what is now Pakistan enjoyed such a significant blossoming of Islamic culture as here on the Ravi river in the fertile Punjab in the "land of the five rivers" formed by the Indus and its tributaries.

The Moguls had a wall built around the place with twelve towers. Within these walls they built the Royal Fort that still exists as a grand residence with palaces, quiet courtyards, and bath houses. These were later followed by the three white pearl-form domes of the "Pearl Mosque." The main entrance to the Royal Fort area is formed by the gigantic Shah Buri gate that needed to be high enough and wide enough for the emperor to pass through when seated on an elephant. There is also an elephant's staircase constructed of solid timber that leads diagonally towards the Shish Mahal. The walls of this mirrored palace are decorated with mosaic of various colors of mirror glass and larger mirrors that are set within incrustations of gold and gemstones.

While the mirrored palace served as the emperor's home at the beginning of the seventeenth century, the Great Mughal even had palace districts within the fortress of a bath house, the "court of the ladies of the harem", and the "house of dreams" or royal sleeping apartment. Feast were held in the "hall of forty pillars". Sports were also important in Lahore according to evidence of picture tiles and frescos on the fortress walls. Riders particularly have high regard for polo which has its origins in Central Asia.

Garden with 412 fountains

Outside the fortified residence the Moguls left behind numerous other fine buildings including above all the largest religious building of Lahore, the red sandstone Badshahi Mosque. It is a picture of perfect harmony with its three white domes and the iwan frontage with its lines of calligraphy and this is further emphasized by the breadth of the inner courtyard with its room for 60,000 believers. A little way outside this city – today of three million people – Shah Jahan left behind for posterity the oriental park created in 1642 of the Shalimar Gardens. The outstanding features of these gardens on three levels are the 195 foot (60 m) long water rills with their 412 fountains, artificial islands, pavilions, and marble sides.

The numerous mausoleums in Lahore are the stuff of legends. In one tomb, that was later used as a Christian chapel, Anarkali ("Pomegranate Blossom"), a concubine of Akbar the Great is said to have been laid to rest. When the ruler noticed in a mirror the beauty cast a glance at another lover he had her bricked in the tomb alive and then mournfully added an inscription: "Oh dear, I can still see that beloved countenance."

Two less important tombs in terms of their architecture outside the city are reminders of two men who are famous in Pakistan. One of these is the scholar Ali Makdum Al Hujwiri who died in 1072, a universal genius of such intellectual ability that he can still inspire from the grave. In the second tomb Hasrat Mian Mir has lain since 1635, who was well over a hundred years old and yet seldom breathed: at night just two or three times and in his final years just four times in all.

Three bright and shiny marble domes crown the red sandstone prayer hall of the Badshahi Mosque. On special Fridays up to 60,000 people gather in the inner courtyard. (top)

Magnificent royal building atop the city wall (bottom left)

A plasterer restoring a tile (bottom center)

Building facade in need of restoration in the old town

GETTING THERE
International flights from all over the world

ACCOMMODATION
From inexpensive places to the most luxurious hotels

BEST TIME
November–April. It can be unpleasantly cold in December and January

TIPPING
Bills are rounded up to include service but give additional tips for small acts of helpfulness

EXCURSIONS
To Agra to visit the Taj Mahal

Delhi – football of the powers

Palaces and tombs tell of dramatic events in India's capital

It is not the Red Fort with its white domes, nor the pomp and ceremony of parades, or yet a Hindu temple festival, let alone a colorful market that brings tens of thousands of pilgrims each 30th of January but a simple monument for a unique man: Mohandas Karamchand Gandhi, better known as Mahatma, great mind. It was on the 30th of January that the proponent of non-violence was shot by a political fanatic while he was engaged in his evening prayers in front of his house in Delhi.

It is part of the tragedy of this otherwise joyful city of two faces: old and new, that amid its history of progress there is frequently horror. Here in the north of India, close to where the fertile flood plains spread out at the foot of the Himalayas, cultures and religions have lived alongside one another in friendly competitiveness for three thousand years but also frequently at war.

The 230 foot (71 m) high Kutab Minar sandstone tower that is lit at night by floodlights is not just Delhi's oldest landmark but also a symbol of clearly contrasting worlds. Muslims erected the minaret-like building as a victory memorial to mark Delhi coming under Islamic rule in 1206. The tower reminds Hindus of the last Hindu king, Phrithviraj who fell in the battle with the Muslims. The imposing remains of the first mosque in Delhi are close to the Kutab Minar, which according to an inscription on its eastern portal was built using stones from twenty-seven temples of the Hindu and Jaina religions that were demolished. Other religious sites that stood after this time were leveled by 1398 at the latest when the Mongol war lord Tamurlane plundered the city and according to tradition killed 100,000.

Artistic Mughal emperor

Fortunately there were also Muslim rulers who did not destroy but built. Hence a Mughal emperor with artistic taste had the Red Fort built on the western bank of the Yamuna in the seventeenth century with its complete array of superbly finished marble palaces, bath houses, courtyard gardens, and heated apartments. Beneath the canopy supported by snow-white marble columns the Shah of Persia sociably smoked a hookah here in 1739 with the Indian King Bahadur before his soldiers massacred the civil population, taking the Indian peacock throne and

other treasures before returning back in the direction of Teheran.

The palatial assemblage of the Red Fort has meanwhile become Delhi's principal tourist attraction. The residence is surrounded by a semi-circle of high wall that protects the royal town of Shah Jahanabad which today is the oldest part of Delhi. The time of the Muslim overlords finally ended when India was absorbed into the British Empire in the nineteenth century.

The two faces of Delhi

Close to the Red Fort is the outstandingly restored Jama Mashid Mosque that was completed in 1658 and of such enormous proportions that up to 25,000 believers can find room in its courtyard. Its twin 140 foot (40 m) high minarets make it possible to gain a bird's eye view of the two faces of Delhi. To the north there is the metropolis of Old Delhi with its oriental bazaars and the striking buildings of the Mughals while to the south there is New Delhi with its government buildings that looks as English as London, but slightly newer.

New Delhi was built in the 1920s according to plans of British town planners and architects to form a modern center of power for the Empire. Dead straight streets connect circular places and dozens of gardens with one another. From the triumphal-style arch of India Gate the central axis is a grand avenue, the Rajpath which leads to the former Viceroy's Palace that has been home to the Indian President since 1947.

Outside the commercial areas of both Old and New Delhi one finds one of the most grief-stricken sites of recent Indian history. It is the Indira Gandhi House, final home of the daughter of Jawaharlal Nehru, who like her father served India as Prime Minister until on 31 October, 1984 during a morning stroll in her garden she was shot by two of her own guards. Indira Gandhi's home has been left just as it was on the morning of her death. The spot on which she was killed is marked by a glass shrine.

The Mandhir Temple is one of the most impressive cultural sites of Delhi

View from the Jama Mashid Mosque across the roofs of the city (top)

The large open space in front of the mosque shows the overall grand scale of the structure with its domes (bottom left)

The Humayun Mausoleum also has enormous proportions

Many gods in Kathmandu

The fantastic world of temples of Nepal's capital

Katmandu takes on a complete air of mysticism when the early morning mist in the high valleys all around rises up to the icy ridges of the Himalayas. Temples and images of the gods are swallowed up in a sea of white, one imagines hearing distant muffled sounds of gongs and detecting a cold whiff of decay and charred wood. In these unreal moments the Newar people believe they find spiritual cleansing, with all sins and bad thoughts being freed and born away by the mist.

This does not last long because in the modern parts of the "city of a thousand temples" the cleansing mist is replaced by smelly gases from car and moped exhausts. The large volume of foreign visitors has long since changed the isolated town in the Himalayas into a noisy major city with a sudden rise in population – from 123,000 to 450,000 within four years. But in the midst of modern Kathmandu there is still the virtually undisturbed age old scene of many shrines, images of gods, and palaces.

A demigod hits back

The 4,225 foot (1,300 m) high valley of Kathmandu is the relic of a mountain lake that a mere 10,000 years ago suddenly released its water through the Chobar Gorge in the south. Geologists believe the outflow was caused by an earthquake but the Newar who have lived here for centuries know better: the demigod Manjushri performed the miracle with a single blow from his sword of light. The Nevar people's religions are Hindu and nature and talented wood carvers among them have created works of art that can be admired at many temples.

Kathmandu ("house of wood") probably dates from the tenth century when a number of villages on the old caravan and pilgrim trails between Tibet and India joined together. Monks and merchants brought their religions with them to the valley, first Buddhism, followed by Hinduism, and then the teachings of the Tibetan Lamas. Hence a variety of different religious buildings have come to be built in Kathmandu and shown by hard-working builders in the sixteenth and seventeenth centuries for the Newar kings. Dozens of shrines alone date back to King Pratapa Malla (1641–1674), an undogmatic mystic.

Away from the noisy streets there are old parts of Kathmandu that appear not to have been changed for centuries where sacred cows chew at the garbage lying around and scraggy dogs chase one another. Ancient merchant's houses stand cheek by jowl in the narrow streets with artistically carved showcases and together form monuments from the time of the Malla kings that are an open air museum of Nepalese and Tibetan architecture. Hindu shrines with rectangular bases and triple-winged roofs alternate with rounded Buddhist pagodas, elongated prayer halls, and pavilions with images of the gods and masks of demons.

In the center of Durbar Square stands the old Hanuman Dhoka royal palace built on nine storeys with temples, and large reception halls. The structure is dedicated to the ape king Hanuman who protects against illness. Within there is reverence too for the elephant head of Ganesh, god of wisdom and wealth. A golden gate leads to the coronation courtyard of the Nepalese ruler. In a further courtyard, the Mul Chowk, buffalo, billy-goat, and cockerel are given up in order to make the mother god Durga gracious.

Sex versus lightning

Some of the sites of the cults are intertwined with quite astonishing stories. The representation of a copulating couple on the roof trusses of a Tantric Jaganath (Krishna) temple are said to protect the building from the still virginal goddess Jaganath who comes to earth as lightning and will be so shocked by such images that she will not strike the building. In the Tibetan Bonpo monastery fifty monks and mystics await the paradise on earth kingdom of Olmo Lungring prophesied for 18,000 years. Devout Newars take care of a jeweled waistcoat that the serpent god once stole from a demon and the sight of which will now protect against theft. And a giant statue represents the frightening Kal Bhairab, god of truth, that will destroy all who lie to him.

Kathmandu is a place of wonders. Every lane contains a little secret, every temple a myth. This place of many religions in the bright clear light of the high Himalayas is a perfect travel destination for westerners provided they suspend the pure reason of their own world.

GETTING THERE
Direct flights from various airports. Bus travel between Delhi and Kathmandu with change of buses at the border takes three days. Travel in own car requires Carnet de Passage (international registration) and an international driver's license.

ACCOMMODATION
Private rooms and simple lodges for a few dollars per night. Many hotels from mid-range to luxury class

BEST TIME
October–November and February–April

TIPPING
Restaurants and hotels providing bills add 10 % for service. Give extra tips for good service. Porters, travel guides, and hotel service staff expect tips

ALSO WORTH SEEING
The Lion Palace of Singha Durbar, an enormous building from the twentieth century. The Narayan Hiti royal palace is still occupied. The 195 ft (60 m) high Bhimsen Tower for its views

Pagodas with triple wing roofs and all manner of holy shrines as here in Patan are typical of the historic center of Nepalese towns (left)

A Hindu begging monk in front of a temple in Durbar Square (bottom left)

A Buddhist shrine or Stupa with sacred figures and mythical animals

Desecrated holy place of Lhasa

China took their land from the Tibetans and destroyed their culture

GETTING THERE
Regular flight connections to Chengdu in China and athmandu in Nepal with Gonkar Airport, Tibet about 30 miles (90 km) south of Lhasa. There are also buses to Lhasa from Kathmandu

ACCOMMODATION
Very basic Tibetan accommodation and a few medium class hotels to western standards

BEST TIME
April-June, September-October

TIPPING
Officially forbidden but frequently and happily accepted

SPECIAL HINT
Unless you go with an organized group it is very important before the start of the journey to make inquiries about Visa requirements and to plan the trip very carefully

According to one version of many ancient legends an invisible demoness lay herself across the mountains of Tibet in the seventh century to hinder the initiation into Buddhism of the thirty-third Tibetan king, Songsten Gampo. The magical daughter of the king, Princess Wencheng, knew what to do though: a Buddhist shrine was erected over the demon and the evil spirit was forced to give up her resistance.

The ground chosen was so fairytale like that the king, who reigned from 629–649, made Lhasa, at a height of over 12,000 feet (3,700 m), his capital and built his Jokhang Temple there. A mixture of Buddhism and ancient beliefs in demons developed in the course of time into Lamaism or Vajrayana Buddhism. The senior representatives of the religion are the god kings or Dalai Lamas who are reincarnated after their death according to Tibetan beliefs.

The twin roles of religious and worldly leader of this Himalayan state were assumed first in the seventeenth century by the "Great" fifth Dalai Lama Ngawang Lozang Gyatso. This charismatic holy man had the high-walled Potala Palace built on the remains of the residence of Songtsen Gampo on the edge of Lhasa, as a sort of Tibetan Buddhist Vatican. Extended several times, the thirteen storey Potala Palace with its unbridled architecture became one of the largest structures of Asia. It remains impressive today for its enormous proportions, pure beauty, and radiance of spirituality.

Strangers threatened with death

The god king is also responsible for the conservation of the Jokhang Temple that was formerly known as Tsug Lha Khang or the "central cathedral" and in Tibetan is often referred to as Trulnang or "temple." The current name is derived from the fact that the temple houses a priceless statue of Buddha Shakyamuni that was created in Jowo Shakyamuni's lifetime. This central figure in Buddhism, is founder of the Tibetan tradition of Buddhism. The Buddha has a five pointed diadem and is heaped with gemstones, turquoises, moonstones, coral, and amulets.

Up to the early twentieth century Lhasa was the "home of the gods" and one of the most isolated royal residences on earth. Most Tibetan pilgrims could only reach their capital by arduous mountain paths or snow-covered caravan routes and strangers were forbidden on pain of death to approach the holy city. The Swedish explorer of Asia, Sven Hedin, who was one of the first Europeans to penetrate into Tibet, only dared to view Lhasa – the real objective of his expedition – from afar.

Rebellion put down

The fear of foreigners by the Dalai Lamas was well-founded was proven in 1950 when the Chinese, in breach of international law, marched its army into eastern Tibet and eventually managed to occupy the entire land in spite of increasing resistance. The government in Beijing spoke of a "liberation" of Tibet from its Medieval feudal ruler but was treated by the population as an enemy. A number of rebellions were savagely put down. Around 100,000 Tibetans fled the country as in 1959 did the Dalai Lama, to India.

Soon a systematic eradication of Tibetan culture got under way. The big colorful festivities of the Tibetans were forbidden as "too costly," the monasteries were disbanded and plundered. What was not destroyed during the "liberation" while the United Nations stood idly by, succumbed later during the Chinese cultural revolution. Mao Zedong destroyed ten thousand statues of Buddhas, and burnt pictures and writings. Entire monasteries were cleared away stone for stone.

In the meantime Lhasa is now a provincial capital of a "Chinese autonomous region" and the last bastion of Tibetan culture, although the majority of the inhabitants are Chinese. While of four thousand religious sites elsewhere in Tibet believers have a mere one hundred at their disposal it has been permitted in Lhasa to restore the badly damaged Jokhang Temple and make it a focal point once more for processions. At the same time the Potala Palace has been turned into a folklore museum that after a long ban is open once more for western tourists.

With its unbridled architecture, the Potala Palace of the Tibetan capital is one of the most magnificent buildings of Asia. This was home to the god king, the 14th Dalai Lama until his flight following the Chinese occupation (top)

The people of Lhasa dressed in traditional costume during horse races (bottom left)

A Lamaist monk outside a monastery in the old town

Buddha's hair kept in shrine

Former **RANGOON** welcomes foreigners again

Around midday the light of the sun on the Yangon river dazzles the graceful inhabitants of Yangon from two directions at the same time. One sun is high above the Andaman lake, the other glistens as its reflection in the golden Shwedagon Pagoda 318 foot (98 m) high above the harbor. This is one of the finest Buddhist temples in the world that Jungle Book author Rudyard Kipling once described as "a beautiful, winking wonder that blazed in the sun."

Western literature associates Rangoon – known again by its original name of Yangon – with oriental magic and lurking danger. Because since Great Britain extended its colonial reach in the early nineteenth century to the territory of Burma that was populated by hostile tribes, Europeans were not welcome in the interior of the deepest parts of the Indian sub-continent. Even after independence following World War II when the country became Myanmar it closed itself off against the west for a long time. It is only in the past two decades that secretive Yangon has become open as a tourist destination.

Living with composure

Despite four million inhabitants the street life of Yangon today still exhibits a certain calm composure that has long since been lost in other major Asian cities. Well-traveled people are pleasantly surprised by the charm of the people living on the Yangon river, their traditional courtesy and good manners, respect for women, and their endeavor never to raise their voice or act insistently.

The city's buildings are from a variety of different eras. On the river front wooden houseboats in the form of gracefully curved shallops swing at their moorings. Their shape has not changed for centuries. Buildings with Victorian facades recall colonial times with unusual balconies and temple like ornamentation. The recently re-opened luxury Strand Hotel is a pleasing legacy from the British.

The city's atmosphere is helped by the many trees and smiling Buddhas. Not far from the airport the many manifestations and incarnations of Buddhas are displayed. A seated "five-storey" Buddha of the Ashay Tawya monastery is almost 100-feet high (20 m) but is outdone for size by the Reclining Buddha a few streets away. The stupas or upright bells with elongated points are a typical sight of Yangon. There are some Buddhist relics, most of which recall certain religious events.

The Shwedagon Pagoda that is Yangon's main landmark sits on Singuttura hill is also shaped like a stupa. In a legend of its origin two merchants were granted the favor of eight of Buddha's hairs 2,500 years ago to be kept for posterity in a shrine. When the men placed the Buddha's hair as instructed in a shrine, a miracle occurred. Sparkling beams emanated from the hairs, the blind could suddenly see, the deaf hear, the dumb began to speak, the earth shook, it rained gemstones, all the flowers bloomed, and all simultaneously bore fruit.

Weight in gold

In reality the golden bell-form pagoda was erected by the Mon people between the sixth and tenth centuries. According to archaeologists the shrine of the relics was originally only a few feet high and was covered with jungle vegetation for a long time. Centuries later a Burmese king had the shrine uncovered and enlarged to its present proportions. The Mon king Shinsawbu ordained his body weight of approx. eighty-eight pounds of gold for gilding the stupa, whereupon his daughter and son-in-law even gave four times their body weights in gold. Meanwhile the weight of gold of the massive stupa of the pagoda is around fifty-eight tons.

The Golden Pagoda, which is surrounded by dreamlike temples, monasteries, impressive sculpture, and smaller stupas, is today a national shrine. Freedom fighters first engaged the British troops here high above the town in 1824. In 1929 the British relinquished control of the holy hill and finally handed back the whole of Burma in 1947. The adoption once more of the former name of Yangon with the disappearance of the colonial power has a certain poignancy for yangon means "end of strife."

MYANAMAR (BURMA)
Rangoon

Pacific Ocean
South China Sea

GETTING THERE
Direct flights from Bangkok

BEST TIME
November–February

ACCOMMODATION
Inns and hotels in all categories up to the legendary 5-star Strand Hotel

TIPPING
Tipping in the western sense is unknown but small gifts in the form of money, cigarettes, or lighters are a good way to remove bureaucratic delays or acquire "sold out" tickets

The Shwedagon Pagoda is particularly atmospheric in the evening (left)

The head of the Reclining Buddha in the Chaukhtatgyi Pagoda (bottom left)

Devout monks in their red habit kneel before the golden Buddha of the Shwedagon Pagoda

THAILAND
Bangkok

GETTING THERE
International flight connections. Many package offers

ACCOMMODATION
Hotels for all tastes. Best address: Hotel Oriental right on the Menam

BEST TIME
November to February

TIPPING
No fixed rules. It is as well not to be miserly with tips for the usually badly paid serving staff

Bangkok - the city of angels

Elaborate royal palaces and variety of life on the "floating markets"

On their last reach to the Gulf of Thailand the olive-green masses of water of the Menam roll through flat land past mango groves, rice plantations and fields of betel nuts. Then, only 22 miles (35 km) from the sea, in a bend of the river, holy shrines with points like needles, temples with golden roofs, industrial chimneys, high-rise buildings and hotel palaces appear on the east bank. This is the capital of Thailand, Bangkok, with its seven million inhabitants, in the language of the natives Krung Thep, city of angels.

Its history began with the murder of a tyrant. After the destruction of the former capital Ayutthaya by Burmese troops, in 1767 the defeated Thai general Taksin had appointed himself king and made a village on the west bank of the Menam his royal seat. But he suffered increasingly from delusions of grandeur, passed himself off as the coming Buddha and bullied his followers. A palace revolt ensued, in which the mad king was killed by his own officers.

The abandoned throne was taken over by a general involved in the murder conspiracy, Chakri by name. As Rama I, the new ruler founded the Chakri dynasty, which has since reigned in uninterrupted succession and from which the present king Bhumibol also originates. To avoid being exposed to a bad omen, Rama I moved the royal seat from the scene of the crime on the west bank to the opposite side of the Menam and there developed little Bangkok (village of olives) into the new capital of Thailand. Under Rama and his successors magnificent residential palaces, coronation halls, ministries and a Buddhist monastery complex developed on a square of open country by the river there. Part of it is still used by the royal family, but, apart from a few exceptions, the temples and palaces are open to the public.

Before the black throne

One of the oldest buildings in the complex is the coronation palace of Rama I, erected in 1783, with its black throne decorated with mother-of-pearl inlays. On the green and gold gleaming walls are angels, floating upwards out of lotus flowers – possibly the original reason for the name "city of angels". In a second palace of the first Chakri ruler is the golden Busabok Mala throne, which is shaped like a boat.

Of four further palace buildings the "Great Palace of the Chakri Dynasty" is the most imposing. British master builders erected it in 1876 as a kind of Renaissance castle with Thai stepped gables, from which carved celestial snakes jut out. Inside, huge crystal chandeliers illuminate the throne room with Bhumibol's throne under an overhanging white screen.

And Buddha greets you everywhere

Six entrance gates, each guarded by two giant yak sculptures, lead into the adjacent monastery complex Wat Phra Keo, which is one of the most beautiful ever created by Thai artists. A rectangular hall, surrounded by golden Chedi shrines and animal sculptures, here shelters one of the greatest holy relics in Thailand: the "Emerald Buddha", enthroned on a 33-foot (10 m) high plinth. The jade figure, according to myth created by gods, is the tutelary god of the Chakri dynasty.

The 46-foot (14 m) high and 151-foot (46 m) long "Reclining Buddha" of Wat Po enjoys particular popularity with the people of Bangkok. Devotees have stuck layers of little gold plates all over the body of the giant figure.

Perhaps the most colorful area is on the west bank of the Menam in the klongs, a maze of canals and tributaries, where from time immemorial the "river people" have lived their lives. They live in stilt buildings between ancient trees and their means of transport are canoes and sampans, which are also used to convey large freights. In the mornings you will see many klong residents in colored garments taking fruit and vegetables from tropical gardens to the " floating markets", where everything the surrounding fertile alluvial soil produces is traded. A wonderful sight!

In the evening many tourists are drawn to the traditional Thai dances performed by ballerinas or to a stroll through the entertainment's area. Visitors come from far and wide to the city of angels, not least because of the beautiful Thai women.

In front of the temple complex of Wat Phra Keo is Sacrifice Square, where flowers and candles are offered to the gods (above)

The food market in the "klongs", where fresh vegetables are sold on boats, is a riot of color (below left)

Praying monks – as here at Wat Indraviharn Temple – are to be found all over the city

The temple figures of Wat Phra Keo are world-famous (left)

Parisian life in Saigon

The former colonial city has retained its charm

VIETNAM

Saigon

Pacific Ocean

South China Sea

GETTING THERE
Via Saigon international airport

ACCOMMODATION
Good average class and luxury hotels

BEST TIME
November to January

TIPPING
Not customary in Vietnam, though small gifts for special services are of course welcome

SPECIAL TIP
If you don't haggle you will be paying too much

Freight ships and wooden houses on the riverbanks in the district of Ben Nghe (above left)

Ho Chi Minh memorial in front of the city hall in Saigon (below right)

So, what region of Europe are we in? The ochre-yellow city hall with its ornate clock tower looks like an hôtel de ville in Provence. The villa with the pillared portico extending up to the roof is like those seen in London, while the Hotel Majestic could be on the French Riviera. And Notre Dame Cathedral with its red brick would be at home in Normandy. In reality all four are in southeast Asia, more precisely in Saigon, which has been named Ho Chi Minh city since 1975, but is still called Saigon by its inhabitants.

Although a few high-rise giants and the memorials to Viet Cong heroes do not fit so well into the image, in the center of the second-largest city in Vietnam you have the feeling of being in a French colonial city a hundred years ago. Official buildings and churches, the opera house and the larger hotels were all built by Parisian architects. And the "Paris of the East" still has its wide avenues in common with the city on the Seine. The major part of life is played out under eucalyptus trees and the delicate green umbrellas of tamarinds. There are thousands of folding chairs on the boulevards inviting you to sit down.

In the language of the Khmer Saigon means kapok forest. For giant kapok trees once lined the Saigon River, on whose banks houseboats and restaurant ships are now moored. A thousand years ago Khmer were the first settlers in the subsequent area of the metropolis, joined at the end of the seventeenth century by Vietnamese from the region of Hue. With refugees from China all then became mixed together as Saigonese, a petite race of people full of vitality.

Missionaries followed by soldiers

Christian missionaries from France were mostly given a friendly reception in Saigon at the beginning of the nineteenth century. No one suspected that the religious brothers would be followed in 1859 by eight battleships full of French soldiers. In a short time the foreigners conquered the south of Vietnam and declared Saigon capital of the French colony of Indochina. On the one hand the colonial lords began to exploit the land and on the other, especially in Saigon, they also did some good by draining the swampy subsoil by means of canals and adding valuable

Parisian touches to the still shabby cityscape. After World War II first the French and then the Americans waged a bloody war to prevent South Vietnam being united with the communist North. But the North won. Since 1976 the country has been constitutionally one again.

Whole battalions of communist party functionaries arrived from the capital Hanoi to re-educate the residents of Saigon, whom they regarded as western decadents, into becoming good communists. It now

looks more as if the Saigonese have re-educated the communists.

Anyway, in the city on the Saigon River national socialist uniformity has not become widespread, but the citizens have retained their cosmopolitan spirit, their flair and their tendency to be easy-going by nature. Saigon has long been the "boom town" of Vietnam, the city with the greatest economic growth, the most important harbor and record rates of increase in tourism.

A popular meeting point for foreigners is the roof terrace of the Hotel Rex with its bamboo cages full of twittering birds and bonsai trees hung with strings of lights. Here tips are exchanged as to what, apart from the colonial architecture, is worth seeing. The somberly beautiful Glac Lam Pagoda, for example, with its tower of seven levels, the boulevard Don Khoi, lined with street cafés, or the war relics museum with horrifying photographic documents.

New Cholon

The Chinese quarter Cholon is a city within a city. For 300 years primarily merchants have lived here, who trade in practically everything that brings in money. For a long time the area was notorious for its opium dens and at the same time a magnet for brothel visitors. Neither of these services is offered any longer in communist times, but instead you can get cheap haircuts by street hairdressers, singing birds, amulets and medicines for boosting male potency. In addition Cholon can offer at least a dozen secret Tao shrines, including the superb "Temple of the Divine Lady" with its countless colored ceramic figures and sacrificial altars, where paper money is burned for dead relations.

The area around Ho Chi Minh city also has many diversions to offer those who are tired of the streets. In the south there is the beach resort of Vung Tau on the South China Sea and in the north the extensive Cat Tien National Park.

The streets of the city center are still dominated by the traditional trishaws (top right)

The wide boulevard on which the Hotel Rex is situated symbolizes modern Saigon

The decorative Kuala Lumpur

A hot and humid mining village has risen to become the super-modern capital of Malaysia

In the year 1857 a group of Chinese mining experts from the west coast of Malaysia penetrated the interior of the country and discovered at the foot of the Banjaran mountain range a large tin deposit. A few miles away the expedition set up a supply station with accommodation for mine workers at the confluence of the jungle waters Klang and Gombak. It was a swamp region infested with malaria, which they named "Dirty Confluence": Kuala Lumpur.

In spite of its off-putting name in a few years the tropical settlement had developed into a prosperous city, owing to the tin, which at that time could be traded for a good price. Soon gigantic coffee and rubber plantations, wrested from the rain forest, were contributing to Kuala Lumpur's economic upturn. The population consisted – as still today – principally of three groups: Chinese mine workers and merchants, Malayan farmers and numerous Indians, mainly employed in constructing the railroad and on the plantations. In 1896 "Dirty Confluence" was appointed capital of the Federation of Malaya.

Sultans elect the king

With the beginning of the twentieth century and the triumphal progress of cars – reliant on rubber wheels – Kuala Lumpur profited from the worldwide demand for rubber, which from now on took over first place in foreign trade ahead of tin. From southern India and Sri Lanka a new wave of immigrants began and caused the number of the city's inhabitants to rise at the beginning of the 1930s to approximately four million.

The first severe setbacks came during World War II, when the British colonial power withdrew in the face of the Japanese, who were advancing into Malaysia. After 1945 life was adversely affected by battles between nationalist and communist groups for supremacy in Malaysia. When the wrangling was over the state of Malaysia emerged in its present form as a democratic, parliamentary monarchy, whose royal head of state is elected by sultans. The capital and seat of the king is Kuala Lumpur.

The comparatively very young capital achieved a worldwide degree of recognition at the latest in 1977 with the completion of the twin skyscraper Petronas Tower, the two towers of which, at 1,480 feet (452 m), stand out above everything so far built by man. With the advantages of the economic boom of the ASEAN states, in Kuala Lumpur at the end of the twentieth century dozens of further gigantic buildings have appeared overnight. The television tower is the fourth-tallest in the world and the Linear City, which leads over the Klang River and beyond for almost a mile and a quarter apparently represents a world record in the horizontal. However, the growing stream of Malaysia tourists are more enthusiastic about the traditional and the typically Asian.

A large building with 98-foot (30 m) high minarets, arches and decorative domes turns out, as one gets closer, to be the main train station, from where the prestigious "Eastern & Oriental Express" steams off towards Bangkok and Singapore. The main post office and the railway administration building give the impression of oriental dream castles, at least externally. The Old City Hall, the Sultan Abdul Samad office building and the Supreme Court are also in Moorish style.

Cave temple of the Hindus

As Islam is the chief religion of the Malays, in the city area there are also numerous genuine mosques. The spit of land at the confluence of Klang and Gombak has since 1909 been the picturesque location of the Friday Mosque, Masjid Jame, whose white domes are reminiscent of the Pearl Mosque of Old Delhi. It is exceeded in size by the Masjid Negara National Mosque, a modern marble building with a 240 foot (73 m) tall minaret and space for around 8,000 devotees.

There are temples of Asiatic religions in the colorful shopping alleys of the Chinese city and the old Indian quarter. In Sze Yeoh Temple Chinese pay homage to the god of pioneers, Sen Sze Ya and the popular deity Kuan Yin. Not far from the night market is the Hindu temple, Sri Maha Mariamman, erected in 1873 in the form of a blue and gold painted five-storey mountain of gods. A little way outside the city 272 steps of a wide staircase lead up to the Batu Caves, a gigantic cave temple. Up to 100,000 Hindus gather on important holidays in the 1,310-foot (400 m) long and around 390-foot (120 m) tall caverns to honor Shiva and his son Subramaniam.

The 1,480-ft (452 m) high Petronas Towers (left) in the Malaysian capital are a delightful contrast to old Chinese shrines like the Thoan Hou Temple (below left) or the Hindu shrine Sri Maha Mariamman, in the form of a mountain of gods

Clinical beauty

The island state of **SINGAPORE** is a classic example of multi-cultural life

GETTING THERE
Direct international flights. Passage on freighters also possible

ACCOMMODATION
Many possibilities, from sailors' homes to luxury hotels. Suites in the restored Raffles colonial hotel are extremely expensive

TIPPING
Tips are not customary. Hotel and restaurant bills usually include 10 % service charge

BEST TIME
Best time to travel March to June. However, with an average daytime temperature of 86 °F (30 °C), the other seasons are bearable

At first sight the high-rise district on both sides of the deep green Singapore River is identical to the inner city area of most modern metropolises. But only here at the southern tip of the Malaysian peninsula do streets, parks and quay-sides give the overriding impression of clinical cleanliness. Houses and bridges look freshly painted, the riverbank promenades freshly sprayed with water and the flower beds freshly raked. Nothing seems to be more repugnant to the strict city council of Singapore than dirt and untidiness.

The history of this city state, extending over one large and fifty four smaller islands, began, according to legend, in the eighth century with the appearance of a sea monster, half fish and half lion. A Malayan prince standing on the bank was supposedly so impressed by the monstrous creature that he changed the name of a fishing village from Temasek (place by the sea) to Singa Pura (lion city). In fact the lion-mouthed water dragon today not only adorns stamps, but can also be admired as a 26-foot (8 m) tall statue in Merlion Park.

The British arrive

Although Singapore is on the Strait of Malacca, the much traveled shipping route between the Indian Ocean and the South China Sea, during the next thousand years it did not play any role in world politics with its fishing port. This did not change until the Englishman Thomas Stafford Raffles went ashore near the mouth of the river on 29 January, 1819. The British East India Company agent founded a branch of the organization and five years later bought from the Malayan sultan Hussein Mohammed Shah the entire group of islands for a life annuity of 5,000 Spanish dollars a year.

Singapore thus became a British crown colony.

Now whole fleets of large sailing ships made for the harbor city and gave it an unprecedented economic boom. Chinese, Indians and Malays immigrated to Singapore, where workers were being sought, in their thousands. British trading companies opened one branch after another and erected residences for themselves in the most lavish colonial style.

After World War II Singapore became independent and in 1965 adopted the status of a republic. All governing power is now wielded by the People's Action Party. It was founded by the lawyer Lee Kuan Yew, who as city president for many years pursued a strict law-and-order policy, but also created the conditions for Singapore to be able to rise to become the second largest economic power in southeast Asia.

Peaceful interaction

The ethnic mix of its inhabitants has benefited Singapore's development into a classic example of cultural juxtaposition and religious tolerance. At the same time the architectural influence of the immigrant countries has been preserved in the areas of ethnic character. In the Chinese quarter, for instance, you come across a great variety of stylistic elements from the Middle Kingdom: pagoda-shaped towers, ancient Chinese dragon structures and carvings, a great deal of red and gold on the façades of buildings. Chinese immigrants also built the largest and most beautiful Buddha shrine in the place, the temple of the twin grotto of the lotus mountain, Siong Lim.

The Little India quarter, with its two to three storey shops combined with houses is similar to a southern Indian small city. The colorfully painted Hindu temple Sri Mariammam with its five-storey tower and its facade, decorated with layer upon layer of figures of animal and gods, also fits in here. In the Arab quarter with its typical hot food stalls Moslems have donated a great deal of money for the restoration of the large Sultan Mosque, whose style is reminiscent of the architecture of the Saracens.

Malayan Singalese are proud of their Sakaya Muni Buddha Gaya

temple, designed on a Thai model. Its focal point is formed by a 49-foot (15 m) tall Buddha weighing 249 tons, which is illuminated at night by 1,000 electric light bulbs. The main church of Christians of British origin is Saint Andrew's Anglican Cathedral, erected in the mid nineteenth

century by Indian laborers, with its unusual exterior plaster of egg white, grated shells and coconut fibers.

At night hordes of city workers are attracted to the nearby Boot Quay and to Clarke Quay. Here whole rows of old two-storey office buildings and warehouses were saved at the last moment from being torn down and have been redesigned into restaurants and bars. You can taste the quality of the food immediately and you can be sure of cleanliness in the kitchens, since, quite apart from trouble from the town clerk's office, a landlord who is not careful about cleanliness is threatened with the far worse danger of being denounced in the "Straits Times", which has a very large circulation, with full name and photo as "Dirty Pig of the Week".

Glass palaces characterize the skyline on Singapore River (above)

The venerable Raffles Hotel with its luxurious suites (below left)

Colorful dragon dance at the traditional Chingay Parade

The rich bride Hong Kong

China leaves the former crown colony to its own devices

Looking down 1,820 feet (554 m) from Victoria Peak on a still evening on to the bays and islands of the Hong Kong region is an amazing sight. The helicopter landing pads on the brightly illuminated skyscrapers, the lamps in the hotel windows and the floodlit Bank of China, easily recognizable from its facade divided up into enormous squares and triangles, are almost close enough to grasp.

Navigation lights and the lights along the water's edge in Kowloon are reflected in the sea water of the harbor. And right in the distance the romantic silhouettes of the mountains can be seen – Tai Mo Shan, Lion Rock, Diamond Hill, Man O Shan – in the reflection of glittering satellite towns.

After the Opium War China had to cede the 236 islands and the district of Kowloon to Great Britain – according to a ninety-nine year lease following later in 1889. Most of the land was deserted and uninhabited, but the British were aware of the great significance of the natural deep water harbor in front of Hong Kong peninsula (Fragrant Harbor) for the politics of trade and began to build quay sides and freight sheds. It was the beginning of an unprecedented history of success. When the crown colony was reunited with China a year prematurely in 1987, with almost seven million inhabitants it was one of the most densely built-on regions on earth and had a dowry of eighty-five billion US dollar foreign currency reserves.

In line with the motto "one country – two systems", China is allowing the rich bride the special status of a largely self-administered free trade zone for the next fifty years. In fact since then a brutal capitalism has reigned unchanged in Hong Kong, rewarding the clever, giving the hard-working a chance and allowing the weak not to starve completely. The economy is flourishing and hordes of tourists land daily at the new major airport Chek Lap Kok.

Irresistible exoticism

It is not a bad idea if, as a stranger, you let yourself be guided aimlessly by the crowd in densely populated districts like Kowloon. You may be pushed towards the Jade Market, where huge lumps of this semi-precious stone are haggled over, or straight into a hot food stall with soup made of snake meat. The sweet scent of incense cones entices you into the Wong Tai Sin temple, whose Taoist chief saint is responsible for winning bets in horse-racing. A Chinese apothecary has stocks of tiger penises, dried seahorses and pulverized rhinoceros horn on long shelves, all doubtless potency medicines. You know by the many different sounds that you are approaching the bird market even before you can see it.

In spite of two new vehicle tunnels, the finest connection between the mainland and the Central District on Hong Kong Island is by water. In no more than a quarter of an hour the Star Ferry reaches the capital Victoria, where mountainous skyscrapers now obscure most of the buildings from the early colonial days. Housing is very varied here. About one thousand Hong Kong residents still live, like their ancestors, on boats and junks, while successful business people pay a monthly rent of up to $17,000 dollars for one of the scarce luxury apartments. The villas on Victoria Peak with a sea view are impossibly priced.

Idyll and magic

Hong Kong is connected to all the larger neighboring islands by ferries. You can escape the noise of the teeming streets to Lamma Island, whose 8,500 inhabitants do not tolerate cars, but instead have beautiful swimming beaches. On the southern tip of Kowloon the fishing village of Lei Yue Mun has preserved a touch of originality. Everyone buys fish daily at the well-stocked market and has it cooked in one of the restaurants.

Magic worlds are also among the unusual features of the former colony. At the jagged Lovers Rock courting couples lay down lotus flowers to make the gods favorably disposed towards them. In the temples you can discover your future from soothsayers, astrologers and palm-readers. The most important magic role is played by Taoist feng shui experts, without whose advice a superstitious Chinese person would not buy a plot of land or build a house.

Sometimes it is sufficient to block the path of evil spirits through a chimney, but occasionally more extensive measures are necessary. For instance, one feng shui expert gave warning just in time when a high-rise block was being erected on the beach of Repulse Bay that a dragon living behind it on a mountain would have his view of the sea blocked. The cautious building contractor changed his plans and left a seven-storey high, 59 foot (18 m) wide peephole open at the correct place for the dragon in the reinforced concrete building.

GETTING THERE
International and Chinese internal flight connections. Also possible to get there by ship

ACCOMMODATION
All hotel categories. Traditional establishments like The Mandarin on Hong Kong and Peninsula in Kowloon

BEST TIME
Spring and fall

TIPPING
Restaurant bills are rounded up by 5 to 10 %. This also applies to taxi prices. In hotels an appropriate tip is left when you depart

EXCURSIONS
By ship to Macau and Canton

Panoramic view of the hyper-modern skyline of Hong Kong and the mainland with Kowloon (left)

Tram in the bustling shopping district (above)

Traditional Chinese junks against Hong Kong's modern glass palaces

The miracle of Shanghai

A forest of futuristic skyscrapers has grown up on the Huangpu

CHINA
Shanghai

Pacific Ocean

GETTING THERE
International and Chinese internal flight connections. Numerous package deals

ACCOMMODATION
Hotel accommodation from around $30 upwards. Luxury hotels from $200

BEST TIME
May to June, September to November

TIPPING
Tips are not customary. Exception: non-state tourist guides and chauffeurs. Porters receive a small remuneration according to the number of pieces of baggage

EXCURSIONS
The ancient village of Zhouzhuang. Sheshan National Park. The garden city of Suzhou.

Shanghai is living half in the past and half in the future. While the grand buildings of European colonial powers still stretch out along the west bank of the Huangpu, modern architects and daring building contractors have conjured up on the eastern side a forest of skyscrapers and miraculous towers, on the outskirts of which enormous cranes are laying the foundations for new superlatives. The magnetic cable railway, developed in Germany, will soon connect this Chinese Manhattan to the new airport.

Over the course of a millennium the development of Shanghai from a fishing village to a high seas port has been largely peaceful. However, in the nineteenth century Great Britain suddenly waged war on China, because the country had opposed illegal deliveries of opium by English trading houses. In 1842 British warships set fire to Shanghai, advanced over the Yangtse to Nanking and forced their opponents to capitulate. China not only had to allow the import of opium, but also to lease Hong Kong to the British and grant western trading nations sovereignty rights to part of Shanghai.

It all started with opium

From then on huge fortunes were made in Shanghai with opium. The bosses built themselves private castles and invested in casinos, pleasure houses and opium dens. Even more than drug trafficking, though, honest trade also soon began to boom – export of silk, cotton and porcelain from China and import of machinery, engines and household technology from the west.

British, Americans, French and Germans established their businesses, banks, hotel palaces and clubhouses on the riverbank promenade called The Bund. But in World War II the foreigners lost their concessions. Shanghai was now ruled from Beijing by Communists – and financially exploited. Even worse: between 1966 and 1976 Shanghai was forced to act as the launching pad for Mao's Cultural Revolution. The economy broke down. Red guards forced the engineers of the Shanghai Wharf out of their bosses chairs by beating them and downgraded them to latrine cleaners.

It was when the eastern district of Pudong was declared a special economic zone in 1990 that a new upsurge began. With growth rates of up to 17 % Shanghai became the economically most successful city in China. The number of inhabitants in the surrounding area is also exploding - fourteen million, fifteen, seventeen million – tomorrow maybe 20 million people. At the same time the former hotbed of vice enjoys a great influx of tourists. The former show villa of the Iraqi opium tycoon Victor Sassoon, now the Cypress Hotel is one of several offering the height of luxury.

A must for tourists is the Yuyuan Gardens, laid out in 1559, with its five miniature landscapes. The complex includes a picturesque tea pavilion, which can be reached only via the zigzag nine bends bridge. It is supposed to be impassable for demons, because evil spirits can only move in straight lines. Spread out over this district there are temples, which are worth seeing, where Buddhists, Confucians and followers of other religions pursue their cults.

Tradition and modern

The ensemble of colonial buildings on the riverbank promenade still continues to be one of the main architectural sights. Everything considered architecturally beautiful at the time of the opium trade is represented here, from Classicism via variations of Renaissance and Baroque to Art Deco. The building of the former Turf Club is a reminder of the British way of life. On its racetrack the People's Square with the new Shanghai Theater has been built, its construction symbolizing the ancient Chinese idea of a square world under a round heaven.

In the district of Pudong western architects have been able to realize their wildest dreams. Within five years getting on for fifty skyscrapers with extraordinary shapes have shot up overnight. The 1,378-foot (420 m) tall Jin Mao Tower looks like a pagoda, for instance, while the new building of the stock exchange is like a triumphal arch.

The craziest edifice on the east bank is the Oriental Pearl Tower, a 1,535-foot (468 m) tall television tower. Its tubular body is punctuated by eleven spherical floors, containing an entertainment center, restaurants and a luxury hotel.

Ferry in Shanghai's harbor against the varied skyline of the district of Pudong (above)

The riverbank promenade The Bund with relics of the colonial era (below left)

Bustling activity in Nanjing Street

The Forbidden City

In BEIJING people had to keep their distance from the imperial palace and the "center of the world"

GETTING THERE
Airport with connections all over the world

ACCOMMODATION
Good western-style hotels from average to luxury class

BEST TIME
September, October

TIPPING
Has so far been refused. Liberal tourists are gradually causing this custom to waver, however

EXCURSIONS
Daily tours to the Ming Tombs and the Great Wall

The outlay was huge, even by Chinese standards: a million slaves, a hundred thousand building laborers, thousands of wood-carvers, painters, sculptors, bronze-casters, smiths and gilders were employed to construct a new residence for the Ming emperor Zhu Di on the flat land of Beijing. Work began in 1406 and was completed by 1420. It was a show city consisting of palaces, pavilions, halls and courtyards, surrounded by moats and a wall 41 feet (12.5 m) tall.

Although over the course of the centuries some of the wooden buildings have burned down and been rebuilt not quite true to the original, the overall architectural impression has remained unchanged up to the present day. The high wall and the exteriors of the palaces glow crimson in the sun, the roofs with their yellow-glazed tiles, the imperial color, still shine like liquid gold. To this, in the courtyards, is added the dazzling marble white of the many balustrades, open staircases, ornamental bridges and the many staggered terraces.

While the Chinese speak of the Crimson City, in western countries the term Forbidden City has become common usage. During the ruling era of a total of twenty-four emper-

ors, subjects were not in fact so much as allowed to look at the splendor from close quarters unless they worked in the palace or had been invited there. Because here, according to the way the "sons of heaven", as the rulers were called, saw it, was the "center of the world". Anyone approaching without authorization was punished with a beating. The imperial city was not made open to the public until the end of the monarchy.

The Hall of Supreme Harmony

Now that, after the xenophobic period of the Cultural Revolution, China is trying to encourage tourists from abroad, every day vast hordes of visitors throng through the Meridian Gate into the inner area of the palace with the "Hall of Supreme Harmony". This 120-foot (35 m) tall wooden structure dating from the seventeenth century is held together by wooden pegs instead of nails. Beneath the roof, which is supported by twenty-four pillars, is suspended a golden dragon, the symbol of imperial power. Beneath it on a jacaranda podium stands the principal throne, from which the "sons of heaven" announced instructions and laws to the court officials prostrated in front of them.

In all there are about 9,000 rooms inside the palace walls, a considerable proportion of which were reserved for imperial companions and eunuchs. Traditionally each "son of heaven" was allowed to keep up to three principal wives, six so-called favorites and seventy-two concubines of lesser rank. Some emperors, however, had as many as 2,000 concubines. The ladies wore gold labels with their date of birth, which identified them as house-guests.

Outside the residence Beijing, which has existed under various names for 3,000 years, has numerous other historical monuments. The most famous of these is the Temple of Heaven, built in 1420 and renovated many times, a circular building, crowned by a golden globe, with a 125-foot (38 m) tall hall. In the north west of the city on the bank of Kunming lake is the building known as the Summer Palace, Yiheyuan. There was an imperial palace here as early as the tenth century.

Among the most important sights of modern Beijing, with its around 10 million inhabitants, is the Square of Heavenly Peace, Tiananmen, comprising ninety-nine acres, with the mausoleum of Mao Zedong who died in 1976. The embalmed Great Chairman rests in a glass coffin. The features make one suspect, in spite of the heavy make-up, that Mao's death was not an easy one.

A glimpse of Peking man

On the western edge of Tiananmen is the massive building of the People's Congress, with its 1,310 foot (400 m) wide frontage. Most of the space inside is taken up by the banqueting hall, which can comfortably seat several thousand people. Opposite the Congress building on the eastern side is the Historical Museum, also of great interest to tourists. Its prehistoric department proves, with a series of archaeological finds, that Beijing and its surrounding area is one of the oldest inhabited areas of humankind.

The most precious exhibit is the skull of Peking Man, sinanthropus pekinensis, found in a cave south west of the capital. This ancestor of homo sapiens was probably around in China as much as 500,000 years ago.

Entrance to the Forbidden City. The ancient imperial palace is today a favored destination for tourists from all over the world (right)

At the Square of Heavenly Peace, the traditional square for political demonstrations, a photograph and the mausoleum are reminders of Mao Zedong, the founder of communist China (above)

To the west of Beijing the Great Wall of China is a place of pilgrimage for visitors from all over the world (below left)

If you wish to experience the music of the Middle Kingdom, you will have the opportunity at a performance of the Beijing Opera

The last palaces of Seoul

A major city has grown out of the desert of rubble left by the Korean war

GETTING THERE
Several airlines offer
direct flights to Seoul

ACCOMMODATION
Numerous hotels from
tourist to luxury class
with English-speaking
staff

BEST TIME
All year, except for the
hot and humid period
from July to mid
September

TIPPING
Is not customary, but is
willingly accepted by
staff in larger hotels and
by taxi drivers as reward
for good service

SPECIAL TIP
Great importance is
attached to conventional
clothing in social
situations

The royal residence
Kyongbok-kung dating
from the fourteenth
century has been
rebuilt true to the
original style after a
major fire (above)

A pedestrian precinct
in the shopping center
of Seoul (below left)

The south gate
Namdaemun has
forfeited its dominant
role to high-rise
buildings

Large has suddenly become small in Seoul and small large. The south gate Namdaemun stood out, visible for miles, above all the surrounding buildings for centuries. Carefully built up of light gray squares and crowned by two beautifully shaped roofs, it represented a dignified entrance to the capital and at the same time opened up the way to the royal residence in the opposite direction. There is no question of this any more. Encircled by a fence, the neat tower is now just a traffic island at a noisy main road crossroads and looks very small – at any rate in comparison with the neighboring high-rise buildings.

Within a few decades Seoul has grown out of all recognition, more radically and faster than any other east Asian metropolis. The desert of rubble left by the Korean war of 1950-1951 has been transformed into a major city with twelve, or maybe even fourteen million inhabitants, into a human ant colony within the state. 25-30 % of Korea's entire population work in Seoul, on just under one percent of the country's surface area. In spite of the hubris it is worth visiting Seoul, even if only for the historic buildings from the early era of the former kingdom. In the north and east ranges of hills protect the city from cold winds, while the Han River enables shipping traffic to reach the Yellow Sea. In 1392 Seoul became the royal seat of the Yi dynasty and therefore capital of Korea. The first royal residence, the Kyongbok-kung (Palace of Shining Happiness) fell victim to a devastating major fire in 1592, but has been rebuilt true to the original style and is now open to visitors from all over the world.

The missionaries' deception
Religious thought in Korea used to be under the influence of Buddhism, Confucianism and Taoism. Devotion to god and admiration of nature, ancestor worship and also delight in bright colors when painting temples or choosing a festive wardrobe are characteristic of traditional life in Korea. The Yi dynasty which ruled in Seoul tried in vain to isolate their country and way of life from foreigners. Although in the seventeenth and eighteenth centuries unpermitted entry was even threatened with the death penalty, Christian missionaries managed to reach Seoul – because, pretending to

be "mourners", they deceptively hid their long nosed faces under scarves. Today Korea's Catholic church is the second largest faith after the Buddhists. The Land of Morning Freshness, as an old name for Korea goes, was most persistently exposed to foreign influences by the Japanese, who occupied the country for forty years at the beginning of the twentieth century and made Seoul the capital of a Japanese province.

Lights for Buddha's birthday
Seoul has lost entire historical districts under Japanese rule, due to clashes in the war with North Korea and due to "being restored to death" in the hectic years of reconstruction. But anything that was still able to be saved after all this has now been rescued. As well as the Palace of Shining Happiness three other impressive royal palaces have been preserved: the Toksukung, the Changgyong-kung and the Changdok-kung with the throne room of the Yi dynasty, which died out in 1910. The palace complexes – partly reproduction – mainly consist of red and gold wooden houses, with slightly curved and ornately decorated roofs.

There are still traditional houses with black tiled roofs in some of the old alleys of the Chongno-Gu district. In a small park on Insadong Street an interesting pagoda from the Koryo period (918-1392) has survived the era of major construction. The ancestor shrine of Chongmyo Temple is the focal point of a magnificent ceremony every first Sunday in May, when the descendants of the royal house, shrouded in crimson garments, commemorate the twenty-six dead rulers of the Yi dynasty. Also in May, Buddha's birthday is celebrated with processions of lights in Buddhist temples such as Chogyesa in the city center. The meeting point for Seoul's Christians is the Neo-Gothic Myongdonk Cathedral.

Among the attractions of modern Seoul are the sixty-three storey high skyscraper of the Dae-Han Insurance Company on the bank of the Han and Seoul Tower, high up on the Mansan (southern mountain). In Seoul they are particularly proud of an extremely exotic sight: the reproduction of the Bavarian castle of Neuschwanstein next to Lotte amusement park.

The world's largest village

In Japan's capital, **TOKYO**, there are not only skyscrapers

JAPAN
Tokyo

Pacific Ocean

GETTING THERE
International flight connections to Tokyo International Airport

ACCOMMODATION
Western-style hotels. Staying at ryokans, Japanese style hotels, is more informal. Beware of "capsule hotels" which accommodate their guests in narrow containers

BEST TIME
Best times to travel are spring and fall

TIPPING
Customary only for porters in hotels and attendants in ryokans. Discretion is expected when handing over tips

SPECIAL TIPS
It is advisable to take plenty of business cards. Watch out for traffic on the left

Every description of Tokyo suffers from the speed at which this superlative metropolis unintentionally surpasses itself. Whereas yesterday twelve million people were living on 828 square miles (2,145 squared km), today it is possibly already fourteen million. Whereas the Sunshine City skyscraper with its 787 feet (240 m) was until recently the tallest concrete building, a short time later the twin towers of the New City Hall have achieved a further 10 feet (3 m). And if it is rumbling more than usual in the Tokyo underground, this can just as suddenly completely change.

Earthquakes and conflagrations have contributed to the fact that in the Japanese metropolis there is nothing that could be called an historic old city. No longer any trace of the dwellings of early twelfth century aristocratic settlers. No shops from the eighteenth century when Tokyo was still known as Edo, but already had a million inhabitants. Everything burnt down, collapsed, was pulled down or built over long ago. In 1923 140,000 people, almost all the principal buildings and 700,000 houses fell victim to the worst tremor to date. A similar inferno with more than 80,000 dead was the result of an American air attack in 1945.

After each catastrophe the rebuilding of Tokyo, if not more beautiful, is at least on a larger scale and more modern. Nor are they afraid to imitate western models. In the district of Minato-ku, for instance, engineers have erected a second Eiffel Tower, quite similar to the Parisian one, except that at 1,092 feet (333 m) it is 43 feet (13 m) taller.

From its two viewing platforms you can look out over the overdeveloped landscape as far as the holy mountain of Fujisan. The conurbation of Tokyo reveals itself as an accumulation of dozens of individual towns with their own high-rise inner cities, embedded in a maze of village-like living quarters with one and a half million low wooden houses.

In the center of this ocean of roofs, seen from a bird's perspective is a green oasis bordered by ramparts and moats. Here, amidst well-tended gardens, live the emperor and his family. The palace buildings in ancient Japanese style stand on the remains of a Samurai castle dating from the fifteenth century, once the first permanent building far and wide. The grounds were extended to become the imperial residence in 1868 when the current Tenno moved from Kyoto to Tokyo.

Most of Tokyo's religious buildings that are worth seeing, including the Hie shrine of Kyoto's tutelary goddess, many times rebuilt, and the Gokokuji Temple with a statue of Kannon, the goddess of mercy are also located in the middle of stretches of green. The temple and the "scarlet Pagoda" of Asakura are also dedicated to the same goddess.

For larger purchases there are multi-storey super-gigantic shopping centers under most of the stations. The most popular shopping

zone is as always the famous Ginza with its department store palaces and classy shops, but also theaters and restaurants. Bookworms can rummage through more than a hundred antiquarian bookstores in the Kanda district. And in the district of Akihabara tiny shops and technical markets overflow with entertainment electronics and computer goods.

Bonsai gardens next door

At anytime and anywhere you can escape the noisy shopping streets with their ridiculous neon advertisements for a quieter Tokyo. Often only a hundred yards from the concrete monsters with their thousands of windows there are small court-

yards and narrow alleys with corner stores, mini-restaurants, fast food stalls and bonsai gardens. Away from the main streets there are also many hospitable ryokans, traditional hotels with straw mats on the floor and sliding walls to divide the rooms. As soon as they enter guests change their street clothes for slippers and a light kimono, to make them feel at home.

Cheaper than the informal ryokans are the Japanese capsule hotels, where guests crawl into prefabricated containers with only a mattress and a television in them. It would be impossible anyway to put any more into a space three and a half feet wide, seven feet long and

about four feet high. Of the – admittedly far more expensive – luxury hotels in Tokyo the Imperial Hotel, designed by star architect Frank Lloyd Wright in 1922, is worthy of mention. To make the five-star hotel secure against earthquakes the American placed it on sliding rails.

The most popular meeting point in Tokyo is the memorial to the faithful dog Hachiko, who waited at Shibuya station for his master for many years and ultimately died there. Sometimes a slight shudder goes through the memorial and the station and the surface of the street and the high-rise buildings seem to tremble. But don't worry: after a second or two the tremor is over.

People meet for picnics at the cherry blossom festival in Ueno Park (above left)

Hectic activity and street cafés in the famous Ginza shopping street (top right)

Nijubashi Bridge in front of the imperial palace

The emperors were gods in Kyoto

Every year ten million Japanese visit the ancient temple city

As far back as the Middle Ages court poets sang about the beauty of the temple city of Kyoto. Early silk paintings show its tea pavilions at the foot of green mountains and yellowing chronicles tell of the Japanese emperors who held court in Kyoto in great splendor in the eighth and ninth centuries and encouraged the arts. Nowhere else in the Land of the Rising Sun were so many art treasures collected at this time, nor did so many palaces, magnificent gates, Shinto shrines, Buddhist temples and Zen gardens arise as here 310 miles (500 km) from Tokyo.

In 794 the first Tenno, Emperor Kammu, chose a flat area of land not far from the village of Uda to build a residence, which he called Heiankyo, capital of peace, which later became Kyoto, capital. On Chinese lines it was given a square outline. The street network was divided up like a chessboard, with a 272-foot (83 m) wide main street dividing the district into two sections.

Sons of the sun goddess

North of the wooden city with its estimated 400,000 inhabitants arose the imperial palace with the coronation hall and the celestial throne vaulted by a canopy. According to Shinto faith Kammu was a direct descendant of the sun goddess Amaterasu Omikami and he was therefore himself to be worshipped as a god. The emperors of Japan who followed Kammu also regarded the sun goddess as their progenitrix. It was not until after World War II that the reigning Tenno renounced the status of god.

Of Kammu's residence city only the rectangular street system has survived conflagrations and earthquakes. The imperial palace also burnt down many times, but was always rebuilt, the last time in 1855. The complex, consisting of eighteen buildings, is open to visitors today and known as the Old Imperial Palace. The rectangular area is surrounded by a rampart, of whose four towers one was reserved for the royal couple and another for the concubines. In the ceremonial hall a piece of floor has been left out so that the Tenno could stand on the bare earth when worshipping his ancestors, as prescribed.

As well as numerous other palaces, pavilions and imperial gardens, among the major sights of Kyoto are getting on for two hundred Shinto shrines, dedicated to particular gods of nature, of which the former state religion of Shintoism has no less than 800,000, including

animals, mountains and lakes. The oldest Shinto shrine is the Fushimi Inari Shrine with thousands of toriis, the traditional arched gateways with black beams on top of red pillars, following on from one another. The almost two mile (3 km) long row of toriis was constructed by devotees in 711 to thank the goddess Inari for a good rice harvest.

Buddhist art

Kyoto owes the most elaborate masterpieces of religious art to rich forerunners of Buddhism, which was brought to Japan at the end of the first millennium and particularly impressed the aristocracy. There are thirty ancient temple buildings, in which a whole variety of cults of Japanese-style Buddhism are celebrated. Compared with the simplicity of Shintoist edifices, the Buddhist ones stand out with a large number of gilded statues and rich carving. The oldest Buddhist edifice on the site, the Shionin Temple, originates from the thirteenth century.

Efforts to attain the utmost aesthetic sophistication, typical of Japanese art, are expressed in the world-famous gardens of Kyoto. They are for the most part creations by Zen masters, who wanted to produce ideal areas for meditation in the open air by means of a symbiosis of nature and art. Good examples of this are the stone gardens, where carefully raked areas of sand, mythological lakes and cone-shaped stones symbolize the holy mountain of Fujijama.

The garden of Saiho Ji, laid out by the Zen priest Muso Kokushi in the fourteenth century, is also worthy of note. With the aid of more than a hundred different types of moss the illusion is conveyed to visitors that a mountain landscape with waterfalls, grottos and seas of flowers is unfolding at their feet.

After the imperial residence was moved to Tokyo in 1868, many architects in Kyoto attempted to create attractive connections between traditional and modern. Parts of the new city hall, for instance, are reminiscent of the beautifully simple structures of Shinto shrines. From the viewing platform of the 430-foot (131 m) tall Kyoto Tower there is a worthwhile panoramic view of the old and the young city – an ensemble that entices ten million Japanese every year.

GETTING THERE
From Tokyo by the Shinkansen high-speed train. It covers the 320-mile stretch to Kyoto in just under three hours

BEST TIME
October to December

ACCOMMODATION
Hotels and pensions in all price categories. With cheap offers sometimes the rooms are very tiny - not much larger than a camp bed

TIPPING
Not customary in Japan. Except for porters in western hotels and attendants in ryokans (ancient Japanese-style accommodation)

OTHER
Watch out for traffic on the left. Have business cards handy

Kinkakuji, the Golden Pavilion, is illustrious in appearance (left)

Katsura Villa in Kyoto Garden with fall colors (above right)

Shijo village is the commercial heart of the city

AUSTRALIA

Two emblems of Sydney

Australia's great harbor city founded by English deportees

It was the most unusual cargo Captain Arthur Phillip had ever had to transport. The fleet commander set out on the seven-month long voyage from England to the east coast of Australia with 700 convicts deported from England and 450 seamen on board eleven ships. On 18 January, 1788 the sailing convoy reached a spit recommended as a mooring place by other seafarers and the exhausted prisoners, also including women, were allowed to disembark as free people.

The new settlers found a fertile coastal region, apparently devoid of people, with ocean bays carved deep into the land. While the sailing ships remained anchored for some time in a natural harbor, Botany Bay, some of the deportees made themselves initial shelters on a rocky high bank, which they called The Rocks. This was the start of the colonization of Australia by Europeans and at the same time of the history of the harbor city of Sydney that grew up on this site.

If you approach this historic land site from the sea today, the first thing you will see is the imposing skyline of slender skyscrapers. Modern Sydney is a world city with around four million inhabitants, street ravines like those in New York and a lively natural harbor of exceptional beauty. By contrast with the noisy city center, in the many green suburbs, with tens of thousands of individual bungalows with gardens and swimming pools, there is a peaceful atmosphere and a holiday feel.

The Sydney Opera House

The emblem of Australia's largest city is Sydney Opera House, built on a spit of land at the edge of the harbor far out into the sea, the bold roof structure reminiscent of giant shells or sails. In 1957 the Danish architect Jørn Utzon won an architectural competition with his design for an avant-garde music theater. However, there were such great technical and financial difficulties in implementing the project that the Dane resigned as its project architect. Australian architects finally completed the work, though the costs rose from an estimated seven to 102 million dollars and the construction time was extended from five to fourteen years.

In the city it is worth taking the 1,000 foot (305 m) high lift to the viewing platform of the Sydney Tower. From here not only is there a view of the city with its many bays, but in clear weather it is possible to see the beaches on the Pacific Ocean, washed by tall breakers, and in the opposite direction, the Blue Mountains. Below, dense crowds jostle in the shopping area of Pitt Street, whose streets of

A continuous stream of motor vehicles passes daily over the Harbor Bridge, completed in 1932, with its eight car lanes, two railway tracks and cycle and pedestrian paths. Until the new opera house was built the Old Coathanger was Sydney's emblem.

It's better by water

A large part of the downtown traffic can only be coped with by ship. Fast catamarans, and also older ferries with smoking funnels, travel constantly from one shore of the harbor to the other and between the city center and more distant suburbs. The chief mooring place is the Circular Quay, on which street performers, acrobats and musicians give a taste of urban life. Close by, a replica of the mutiny ship "Bounty" lies at anchor, available for sightseeing and short trips round the harbor.

From the Circular Quay a few minutes on foot brings you to "The Rocks", the first shore settlement founded by the deportees in 1788. For the 200th anniversary celebration the city council had the old houses rebuilt and incorporated into a tourist pub and shopping area. Among these is "Cadman's Cottage", the oldest house in Sydney, opened in 1816.

A little further on, at Botany Bay, memorial stones commemorate Captain James Cook, who in 1770 first trod on Australian soil and took possession of the entire east coast as New South Wales for the English crown. It is the same mooring place at which, eighteen years later, the first settlers and their fleet captain Phillip went ashore.

The shell-shaped roof structure makes the Sydney Opera House the unmistakable emblem of the city (left)

The modern skyline at Sydney Harbor

shops are covered with enormous lengths of sailcloth as a protection against the usually scorching sun. The monorail, a modern track railway, glides almost silently through the center of the city.

Sydney Harbor Bridge, also affectionately called "The Old Coathanger" by the inhabitants, owing to its arch-shaped steel structure, provides fast connection between the southern and northern districts of the city.

The race to Melbourne

Love of the distant homeland has left its mark on Australia's second largest city

Farmers, cattle breeders and gold-diggers were among the founding generations of Melbourne, the second largest Australian city and eternal rival of Sydney. Judging by their history the two coastal resorts could be called sisters, with Melbourne the younger, although it looks older. For decades the two fought for the honor of becoming Australia's capital city, until in 1913 neither of these two, but Canberra, became the seat of government.

Fifteen years after the arrival of the first settlers in Sydney, in 1802 landowners from England established themselves 435 miles (700 km) further south at Phillips Bay, where Melbourne later developed. But tilling of the land did not go as well as

anticipated and it was difficult to engender any enthusiasm for field work in the curly-haired, dark-skinned aboriginal people, so many farmers went on to try their luck in the interior of the continent. It was not until 1835 that cattle breeders made their homes in the fertile Melbourne region and soon brought hordes of further settlers in their wake. Around 1850 a real race of strong men started when gold was discovered in the area. This was the start of the unstoppable ascent of the city of Melbourne.

Today the former gold-digger city has around three and a half million inhabitants and in its older districts is reminiscent of the Victorian and Edwardian architectural style of

London in the nineteenth and early twentieth centuries, even if no-frills new tower blocks are gradually stepping into the foreground.

In an effort to create tradition in a place without tradition, in 1840 Melbourne imported the residence for the governor of the region of Victoria straight from England and rebuilt the country house, which had been split up into individual sections, stone by stone. It is known as "La Trobes Cottage" and is open for tours. In 1934 the parental home of the famous seafarer and discoverer James Cook was brought across the waters from the British county of Yorkshire to Melbourne, where, as "Captain Cook's Cottage", it now adorns a car park.

Diverse cultural influences

Other cultures also left their mark on Melbourne. Incomers from the Middle Kingdom enriched the city with a colorful Chinese quarter and the "See Yup Joss House" temple of 1856. The Little Italy area with its many pizza bakeries, ice-cream parlors and pasta shops offers a Mediterranean way of life. Melbourne's Richmond area has such a large

Greek population that it is regarded as the third largest Greek city, after Athens and Thessaloniki. Here too is Little Saigon, Richmond Street, dominated by Vietnamese shops, restaurants and subcultural pubs.

It is these strong ethnic influences that give Melbourne its liveliness and its endearing character. The city center with its pedestrian precincts and shopping arcades, its large squares and numerous green areas is the showplace of a thriving urban culture.

Entertainment for all

In City Square refreshing decorative fountains splash, acrobats and mime artists perform and a colorful ethnic mix enjoys itself in tavernas and outdoor restaurants. Young people, in particular, are attracted by the free entertainment, the rock concerts, dance and theater performances taking place in the open-air with free entry.

Adding to the charm of the city are the trams, threatened with extinction in western Europe, though not so much the smart modern ones as the old rattling ones with their hard wooden seats, constant draught

and – in most cases – green paint. When visiting Melbourne, the pop star Elton John fell so much in love with a hundred-year-old tram that he bought it on the spot, shipped it to San Francisco and had it installed there in the garden of his house.

Works by Australian painters, including Aborigines and members of a group known as the Heidelberg School are exhibited in the Victorian Arts Center. Among the museum treasures of the city are veteran airplanes, the stuffed miracle racehorse Phar Lap and the sailing ship Polly Woodside built in Belfast, Ireland, in 1885.

Each year in March Melbourne celebrates its popular Moomba Festival with street processions, competitions, theater and music. The word "Moomba" originates from the language of the Aborigines and means "come and have fun!" The native in-

habitants have virtually disappeared from the streets of the city, though. The diseases and liquor of the white people have decimated their numbers. The Aborigines came to Australia about 40,000 years ago on rafts or over long submerged land bridges and were the real lords of the continent.

Melbourne's imposing skyline by the Yarra River (top left)

The modern Southgate Center on the bank of the Yarra River (top right)

Elderly trams add to the charm of the city outside Flinders Street Station (middle right)

Picturesque beach huts grace Melbourne's Brighton Beach

AFRICA

The magic of the Orient

MARRAKECH and a rendezvous with traveling entertainers and snake-charmers outside the gates of the old city

When the sun sinks behind the emblem of Marrakech, the minaret of the Koutoubia Mosque, in the late afternoon and the shadows lengthen, the smell of countless barbecue fires rises from the long rows of the food stands in Djemaa el Fna Square. It is almost unbelievable that the bustle of the day can actually increase. For, with rapidly falling darkness, musicians, snake-charmers, magicians, acrobats, story-tellers, fire-eaters and pickpockets pop up from all over the place and mingle with friendly lunatics, aged water-sellers and distraught tourists.

You are fortunate if you can grab a seat in one of the numerous cafes framing the square or even have the luck to find a ringside seat on a roof terrace from which to watch the exciting comings and goings in the glow of the countless lights and to abandon yourself to the cacophony of voices, animal cries, drums, bells, flutes, mopeds and car horns.

The square in front of the Medina

Djemaa el Fna is Marrakech's most famous square. At one time farmers came with their products from the fertile Haouz Plain outside the city to meet traders here. But this Square of the Beheaded was also where the rulers displayed the heads of beheaded sinners, criminals and Christians on spikes.

From here the streets, become increasingly narrow, leading on all sides into the labyrinth of the old city, in which are hidden sultans' palaces, ornate villas of rich merchants and some of the most colorful of Arabian bazaars. A massive 39-foot (12 km) long rampart dating from the twelfth century surrounds the Medina, with cypresses, date palms and pine trees standing out above. Through eleven ancient gates, the most beautiful of which is the Bab Aguenaou, a constant stream of traders, craftsmen, auxiliary workers and visitors, mopeds and donkeys floods into the maze of narrow alleys, above which colored silk often hangs to dry.

In the mid eleventh century the dynasty of the Almoravids built a settlement here, which soon became an important trading and resting place for the caravans. Around a hundred years later the Almohads took over government and made Marrakech their capital. They further extended the city and left their mark on the old Moorish architectural style of Marrakech's Medina.

Also from the time of the Almoravids comes the ingenious irrigation system that today still supplies the parks for which Marrakech is so famous, including the Menara olive grove and the Agdal gardens, which are more than one thousand acres in size.

The Koutoubia Mosque, dating from the twelfth century, to the west of Djemaa el Fna, on the other hand, is a product of the Almohads. Its 253-foot (77 m) high minaret, the oldest and best preserved of its kind, is Marrakech's emblem.

In 1269 the Merinids took over the rule of Marrakech, after having conquered Fes 20 years previously and ended the rule of the Almohads in Morocco.

From this time also originates the jewel of the old city architecture in the north Medina, the madrasah or Koran school of Medersa Ben Youssef, next to the mosque of the same name. It was founded in the fourteenth century by the Merinid sultan, Abou el Hassan, and extended into the largest Islamic theological college in the Maghreb in 1570 by the Saadian Abdallah El Ghalib. Up to nine hundred students and teachers are said to have lived there in its hey-days, in the 150 cramped chambers opening on to the inner courtyard. The madrasah has been extensively renovated in recent years and today visitors can again admire the finely chased stucco decorations, mosaics and carvings.

Sub-tropical ambiance

Gueliz, constructed in 1916 under the French protectorate, more than any other modern city, entrances with its opulent wealth of palms and sub-tropical plants. Avenues of orange and jacaranda trees line the broad streets with their office buildings, modern shops and street cafés.

In the midst of this is a botanical fairyland with its beguiling riot of color of bougainvillea, pelargoniums, hibiscus and lotus flowers. It was once the garden of the French painter Jacques Majorelle, who moved to Marrakech in 1923. He built the villa of his dreams and planted a magnificent display of sub-tropical flowers. When he died in 1962 the park ran wild until the French couturier Yves Saint-Laurent made the villa his refuge. He re-designed the garden and gave it to the city of Marrakech. Today in Majorelle's former studio you can marvel at Islamic crafts.

Atlantic Ocean

Marrakech
MAROCCO

GETTING THERE
International direct flights to Marrakech, sometimes with stopover in Casablanca. Good value charter flights to Agadir. From there buses take four hours to drive through the Atlas Mountains to Marrakech

BEST TIME
Year-round season. In July and August it can get very hot. The hotels have heating for cold winter nights

ACCOMMODATION
Most of the hotels are in Gueliz, some exclusive and several very reasonable hotels in the Medina too

TIPPING
Service is normally included in hotel bills. Otherwise taxi drivers, hairdressers, ushers and waiters expect a tip of 5 to 10 %. No extra tip with negotiated prices

Pulsating life in Djemaa el Fna Square (above)

Columns characterize the interior rooms of the Saadian tombs (below left)

The mosaics and fountain of El Bahia Palace invite you to linger

In the bazaars of the Orient

Morocco's **FES** has many faces – and a unique old city

View over the old city of Fès el Bali (above left)

Behind the elaborately tiled gate of Bab Bou Jeloud the old city of Fès el Bali begins (above right)

Hard work has to be done on the dye troughs of the tanners' quarter

When a foreigner enters the old city through the gate of Bab Bou Jeloud, he is immersed in the stories of one thousand and one nights, into the Islamic-Arabian Middle Ages. The ornamental tower, elaborately tiled in blue and yellow, was erected in 1913 in Moorish style and is the main entrance to Fès el Bali, one of the largest medieval cities of our time.

In the narrow, winding alleys and covered bazaars, crammed full of craft shops, restaurants, mosques, markets and potteries, the visitor is in danger of getting lost. Crowds of people and donkeys push busily past one another in the passageways of the old city, which branch off in a confusion of directions.

The streets and quarters are divided according to branches of crafts. For instance, you first pass the grain merchants and go on to the coppersmiths, brass-smiths and goldsmiths before reaching the strongly smelling tanners' quarter, where skins are tanned and dyed using hands and feet in large stone tubs and then dried in the sun.

The Idrisid dynasty

Idris I came here in 789, to escape from Harun al Rashid and to find peace from his enemy. The founder of the Idrisid dynasty began to build his city, still fascinating to today's visitors, on the eastern bank of the Wadi Fès, shortly before it flows into the River Sebou.

Idris I was a descendant of Mohammed and – coming from the east – subjugated the Berber tribes in north Morocco, in part as far

down as the Atlantic coast. Nineteen years later his son Idris II built his own city on the opposite west bank. Although he did not succeed in fortifying and further extending his father's kingdom, Fès, as the capital of the small kingdom, became a religious and political center. The Idrisids were the first to construct a central government in North Africa outside the tribal system of the Berbers.

The Karaouine Mosque in the center of the old city is a sign of the former importance of Fès. With an area of seven and a half acres it is the largest in North Africa. The place of worship, built between 857 and 862, is at the same time one of the oldest Islamic universities. It was extended to its current size in the twelfth century. Twenty-two thousand believers

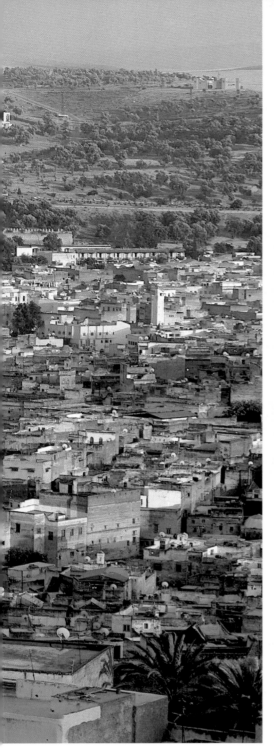

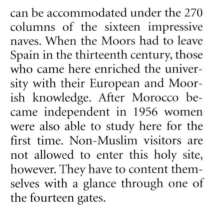

can be accommodated under the 270 columns of the sixteen impressive naves. When the Moors had to leave Spain in the thirteenth century, those who came here enriched the university with their European and Moorish knowledge. After Morocco became independent in 1956 women were also able to study here for the first time. Non-Muslim visitors are not allowed to enter this holy site, however. They have to content themselves with a glance through one of the fourteen gates.

The Berbers are coming

In the eleventh century the Almoravids, two combined Berber tribes, on their victory march through Morocco, Algeria and Spain, also came to Fès. They united the former cities of Idris I and his son Idris II into today's Fès el Bali.

The city reached its zenith in the fourteenth century under the rule of the Merinids, a Berber tribe which had ruled large parts of North Africa since the thirteenth century. They conquered Fès in 1248 and made it

their capital. To the west of the old city yet another new Fès emerged, Fès el Jedid. They erected countless buildings in Arabesque Moorish style. Right next to the imposing royal palace, for example, the brightly colored minaret of the thirteenth century Grand Mosque reaches up to the sky.

Between the palace and the south wall sprawl the alleys of the Mellah, once the quarter of the Jewish goldsmiths, silversmiths and jewelers. When the state of Israel was founded they emigrated there.

The treaty of Fès dating from the year 1912 sealed the sovereignty of the French in Morocco. And yet another new district emerged. In 1916 the French field-marshal L. H. G. Lyautey began to construct the modern Fès Ville Nouvelle on a plateau in the south-west. This Fès also has its charm, if you wander

along the broad Avenue Hassan II, past the many cafés and small shops and boutiques in the old protectorate houses.

Nestling in gentle hills, the city of Fès is surrounded by opulent, green olive groves and orchards. In the north a road leads upwards to Bordj Nord, a sixteenth century castle, today a museum of weaponry, and on to the tombs of the ancient Merinids. From up here there is a stunning view down on to the mysteriously angled alleys inside the walls of both the old and the new city and beyond to the new residential areas.

GETTING THERE
International flights to Casablanca, charter flights to Agadir. Ferries from Spain to Tangier. From there buses, trains and collective taxis to Fès

BEST TIME
It can get very hot when the desert winds blow in the spring. Rainy season from November to January

ACCOMMODATION
Most of the hotels are in Ville Nouvelle. A few luxury and some very simple hotels in the old city area

TIPPING
Service is included in hotel bills. Taxi-drivers, hairdressers, ushers and waiters ask for a tip of 5 to 10 %. No extra tip with negotiated prices

Under the Ez Zitouna

TUNIS and the Medina. An oriental metropolis with a cityscape of both traditional and modern character

The modern up-and-coming capital of Tunisia uniquely combines the traditional and the modern. The new city with its wide shopping streets, proud Art Nouveau houses, Neo-Arabesque glass and concrete buildings and extensive shopping centers, surrounds its precious past, the well preserved, perfectly restored old city, the Medina.

Tunis is probably the most leisurely and most international city in the Orient. Admittedly, as in every world city, here too the metro is jam-packed and cars and overloaded buses struggle through the chaotic traffic, yet even early in the morning the seats outside the numerous cafés in the grand street of Habib Bourguiba are already occupied. People at leisure are even to be found on the benches under the fig trees of the green strip that separates the highways of the wide boulevard.

In the east the Habib Bourguiba leads via the Place d'Afrique down to the Lac de Tunis, the flat coastal lake. At its western end it broadens into the large-scale Independence Square, with its Neo-Romanesque church. In front of it stands the monument to Ibn Khaldoun, the founder of the modern science of history and "Father of Sociology", who was born in Tunis in 1332. The university scholar was political adviser to many princely courts.

Behind Independence Square the now narrow boulevard leads directly to the Bab el Bahr gate, behind which the Medina spreads out.

Rulers and conquerors

Long before the birth of Christ Tunis was ruled and fortified by the Carthaginians. When Carthage was destroyed during the third Punic War in 146 BC, nothing was left of Tunis either. Although the city grew again under Roman rule, it was not until Arab tribes had destroyed Carthage again in 692 that Tunis really began to flourish. The city attained its significance as an oriental metropolis in the reign of the Hafsid dynasty between 1207 and 1574.

In the sixteenth century the pirate "Barbarossa" Khayr ad Din made the Mediterranean unsafe. He rose to admiral of the Ottoman Empire, and in 1534 conquered the whole of Tunisia for the Turks and made Tunis the departure point for pirate attacks on the Italian coast. Attempts by Charles V (1535) and the Spanish (1573) to conquer Tunis failed in the face of Barbarossa's strength. Tunis therefore remained

in the Ottoman Empire from 1574 until 1881 when France made Tunisia its protectorate.

Prosperous merchants and aristocracy formerly lived in the Medina. Gradually, however, they moved into the French new city and the green suburbs, which included Carthage, now an exclusive area of villas. The Medina was in danger of falling into disrepair. But now every effort is being made to preserve the historic city center.

Souks, mosques, palaces

At the Turkish Market, the tourist center of the old city, there is a fairy-tale view from the roof terrace of the richly traditional Café Mrabet over the sea of houses, from which the minarets of the mosques rise up and in which the souks and opulently decorated private houses, palaces, mausoleums and Koran schools are hidden.

Among them, as emblem, is the great mosque of Ez Zitouna, which was first mentioned in 698. It is not, as actually prescribed in Islam, rectangular and built in an east-west direction. It was probably erected on the foundations of a Roman forum, so the architects had no choice but to break with the traditional rules of building. Between the thir-

teenth and fifteenth centuries it was extended into a university complex and the minaret heightened to 143 feet (44 m).

Around Ez Zitouna Mosque are the alleys of the souks, traditionally separated according to crafts. Here there are carpet, wool, spice and perfume traders, felt hat makers, jewelers and, at the former slave market, to the pillars of which at one time human beings were chained as goods to be sold, the goldsmiths. The range of goods today is predominantly oriented towards tourists. Only at a few spots, in the alleys around Bab el Bahr, for instance, foreigners still play almost no part.

The facades of the houses in the Medina appear to be inward looking, in complete accordance with the Islamic tradition. Recessed portals, curved passageways and heavy doors chased in copper are designed to prevent intrusion into private life. In the anthropology museum in the dyers quarter it is possible to peep behind the scenes, however. The impeccably renovated Dar Ben Abdallah house dating from 1796, in which the museum is housed, gives you a good insight into the everyday life of a typical middle-class family in the nineteenth century.

GETTING THERE
Direct and charter flights from all major European cities. Regular ferry connections from Italy and France

BEST TIME
Mediterranean climate, warm all year round. Best times to travel spring and fall. Sometimes wet in winter

ACCOMMODATION
Hotels of all categories in the new city. Simple, good value accommodation in the old city

TIPPING
In all areas of service provision a small tip of 5 to 10 % is expected. Except with previously negotiated prices

SPECIAL RECOMMENDATION
The Bardo Museum is one of the most important archaeological museums in North Africa

The Avenue of the 9th November, elaborately tiled with mosaics (above left)

Oriental roof terrace with Ez Zitouna Mosque in the background (below left)

Sandaled feet of the statue of Jupiter in the Bardo Museum (above right)

Tunisians in their own environment at the arched gateway of Bab el Bahr at the Porte de France

In the land of the
pharaohs: the Pyramids
of Gizeh in front of
Cairo's gates (left)

Modern tower blocks
on the bank of the Nile
define the cityscape.
View of the enormous
city from Cairo Tower

The Egyptian Museum
with its art treasures
dating from the time
of the pharaohs is one
of the most important
museums in the world

In the oriental west

CAIRO preserves testimonies to many cultures and religions – the outskirts of the city extend as far as the pyramids

Only the shimmering heat reminds you that the desert is not far away. At first glance Cairo looks like a modern, western city. Glistening skyscrapers line the bank of the Nile with its opulent tropical vegetation. A maze of streets, freeways, bridges and overpasses crisscrosse the city.

But behind the concrete and glass squares countless minarets, domes of mosques and individual church towers rise to the sky and green parks and avenues shine out of the sea of houses.

Cairo is a major-city of lively contrasts. It is reputed to have close to seven million inhabitants. But it is probably more like fifteen or eighteen million, who actually live here, where antiquity and new era, east and west, Islam and Christianity intermingle.

The foundation stone was laid by the small military camp of Al Fustat, which in AD 641 established Arabian troops here, who brought Islam to the Nile. In 969 followers of the Islamic Fatimids invaded Egypt. Jawhar, general of the conquerors, established a new rectangular city Misr al Kahira, north east of Al Fustat.

Both cities existed until 1168 and then, when the crusaders came threateningly close to Cairo, the unfortified Al Fustat was set on fire, to prevent the European Christian warriors from advancing any further. A Sunnite army drove out the crusaders and the victorious Saladin founded the Ayubid dynasty which in 1260 ceded to the Mamelukes. Under the Mamelukes Cairo reached the peak of its ascendancy. In 1340 around half a million people lived here and Cairo was the largest city in Africa, Europe and Asia Minor. The Al Hazar University, founded in 970, became a center of Islamic teaching way beyond Egypt and the city became the pivotal point in the spice trade with Europe, until, at the end of the fifteenth century Vasco da Gama, with his voyage to India, broke the spice monopoly and Cairo was robbed of its most important economic basis.

The splendor of alabaster

In 1517 the Turks moved in and downgraded the once flourishing metropolis to a provincial capital. After the withdrawal of Napoleon's troops, which had occupied Cairo for three years until 1801, the Turks installed Muhammad Ali as pasha. The last in his dynasty was Farouk I, who abdicated in 1952. Modern Cairo owes its character to the ruler Ismael Pasha, who in the 1830s had a city built in European style, to the west of the medieval center. The historic old city is far more exciting, though.

You come across more than four hundred listed historic buildings in the alleys of Islamic Cairo. Not only do they include evidence from the time of the pharaohs and Islam, but Roman, Greek and Christian architectural styles have also been preserved.

On the far side of the five minarets of the Al Azhar Mosque the emblematic Muhammed Ali Mosque, covered in alabaster, rises from the walls of the thousand-year-old Ayubid citadel. The mosque, built in the early nineteenth century in Turkish style, is one of Cairo's most magnificent buildings; even inside, the walls are covered in white and golden yellow alabaster, relieved by numerous fine gold and mosaic embellishments.

Upriver from the city center and on the far side of the garden city, hidden behind ancient Cairo's old fortification walls, is Babylon, the Coptic quarter. This district has also remained largely intact. Impressive here are the many churches with rich ebony and ivory decorations in their interiors. Especially fascinating is the "hanging church" Al Muállaqa on the south gate. The wide panoramic view from the 623 foot (190 m) high Cairo Tower gives the best picture of the rich variety of the major city of Cairo, right across to the Pyramids of Gizeh in the south west. The filigree tower on the Nile island of Zamalek was erected in the 1960s as a stylized lotus flower stalk.

GETTING THERE
Cairo is connected to the international flight network. Ferry boats travel from Venice and Genoa to Alexandria via Piraeus

BEST TIME
The most pleasant time to travel is between mid October and mid April, with average temperatures of around 68 °F (20 °C). In the summer months temperatures reach 104 °F (40 °C) and above. The very low air humidity makes the high temperatures bearable, however

ACCOMMODATION
As a tourism center Cairo offers accommodation in all categories

TIPPING
Baksheesh is always expected, often even without a service in return. Remain firm. Baksheesh can work wonders in overbooked hotels. In restaurants 10 % on the bill is customary

SPECIAL RECOMMENDATION
Do visit the Egyptian and Islamic Museums

The felucca terminal

ASWAN reservoirs characterize the landscape where caravans once set forth

GETTING THERE
From Cairo, flights via Luxor, many daytime and sleeping-car trains, buses (not recommended), with your own or hired car only in police-escorted convoys, shipping sometimes restricted on the Luxor-Aswan stretch, depending on safety situation

BEST TIME
Best time to travel: from October to March (around 72 °F/22 °C in high season), in summer around 104 °F (40 °C), but bearable as it is dry

ACCOMMODATION
Large choice of hotels in all price categories, youth hostels, simple camping sites

TIPPING
With negotiated prices (feluccas, taxis) no additional tip, in hotels and restaurants 10 %, as internationally customary

Abu Simbel, a popular destination for excursions, with statues of Ramses II (above). Aswan is the starting point for tours to the temple complex, 186 miles further south

The Nile at Aswan – an area of feluccas and sailboats (left)

Frescos in the necropolis of the tomb of Prince Sirenpowet II

Aswan is Egypt's southernmost city. It is situated in the fantastic landscape of a river valley oasis of the Nile below the first of what was originally six rapids between Aswan and Khartoum, the Cataracts. It is a modern city. The planners have succeeded in merging old and new without any great breaches of style. For instance, the local souk has remained one of the most colorful and original in the whole of Egypt.

In spite of the lively hustle-and-bustle, in spite of industrialization and tourism, Aswan is a tranquil, quiet city and since the end of the nineteenth century has even been a health spa for those seeking relaxation. Even traders, travel and boat guides are less insistent than in other tourist centers.

Many people on short breaks are of course attracted in particular to the great sights, such as the relocated Philae Temple on the island of Agilkia, the old Aswan reservoir El Sadd, completed in 1902, the 342 mile long Nasser reservoir behind the Sadd al Ali reservoir, completed in 1970, or even Abu Simbel not far from the border with the Sudan.

From the Corniche, the riverbank promenade with its numerous cafés, there are always new, changing views of the palm-covered islands in the Nile, between which the sails of the feluccas, the Nile boats, pop up and disappear.

The remains of the Fatimids

If you follow the Corniche to the south, past the legendary Old Cataract Hotel, you come, via the Fatimid cemetery and past the Nubian Museum, which is worth seeing, to the famous unfinished obelisk.

The Fatimids were a Shiite-Islamic dynasty, descended from Fatima, the daughter of Mohammed. In the tenth and eleventh centuries they ruled the whole of North Africa from the Atlantic across as far as Syria. Their cemetery is a sea of little domed roofs above low burial structures made of stone.

The stone quarries in the vicinity supplied the granite for many of the ancient Egyptian monuments. The obelisk at the edge of the quarry, which is almost 138 feet (42 m) long and weighs practically 1,320 tons, would certainly have become one of the largest monoliths in ancient Egypt if it had not had a crack

which meant that there was no point in continuing to work on it. To the south of the stone, half buried in the sand, are two sarcophaguses left over from the Greek-Roman era and an unfinished colossus.

Aswan was once the end of the world, the southern border of the Egypt of the pharaohs. For thousands of years it remained a border city. Romans, Turks and the British all maintained their border garrisons here. But the oasis was also a trading place. The trading feluccas had to turn here, as the rapids were impassable. They took the wares of the many caravans from southeast Africa, from the western deserts and even from India and brought them down the Nile.

Originally the Nile islands were also inhabited. There are still two Nubian villages on the largest island, Jazirat Aswan (Elephantine) today. It has been populated since about 3500 BC and the ancient ruins of the former market town of Yet have been carefully excavated. Im-

portant small finds can be seen in the island museum.

At the southern end of Jazirat Aswan ninety steps lead down to the "Nile meter", which was re-discovered in 1870. The pharaoh's officials used it to plan the water distribution, make harvest forecasts and calculate tax payments. A lot of water meant good harvests and therefore high taxes.

In the Garden of Eden

On the island of Geziret el Nabatat, the island of plants, situated further west, a veritable Garden of Eden grows beneath shady mahogany, breadfruit, nutmeg and trumpet trees. Numerous exotic birds nest in the bougainvillea bushes, mallows and oleander. Until 1916 the island belonged to the English officer, Horatio Kitchener, who led the Anglo-Egyptian army in the battle against the Mahdi in 1898.

From the summit of the Tabet el Hawa hill on the west bank of the Nile there is a stupendous view of Aswan. Further down on the slope are several tombs of regional princes and high officials from the ancient and middle kingdoms of the pharaohs more than four thousand years ago.

To the south of this is the mausoleum of the former Aga Khan, who was finally laid to rest here in 1957 in a marble sarcophagus under the granite dome.

Aswan's history is not just one of stone, however. When Nubian musicians and dancers appear in the cultural center every evening, the ancient traditions of the Nile oasis also come to life again.

Abidjan – pearl of the lagoon

This Ivory Coast metropolis is the center of French-speaking West Africa

Atlantic Ocean

CÔTE D'IVOIRE (IVORY COAST)

Abidjan

GETTING THERE
Numerous international scheduled and charter flight connections. Well-developed public transport network

BEST TIME
October to May (rainy season from May to October)

ACCOMMODATION
Abidjan offers the broad spectrum of any city, from luxury, via medium-category hotels and simple lodgings, to good camping sites on the beaches of Petit Bassam

TIPPING
Not customary in street restaurants. Also not if a service charge is shown on bills. Staff in the hotels in Plateau and Cocody expect tips. Escorts and leaders of organized tours receive tips only if service is good

For Europeans it is the Paris and for North Americans the Manhattan of West Africa. However, inhabitants and those who know it call it the "Pearl of the Lagoon". Abidjan, the city of three million, surrounds the inner part of the Ébrié Lagoon. A wide spit, Vridi Plage, protects it from the onslaught of the Atlantic waves. Though since 1983 Abidjan has no longer been the capital of the Ivory Coast – that is the city of Yamoussoukro with 130,000 inhabitants, 155 miles (250 km) to the north in the interior of the country – it is still the seat of government and additionally the business center and main harbor of French-speaking West Africa.

Abidjan has to maintain a balance between its two faces, between the two luxury districts of Plateau and Cocody and the ordinary areas of Treichville and Marcory. In Plateau wide, tree-lined boulevards run between the skyscrapers of local councils, banks and company head offices. Employees spend their midday breaks in the often extensive, shady parks or shop in the numerous French boutiques and supermarkets.

From the clock-tower of modern, imposing St. Paul's Cathedral, which was consecrated by the Pope in 1985, there is an impressive view of the skyline of Plateau. The idiosyncratic architecture of the church fits in perfectly in style with the often markedly futuristic buildings of the center of power.

Gigantic rain forest trees

At night-time life moves into the humbler areas of the city. Two bridges lead from Plateau across to the lagoon island of Petit Bassam, on which Treichville and Marcory are situated.

In the narrow, but clean and modern, streets of Treichville, where the station is too, lively crowds of people push past one another day and night. In numerous shops, street stands and in the colorful markets, as well as native, there are also all kinds of western goods for sale. Nightclubs attract visitors and in the popular, cheap Maquis restaurants you can get anything from Lebanese specialties to authentic West African foods.

A popular excursion destination for the people of Abidjan is the fa-

Panoramic view of Abidjan, a city of three million people and metropolis of the Ivory Coast (top)

Outdoor wash day. Itinerant workers wash the laundry of the city on the Banco River, just under two miles from Abidjan

mous Banco National Park, just under 2 miles (3 km) north west of the city, which is more than 7,500 acres (3,000 ha) in size. Gigantic rainforest trees cover the majority of the park. African civets and genets, bush goats, duikers and monkeys live here in a natural environment in which they hardly ever come into contact with human beings. In the arboretum species of trees and bushes from all over the country grow.

On the way to the park, on the Banco river, you go past what must be the largest open-air laundry in the world. Every day 350 to 400 itinerant workers come here to wash the clothes of the city dwellers.

They are only part of those who daily land up in this city, hoping for a better life. Many come from the famine countries of the Sahel zone, from Mali or Burkina Faso. Abidjan is bursting at the seams.

A hundred years ago this city was a small lagoon fishing village. It was the station, built in 1904, which first made this spot into a trading place and the Vridi canal, which has connected the lagoon to the open Atlantic since 1954, led the city to its present prosperity.

Untouched coast

The Ivory Coast remained for a long time untouched by European influences. The coast was not easily accessible to ships and impenetrable, sparsely populated tropical rainforest covered the hinterland. In the fifteenth century the first Portuguese traders appeared and, after the dissolution of the great kingdoms of Mali and Songhai, numerous tribes moved in from the south and founded important trading sites.

The first French missionaries landed in 1637. From 1840 France began to secure the trade monopoly

for goods and slaves for its traders in the region of the Ivory Coast and in 1893 ultimately declared the country a colony. Abidjan was promoted to capital city in 1934.

After independence in 1960, the "miracle of the Ivory Coast" began. Under its first president, Félix Houp-houet-Boigny, the country's economy grew annually by 10 % – until recession came in the 1980s, due to the world economic crisis and the many years of drought. Today two thirds of the city dwellers live in slums and the HIV virus is spreading rapidly.

As in almost no other city, the bridges of the "Pearl of the Lagoon" are in a fascinating way also bridges between the bubbling life culture of Africa and the glittering facades of the western world of business and leisure, which peaceably complement each other here.

South Africa's resort

In **DURBAN** the Indians determine business life – with the flair of the colonial age

SOUTH AFRICA

Durban

Atlantic Ocean *Indian Ocean*

GETTING THERE
There is an increasing number of direct flights to Durban's airport, sometimes with transfer in Johannesburg. Rail connection from here

BEST TIME
Time to travel all year round. Pleasantly warm in the southern winter, hot and sometimes humid in the sub-tropical summer

ACCOMMODATION
All categories. Most hotels are near the beach

TIPPING
Restaurants and taxis 10 %, porters 2 rand. Rickshaw drivers allow themselves to be photographed, but only for money - they have acute hearing for the clicking of cameras

The beach promenade is part of the city. Panoramic view of Durban from the Indian Ocean (above)

The market in Victoria Street, center of the Indian population (below right)

The city hall with its enormous dome originates from the colonial era. The monument in front of it is dedicated to future generations

Durban is the perfect holiday paradise. Almost 2 miles (3 km) of fine sandy beaches stretch not far from the city center along the Indian Ocean, the impressive breakers of which attract surfers from all over the world. On the beach promenade one luxury hotel follows another and leisure parks, restaurants, cafés and shopping centers line the "Golden Mile". Among the bathers, surfers and promenade walkers Zulu women sell elaborate handmade articles and Zulu men skillfully steer their rickshaws, decorated with skins, ribbons and pearls, through the bustling crowds.

Like Cape Town, Durban is a melting pot of cultures and customs, which give the city its particular flair. Mosques, churches and Hindu temples are witness to the ethnic and religious diversity and not least the tolerance of its population.

The most famous Indian of the city was Mohandas Karamchand Gandhi, called Mahatma, who came to Durban in 1893 as a young solicitor, fought here for twenty-one years for the rights of the Indians and in doing so developed his concept of passive resistance, with which he fought so successfully in his homeland against British colonial rule.

Durban emerged in the nineteenth century. About thirty Europeans settled here first in 1823, founded Port Natal by order of the Farewell trading company and made a living by trading skins and ivory. In 1835 they named the settlement after the governor of the British Cape Colony, Sir Benjamin D'Urban. The Zulu king Shaka had previously granted them rights of settlement.

After his death his successor Dingane tried to drive out the English people and ultimately forced them to flee to the island of Salisbury in the lagoon. He bequeathed the entire country between the rivers Tugela and Umzimkulu to the Boer voortrekkers, who had arrived in a wagon train overland, to escape British supremacy in the Cape.

Driving out the Boers
When in 1842 the British sent a small army and erected the Old Fort, the Boers saw their freedom threatened and besieged the fortress. The subsequent national hero Dick King, however, was able to escape on horseback. After ten days he reached Grahamstown, 620 miles (1,000 km) away, on the East Cape and requested reinforcements. They arrived in 1844 and the Republic of Natal, the land of

the voortrekkers, was incorporated into the British colony. The Boers had to move on and found a new home for themselves in the Transvaal.

The economic upturn came in the middle of the nineteenth century, when new settlers began to cultivate sugar cane. It happened so quickly that the sugar barons brought over thousands of workers from India and sent them into the fields and factories. The descendants of the Indians today represent the second largest population group after the Zulus and, as entrepreneurs and hotelkeepers, have a decisive influence on the city's business life.

In the Snake Park
Mini Town, right on the northern end of the beach promenade, gives you the quickest overview of the numerous sights of Durban. Here, on an area the size of a football pitch, stand more than a hundred of the most important of the city's attractions – albeit as models on a scale of 1:25.

Right next to this is something to give you a thrill: the Fitzsimmons Snake Park contains more than eighty of the 157 types of snake native to South Africa. Serum is extracted from their venom and the inhabitants of Durban can learn here how safely to remove the uninvited guests from their homes and gardens.

Just a few minutes from the palm beach and the high-rises of modern Durban you come upon the small stores, mosques, temples and bazaars of the Indian business quarter, above which the aroma of exotic spices hangs in the air. Not far from the Indian marketplace on Victoria Street are three Hindu temples, of which the Alayam Temple is the oldest and largest in Africa.

Two blocks further rise the minarets of the nineteenth century Juma Mosque, the largest Islamic place of worship in the southern hemisphere. A row of windows lets a great deal of light into the shady inner courtyard, in which five thousand faithful can pray. Filigree Koran texts decorate the walls and a gigantic oriental carpet catches everyone's eye. The close proximity of the Christian Emmanuel Cathedral testifies to the cultural diversity of the city. The Kwa Muhle Museum is also worth a visit. Here the city reappraises its apartheid past and documents the "Durban System", the former policies of suppression and discrimination.

World city on the South Atlantic

CAPE TOWN maintained its tolerance even in dark times.
Table Mountain is a spectacle of nature.

SOUTH AFRICA
Capetown
Atlantic
Ocean
Indian
Ocean

GETTING THERE
International carriers increasingly fly direct to Cape Town's airport, though sometimes it is necessary to transfer in Johannesburg, South Africa's air hub

BEST TIME
Traveling time all year round. Pleasantly warm in the southern winter, hot and sometimes humid in the sub-tropical summer

ACCOMMODATION
All categories. The expensive hotels are near the beach. Numerous good, cheap hotels on Long Street. Pre-booking recommended in the South African holiday season from December to January

TIPPING
Restaurants and taxis 10 %, porters 2 rand

In Cape Town there has always been a more liberal spirit than in the rest of the country. Many of the widely differing cultures of South Africa were not able to continue to develop during the dark days of apartheid and many black, and also white, artists went into exile or were banished. But since the middle of the 1990s the South Africans have been discovering their ancient roots again and in Cape Town a new, exciting cultural scene is flourishing. New galleries and clubs are always being opened, there are concerts everywhere and museums and theaters inspire thousands of visitors daily.

When the Dutch arrived in the Cape as the first white people in the seventeenth century, the Khoikhoi, the Hottentots, were tending their herds of sheep here and the San, the bushmen, roamed as hunters. The first settlers brought over slaves for themselves from East Africa, Madagascar and the countries around the Gulf of Bengal, who brought with them their cultures and their religions, mostly Islam.

Supply station on the Cape

The Portuguese discoverer Bartolomeu Dias was the first white man to see the Cape, in 1488. But it was not until survivors of the ship Haarlem, which ran aground in Table Bay in 1647, sent such enthusiast reports about the Bay that the Dutch East India Company dispatched an expedition under Jan van Riebeeck to set up a station in Table Bay. On 7 April, 1652 Riebeeck hoisted the

Dutch flag and chose the place for a small fortification and a vegetable garden. From now on ships sailing past on the way to Asia could obtain supplies of fresh, vitamin-rich vegetables, fruit, meat and wine.

Gradually other European states also realized the strategically important position of Cape Town. In 1781 the British tried to occupy the Cape, but the French beat them to it and helped the Dutch to defend the land. They triggered a veritable building boom and when Cape Town did eventually fall into the hands of the British in 1795, the two hundred house settlement had already become a city with one thousand houses, mostly in French style.

After the varying turmoils of war, the land on the Cape became a British colony in 1814. The new rulers abolished slavery in 1834 and soon afterwards many of the Boers left the Cape Colony. The liberal British attitude characterized the essence of Cape Town way beyond 1910 when South Africa became independent.

When in 1972 the city could no longer avoid following national apartheid legislation, Cape Town had no less than six colored city councilors. The city council fought time and again against apartheid and in 1985 even formally declared equality for all people. But it was the international economic boycott and the re-

lease of Nelson Mandela from the notorious prison on Robben Island in Table Bay in 1990 that finally led to political changes and brought freedom for blacks and coloreds. Today the prison is a museum.

In the National Gallery numerous photos document the miserable life in the townships of the 1950s, the ghettos of the blacks. But the around 6,500 works by native artists and the alternating exhibitions of modern South African art are also impressive.

Just round the corner from the Gallery is Company's Garden, the vegetable garden formerly laid out by Jan van Riebeeck. Today it is part of the large botanical gardens, which are

worth a visit. Here too is the South African Museum with its impressive exhibition on the history of the development of mankind in Africa.

Waterfront, waterfront

To the north of the garden district, between Strand Street and Wale Street, is a popular shopping center and place to hang out, with beautiful stores, souvenir stalls, pubs and cafés. The central point is Greenmarket, the most lively square in Cape Town, where there is a permanent flea market. All around are fascinating, beautiful art deco houses, including the Market House with its faithful to detail animal and plant ornamentation.

The once neglected harbor area of the Victoria and Albert Waterfront has been newly developed and lovingly restored. Restaurants, bars, jazz clubs and boutiques have been drawn into the lively commercial and shopping center on the marinas, which is also safe at night. The latest attraction is the aquarium of the two oceans, which in two gigantic tanks gives information about the ecosystems of the Indian and Atlantic Oceans.

To the east of the center, on the far side of the station, the castle rises up with its five-pointed outlines. Built between 1666 and 1679, it is the oldest preserved building in South Africa.

Beautiful wide sea world on the southern tip of Africa: view from the 3,560 ft (1,085 m) high Table Mountain over the city and its bay (above)

No less impressive is the view of Camps Bay with the backdrop of the Twelve Apostles rocks (below right) The old Victoria Harbor with its sheds and warehouses has been painstakingly restored and, with its boutiques, bars and restaurants, is today a popular meeting point